Rites
of the Mummy

The K'rla Cell and
the Secret Key to Liber AL

JEFFREY D. EVANS
WITH PETER LEVENDA

To Ruth Marie Keenan-Evans, Soror Maiat ∴ 352

Published in 2021 by Ibis Press, an imprint of Nicolas Hays, Inc.
P. O. Box 540206
Lake Worth, FL 33454-0206
www.nicolashays.com

Distributed to the trade by
Red Wheel/Weiser, LLC
65 Parker St. • Ste. 7
Newburyport, MA 01950
www.redwheelweiser.com

ISBN: 978-089254-198-0
Ebook ISBN: 978-0-89254-690-9

Library of Congress Cataloging-in-Publication Data
available upon request

Book design and production by
SKY PECK DESIGN

Printed in the U.S.A.

MP

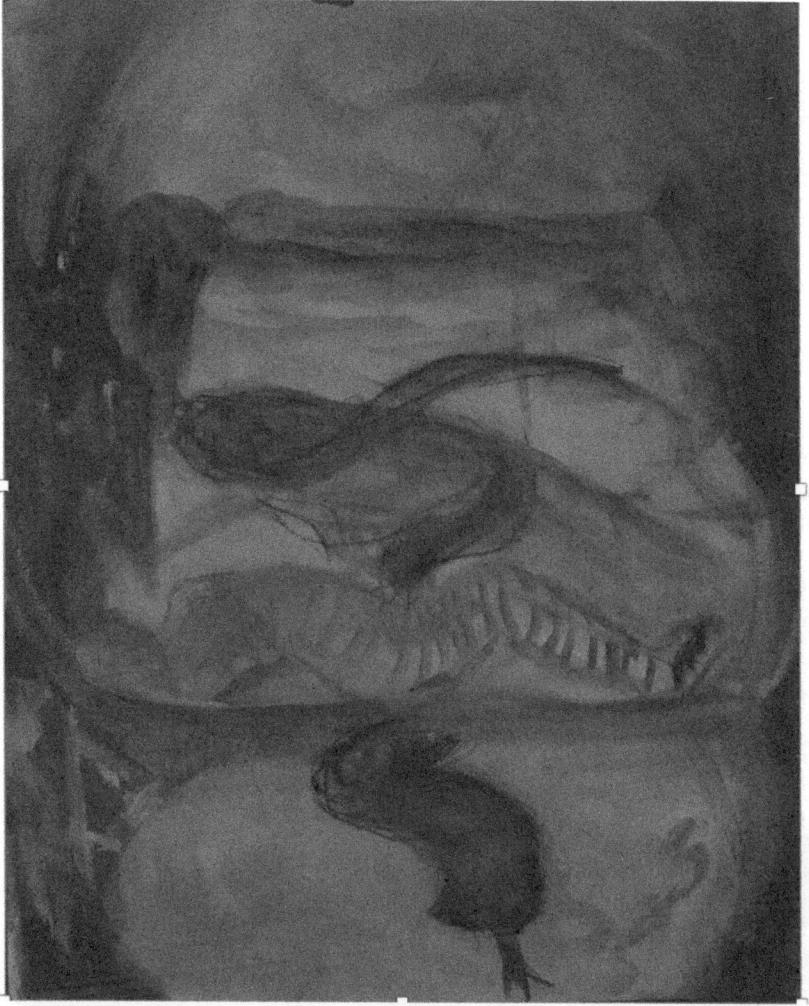

Painting of "The Cell" by Bettina Jeanne Guilbert

Contents

Book Five: The Grimoire of the K'rla Cell

Appendix: Additional Libri

Introduction

W hat follows is an incredible tale based on hundreds of pages of magical records and diaries as well as voluminous correspondence and line after line of mathematical calculations that confirm a fact that Aleister Crowley long suspected but which was never proven in his lifetime: that *Liber AL vel Legis*, the core text of his new philosophy of Thelema, conceals a sophisticated mathematical code within its verses. Moreover, this code is one that has been at the heart of the mystery religions of the world for millennia and is present in the very stones of the Great Pyramid of Gizeh as well as the Gothic cathedrals that are the roots of Freemasonry even as they represent the influence of the Knights Templar. This one mathematical formula is the link that connects the land where *Liber AL* was received—Egypt—with the Order that Crowley inherited—the Order of the Templars of the East—and runs through the esoteric schools of many times and places.

The discovery of this code is directly attributable to an arcane occult lodge operating in the United States, principally in Miami, that was a "power zone" of the Typhonian Order under Kenneth Grant. Grant refers to this lodge in his *Beyond the Mauve Zone*, where he devotes a chapter to its research and hints at its rituals as well as its discoveries. The rituals of the K'rla Cell were replete with correspondences not only to Thelema but to Egyptian religion, the Lovecraft

Mythos, and even to the phenomenon of alien abduction. It represents the Typhonian Current in all its weird and glistening glory, and moreover it demonstrates the power of that Current to reveal the mathematical code that the Beast was certain was concealed within *The Book of the Law*.

As we shall see, there is a further and even more recent development of this investigation that more fully aligns Thelema and *The Book of the Law* with the research of the Typhonian Order under Grant. It is yet another code, hidden in plain sight, and its implications for a new understanding of the "Tantra" of Thelema as well as the structure of the New Aeon are enormous.

This volume is based entirely on the records maintained by Jeffrey Evans and his late wife Ruth Keenan. My contribution solely has been to organize the material, edit it, and clarify its relevance by adding explanatory material. Most occultists in the West are satisfied with the level of mathematical sophistication represented by gematria, notarikon, temurah, and isopsephy: these are all forms of basic arithmetic and substitution cyphers. The New Aeon, however, requires a more ambitious approach utilizing the spaces between the spaces, the numbers between the numbers, and the angles between the angles. We are approaching the world of three-dimensional Qabalah that had always been suggested by the two-dimensional circles, triangles, and sigils of ceremonial magic. The ancients, however, were well-versed in this tradition and accorded it the honor and the reverence it deserved.

We can even find it openly displayed on the Stele of Revealing.

Once you see the inner structure of *Liber AL* (herein after referred to as *AL*), you can never unsee it. It is what Crowley said it was: a form of magic so powerful and so unique that it makes the magic of the previous Aeon seem like a "boomerang in a battle where everyone else has a rifle."[1]

We will study some of the historical background of the K'rla Cell and its founders, and then go on to an examination of the "Death Posture" ritual of the Cell that so fascinated Kenneth Grant.

Finally, we will look at the discovery of the code itself and will append explanations and elucidations of the formula and will demonstrate its relevance to Thelema and to the practices of Thelemic magic in the New Aeon. We will try to make this section as painless as possible, understanding that many readers may have a difficult time with mathematical concepts they may have studied in secondary school but have since all but forgotten.

Regardless of your level of mathematical expertise, however, the importance of this formula will become evident at once and most especially the ingenious way it was encoded in the verses of *AL*. This could not have been done consciously, for reasons that will become quite clear as we go along.

Either Crowley was a mathematical genius all his life—a claim that has no basis in evidence—or the genius that inspired *AL* had access to levels of mathematical intelligence that are only now being understood, more than 100 years after the fact.

We will then explore some of the Lovecraftian elements in the rituals but also in the math and will close with the most recent revelation of a purely Lovecraftian element in *AL*, one which is connected to the deep Tantra of the text. This volume is not only a confirmation of the non-human aspect of *AL*, and thus of Crowley's life work, but also a confirmation of what Kenneth Grant tried so hard throughout his life to explain: the precise correspondence between Thelema and the Lovecraft Mythos.

---

1   Aleister Crowley, "One Star In Sight, Sub Figura CDLXXXIX"

There will be those who will object to my contributing to a book on so recondite a subject as a ritual of sex magic by initiates of the O.T.O. (Typhonian iteration) since I am not an initiate myself. Indeed, I am not an initiate of any secret society or Order. Deliberately so. I have written on Freemasonry, on Tantra, on Crowley and Grant, on Nazis and neo-Nazis, on Satanism, and many other subjects. I have had close proximity to all of these in one way or another; I like to think I am not merely an armchair academic but someone who has spent years "in the field" and who has attended rituals and ceremonies, covens, and conspiracies, in the course of my peripatetic existence. With all of that, however, I cannot claim any sort of "insider's knowledge" regarding the issues before us. I bring only an educated eye to the process. For that reason, the second half of this volume (Book Five) is given over to the written record and statements of the ultimate insider and initiate himself, Jeffrey Evans. Thus, my contribution is merely one of clarifier, explainer, and tour guide for those who cannot boast expertise in all the areas covered by the discoveries of the K'rla Cell. In order to remain true to Jeffrey's discoveries, a deliberate decision was made to not overly edit his voice and thought process in order to maintain the energy of his path and work.

And this is as it should be. In a just world, Evans's discovery would have been recognized and lauded as early as 1984 when he first announced it to the chiefs of the Typhonian Order; as it was, either no one understood it or could not see its relevance within the predominant Hermetic Qabalah/777 tradition in which most Thelemic analysis occurs. To be fair, it most likely was a combination of the two. As the data defied easy categorization it was probably set aside due to the amount of work it would have required to render it comprehensible to non-mathematicians. A similar problem would have been experienced on the other side of that coin: there would have been no way to translate the esoteric, Thelemic context of the material to a traditional mathematician. And so, it languished for decades, even as the K'rla Cell continued to work the system, continue the rituals, and discover additional mathematical clues scattered throughout *AL*.

There exist numerous tables and additional material that the Cell developed over the course of its work in the past 30 years, amounting to thousands of pages. Some of it resists easy description without first understanding the approach in this volume. Some of it is unique to the Cell, such as a textual analysis of *AL* that notes occurrences of specific words, terms, etc., and correspondences to the language and religion of the Yoruba people (for instance). This material may result in future volumes; it is far too early to assess that possibility for now. What is believed is that there is sufficient guidance in these pages to enable the development of a school within Thelemic circles that would focus on the discovery and the implications of it, especially as regards *AL* III:7 and *AL* III:46.

—Peter Levenda

In Quarantine

Miami, Florida 2021

BOOK ONE

Dramatis Personae

CHAPTER ONE

Set and Setting

This is a summary of what happened.

On July 23, 1977, Jeffrey Evans—a IV° member of the Typhonian OTO[2] known as Frater KPhRA-MA-AST, 481∵—was walking on Key Bridge over the Potomac River in Washington, D.C. It was midnight, and for the past five years he had been going through a Dark Night of the Soul. An actor, the job he came to D.C. for had not happened yet (it was supposed to take place during the Bicentennial a year earlier) and when it finally would take place he would be paid only a grand total of one hundred-and-fifty dollars for 18 months of work. He was broke. He lived in a single room with no furniture, and all his books were lined up along the wall, on the floor.[3] He was estranged from his family and friends. There seemed to be no good news anywhere on the horizon. He had just turned 27 years old.

He contemplated jumping from the bridge into the river below.

---

2   For sake of convenience, we will refer to "Typhonian OTO" throughout, with the understanding that it was simply "OTO" until years later when Kenneth Grant changed the name of his Order from O.T.O. to Typhonian O.T.O. (TOTO) or Typhonian Order to differentiate it from the O.T.O. in the United States under, at the time, Grady McMurtry, once known as the "Caliphate." To which we might add, "We're not in Kansas anymore, TOTO."
3   Personal communication Evans to Levenda, email dated July 15, 2020.

He saw a woman walking towards him, materializing out of the whiteness of the fog. She stopped and they exchanged a few words. She said her name was Karla. She was beautiful, confident, and self-possessed. She was blonde, blue-eyed; dressed in denim jeans and a white blouse. She asked him what he was doing, and he unburdened himself of his disappointments, depressions, and anxieties.

She invited herself to Jeffrey's apartment.

The entire encounter was … well, weird.

They spent the night talking, mostly about Aleister Crowley. When she noticed a pile of books that looked like encyclopedias, she asked what it was. Told it was Crowley's *The Equinox*, she gasped, "That's the *Equinox*?" Jeffrey introduced her to the works of Kenneth Grant, particularly *Cults of the Shadow*. She had not heard of Grant but was fascinated, nevertheless.

He pointed her to an episode in the book that quoted a vision by the novelist Joan Grant. It involved a woman bound as a mummy in ancient Egypt and being used "as a kind of battery." Karla was amazed, because she said she had performed that same type of ritual with her (unnamed) boyfriend. What Jeffrey did not tell Karla was that he had the same type of fantasy from an early age.

As the night came to a close and it was near dawn, Karla suddenly had to leave. She got up and Jeffrey offered to accompany her, at least as far as the bridge where they met. She agreed on the condition that he not follow her any further.

They walked back to the bridge, and Karla disappeared back into the mist. Jeffrey never saw her again and, indeed, realized that during the entire evening they had not actually touched.

A few months later, Jeffrey met Ruth Keenan who was to become his magical partner and eventually his wife. That autumn, he was raised to the V° O.T.O. By December of that year, he was in England meeting Kenneth Grant for the first time. Told of the episode with Karla, Grant agreed that the experience with Karla constituted Knowledge and Conversation with Jeffrey's Holy Guardian Angel (HGA), and this became more certain when Jeffrey revealed that he was a cross-dresser and had been since quite young (hence the female persona of his HGA). When told of the idea that the Egyptian mummy experience could be dramatized as a ritual, Grant was certain that Jeffrey was on the right track and proposed a series of rituals that would adapt the mummy concept with an "alien abduction" concept, incorporating elements of the Lovecraftian "Cthulhu Mythos." It was heady stuff.

Jeffrey and Ruth moved to Miami, Florida, in early 1979 after a year in Washington, D.C. and Jeffrey was elevated to VI° O.T.O. and put in charge of the Miami Power Zone. That same year, both became initiated into Santeria.

In early 1980, Jeffrey and Ruth went to England and met with Kenneth Grant, as well as other members of the Typhonian O.T.O. Grant mentioned that there was a member of the Order based in Ithaca, New York that they could look up and they did, moving to Ithaca for about nine months where they conducted various rituals and established a working temple for their own use.

In October 1980, Jeffrey—in his trans-persona of Deborah Davis— was admitted to Olivia Robertson's Fellowship of Isis as a Priestess of Isis.

In 1981 the K'rla Cell rituals began in earnest with Frater 481∴ (Jeffrey Evans) acting as the Priestess: a mummy, bound and gagged, at the mercy of the Priest, Ruth Keenan known as Soror MAIAT.

Ruth had chosen the motto MAIAT due to her immediate fascination with the Egyptian goddess Maat. She had not yet been aware of the idea—promoted by Frater Achad—that the next Aeon would be the Aeon of Maat. Known among her friends as "the goddess of truth" for her characteristic honesty, she gravitated towards Maat when she realized the association. The addition of the "I"—or the Hebrew *yod*—in the middle of the name Maat was her acknowledgment of her role as the Agent (in this case, the Priest) in the rituals of the newly-created

K'rla Cell. The phallic "I" was demonstrative of that fact; thus, for the purposes of the ritual, Ruth was male and a Priest, and Jeffrey was female and a Priestess.

On April 2, 1984 (39 months after the first K'rla Cell ritual), Frater KPhRA-MA-AST 481·٠· discovered the Golden Mean formula hidden within *Liber AL*. It is the date Kenneth Grant says Jeffrey was "impregnated" by the Forces of the Old Ones. (Coincidentally, Frater Achad had proclaimed April 2, 1948, as the date on which the Aeon of Maat had begun.)

And in the year 2020, he would decode the infamous verse *AL* II:76, which connects the Thelema Current with the *Necronomicon*, as Kenneth Grant in his lifetime believed to be the case but could not prove nearly as neatly.

• • •

All the above details are relevant to the case at hand. There is much more, of course, and interested readers will find further details as we go along and in the section entitled "The Grimoire of the K'rla Cell." But for now, attention should be paid to the significance of meeting Karla: the mysterious entity—now known to be Frater KPhRA-MA-AST's Holy Guardian Angel—who gave her name to the Miami Power Zone as the K'rla Cell. A constellation of values confronts us here.

First, the encounter with Karla took place on the day of Rose Kelly's birthday (July 23, 1874). Rose was Aleister Crowley's first wife, and the woman who pointed out Stele 666 in a Cairo museum to Crowley in 1904, thus starting what would become the new religious movement known as Thelema. The meeting with Karla took place on July 23, 1977. On July 23, 1978, a group of occult aficionados (known as StarGroup One) held a party in New York City commemorating Rose Kelly's birthday and a song was composed for her by the lead singer of the band that would become Black 47 a decade later. Neither of these two groups—StarGroup One in New York and the nascent K'rla Cell in D.C.—was aware of the other at any time, but both were well aware of Kenneth Grant and the Typhonian Current.

Further, Jeffrey Evans met Kenneth Grant in December 1977 which is the same month and year that the Schlangekraft recension of the *Necronomicon* was published in New York City; this is a book that would become cited and mentioned frequently by Grant in the Typhonian Trilogies in the years to come, and which was the focus of the first StarGroup One event that same month and year.

Also, Karla, for some reason, was quite familiar with the Joan Grant "female mummy as battery" episode and claimed to have participated in an enactment of that same ritual with a boyfriend. Kenneth Grant would then suggest the context of an alien abduction.

That year—1977—was the year that saw the release of both *Star Wars* and *Close Encounters of the Third Kind*: the first a space-opera that became a cinema franchise comprising nine films (coincidentally, Grant's Typhonian Trilogies also comprise nine volumes), and the second which treated the idea of alien encounters on Earth in a serious way, including alien abduction.

That Jeffrey Evans was a cross-dresser is relevant in several ways. In the first place, his HGA manifested as a woman, Karla. In the second place, he was admitted as a Priestess to the Fellowship of Isis. Finally, when told of his plans for the Ritual, Kenneth Grant thought it was an excellent idea for Jeffrey to occupy the role of Priestess but with a specific requirement: that he abandon cross-dressing altogether except for when he was performing ritual magic. This, Jeffrey accepted, and the rituals proceeded as described in the pages that follow.

There are many other details of significance, including numerological synchronicities and the "deep Qabalah" of plane geometry and of non-Euclidean spaces and they will be discussed as they arise.

The discoveries of the K'rla Cell did not end with the identification of the Golden Mean/Golden Section in *Liber AL*. With the approach of Halley's Comet in the 1980s, Jeffrey Evans found himself strangely moved by the anticipation of its arrival. He spent months studying the heavens and their constellations and made another discovery: this time it had to do with a pattern of constellations and their relevance to the *kalas* so frequently mentioned by Grant and to a mysterious communication from Grant to Jeffrey in December 1977 that "Seventeen is going to become a *very* important number." The analysis of the constellations—the Seventeen Stars—is covered more fully in the section of this volume entitled "The Grimoire of the K'rla Cell," but interested readers also can refer to *Beyond the Mauve Zone* and the chapter[4] devoted to the K'rla Cell for Grant's own discussion of the matter.

This summary introduces some of the most important elements of the discovery, and they will be the subject of considerable expansion in the following pages. The central element is, of course, Thelema with a sharp focus on *Liber AL*. A subset of that is the context of the Typhonian Order, founded by Kenneth Grant, which introduces a more robust discussion of Tantra and "Thelemic sexuality" and non-conforming, transgressive sexual identities in their relation to occult practice.

The mathematics is another, crucial, element and it is the one that will most likely give the reader pause, depending on the level of mathematical knowledge brought to the discussion. We will try to make it as painless as possible. The more one already knows about subjects such as sacred geometry, the Golden Mean, and the Fibonacci series, the easier this discussion becomes.

What may not be so obvious to the casual reader is the importance of sacred geometry to the study of Thelema. Yet sacred geometry has been the underlying foundation of so much Egyptology, Freemasonry, Indian Vaastu, Chinese feng shui, and European alchemy (of the Fulcanelli and Schwaller de Lubicz variety), that the time has come to formally acknowledge its place within an occult tradition that claims it

---

4   Chapter 6, "The Rite of the K'rla Cell," Kenneth Grant, *Beyond the Mauve Zone*, Starfire Publishing, London, 1999.

is the current of a New Aeon. Every other instance of these various and disparate traditions has been embraced by writers on Thelema one way or another—the Egyptian religious environment, the Masonic initiations, South Asian mystical traditions, etc., even astrology and ceremonial magic, including Dr Dee's Enochian system—but the one unifying aspect of all these largely has been ignored. Until now.

A summary of biographical information about Jeffrey Evans and Ruth Keenan follows, and there is an autobiographical essay penned by Jeffrey Evans himself in the "Grimoire" section.

CHAPTER TWO

Frater Kephra-ma-Ast

Jeffrey Evans was born on July 4, 1950, in Washington, D.C. At the age of 7 his family moved to Miami, Florida. His mother was a registered nurse, and his father was a high school dropout who left school to join the service after D-Day but was too young to enlist so he wound up tending chickens on a farm in Virginia.

From an early age, Jeffrey was attracted to science, science-fiction, and religion. He was fascinated by dinosaurs and by Egyptian hieroglyphics (memorizing nearly 200 hieroglyphs by the age of ten) but he missed about a year between second grade and third grade which meant his understanding of mathematics was adversely affected for the rest of his life. He did, however, get accepted into Miami Dade Junior College, majoring in Drama. He performed in community theater and met several well-known actors such as Mal Jones and Karl Redcoff. It was Mal Jones who advised him to drop out of college and find work as an actor, believing that those who got Drama degrees taught acting but did not actually act.

In 1971, Jeffrey saw an ad in a local bookstore in Coconut Grove about contacting the O.T.O. Jeffrey had been studying Thelema ever since finding a copy of Crowley's *Magick In Theory and Practice* at the age of 16, and was excited to see this invitation to contact the actual O.T.O. Although the focus of his attention had been the Golden Dawn up to that point—in 1971, books and articles on the Golden Dawn were far more readily available than Crowley's works, which were often published by small presses in cheap editions—he sent a letter to the address in Fort Myers, Florida, and received a reply. He was told to begin a nine-month period of a magical practice of his own choice and to keep a daily record of it, and then send it back to the Order. He chose *dharana*, succeeded, and in 1973 he became a member of the Typhonian O.T.O. with the motto Kephra-ma-Ast (a phrase meaning "To Come into Being out of Isis") and the number 481.

Jeffrey worked as an assistant manager at the Dadeland Twin movie theater in South Florida, where he met a man who seemed to have been a master of yoga, and a woman who worked as a candy-girl at the concession stand who was British and the child of Wiccans. They eventually decided to work together as magical partners once she had divorced her husband.

But in 1974, he was encouraged to move back to Washington, D.C. to perform in the first ever production of a Shakespeare play sponsored by the U.S. Government. This was to be *Romeo and Juliet*, but the production encountered many difficulties and delays. In the midst of this, Jeffrey became involved with a group that was later to become notorious among conspiracy theorists: the Finders cult.

Astonishingly, Jeffrey was not aware of the connection until Levenda pointed it out to him since the name of his host family in D.C.—Beltz—immediately rang a bell. As it turned out, Jeffrey had not only lived with the Beltz family but had met Marion Pettie—the founder and head of the cult—during the course of his year or so with the group.

The Finders made national news in 1987 when it was revealed that several children were discovered—disheveled and dirty—in a park in Tallahassee, Florida, in the company of two, well-dressed, grown men. Suspicious witnesses called the police, and the entire group was rounded up. The men refused to answer questions, but the children

reported they were on their way to a "secret school" in Mexico. Identification on the men led investigators to an address in Washington,
D.C. and a trove of documents including photographs that showed the
children witnessing acts of animal sacrifice, among other things. There
were copies of telexes and other correspondence with entities throughout the world, some of which seemed to concern trafficking in children.

The news exploded in the mainstream media, but just at that
moment the investigation was quashed by the CIA.

It turned out that Finders did contract work in computer science for
the Agency, and the Petties numbered many CIA and other government
officials among their close friends and associates. A Customs agent,
angry at the way CIA had claimed jurisdiction over what seemed to be
an obvious case of human trafficking, leaked some of the documents
and the police report concerning the Finders, and this material found its
way into the early (1987) Internet and was eventually published. Due
to this investigation, Levenda became aware of the names and affilia-
tions of several of the main personalities of the Finders operation, and
Steve Beltz was one of them, as well as Steve's wife, Judith, who was
a behavior modification specialist. The arrests of the two men in Tallahassee occurred more than ten years after Evans's relationship with the
Beltzes, however, and the FBI had conducted follow-up investigations
of their own in the 1990s.[5]

It is not one hundred percent clear what the Finders were up to.
Marion Pettie has been interviewed and has since published his own
account which painted the group as a collection of latter-day hippies
and the Finders as a kind of commune. This meshes with what Evans
has described as his year or so with the Beltzes, traveling around the
country and into Canada on a converted bus. Evans was not the only
member of the O.T.O. connected with the Finders, however, for one

---

[5]   The FBI file on the Finders has been declassified (although heavily redacted in places) on their
website *vault.fbi.gov*.

of his friends and fellow initiates from Florida had introduced him to the Beltzes in the first place. Information about Pettie and his training in intelligence, his work in Europe, and his contacts everywhere in the world from China to Russia, belie his insistence that he was just a kind of hippie running an open-house commune. Pettie's brief seems to have been to infiltrate the human potential movement of the 1960s and 1970s on behalf of some government agency, or perhaps more than one of them. The O.T.O. organization in the United States in the mid-1970s was not large enough, probably, to merit any close surveillance by the security *apparat* but it is worth mentioning that Grady McMurtry and the O.T.O. came to the attention of the FBI over the "boy in the box" affair of the 1960s. Prior to that, it was Jack Parsons who aroused the suspicion of American intelligence in the 1940s and 1950s. So, there is always the possibility, however slim, that Evans and his circle of friends and associates would have been a target of surveillance or at least of investigation at some point in the 1970s.

Having been abandoned by the Beltzes after a year of living with them, Jeffrey was reduced to a dismal life in an unfurnished studio apartment, trying to find work where he could, always in anticipation of performing in the American Centennial production of *Romeo and Juliet*, which was going nowhere at the time. He maintained his association with the Typhonian O.T.O. and had become a IV° initiate. But he was estranged from his family (who ridiculed his vocation as an actor) and from his friends, was broke, and moved to despair.

And that was when his life changed, abruptly and without warning, as he stood on Key Bridge over the Potomac and contemplated leaping to his death in the waters below.

If what follows seems like a scene out of *It's a Wonderful Life*, the comparison is apt. In both cases there is a potential suicide and an angel. In this case, however, the "angel" was not trying to convince Jeffrey of anything at all but invited herself to his apartment for a chat about

Crowley, ancient Egypt, and ritual magic. The full story is told in "A Brief Biography" which can be found in the "Grimoire" section of this volume, but briefly it was this "Angel"—whose name was Karla—who set Jeffrey Evans back on the path he was to follow for the rest of his life. He eventually realized that he had experienced "Knowledge and Conversation" (K&C) with his "Holy Guardian Angel" (HGA) in the Golden Dawn and A∴A∴ concept, adapted from the *Book of the Sacred Magic of Abramelin the Mage* as translated by MacGregor Mathers. The fact that his HGA was a blue-eyed blond in a white blouse and jeans rather than a male figure was explained by the fact that Jeffrey Evans had always identified with females to the extent of cross-dressing since a young age. Indeed, although they spent hours in each other's company that night, they never physically touched and when Jeffrey offered to walk her home as dawn was approaching, she demurred, but permitted him to accompany her back to the bridge where they met whereupon she disappeared back into the fog.

A few weeks later, he would meet Ruth Keenan and our story develops from there.

CHAPTER THREE

Enter Soror Maiat

As soon as one steps into the Valley Temple from the Causeway, one enters the extraordinary sloping passage known as the Ascending Passage. ... this passage ascends at a slope whose angle is the same as the slope of both the Ascending Passage and the Descending Passage inside the Great Pyramid. It is an angle of 26°33'54," known as the *"golden angle."* It is related to the *"Golden Section"* or *"Golden Proportion,"* which was the geometrical basis of all sacred Egyptian art and architecture. To respect the *"golden angle"* in a sacred ascent or descent was to honour and observe maät, the principle of cosmic order that was thought of as regulating the universe.[6]

S oror Maiat—or Ruth Keenan—was born on November 27, 1953, in Hyattsville, Maryland, a suburb of Washington, D.C. Although she was her mother's tenth pregnancy, she was the only one born alive. Her parents were Roman Catholic and sent Ruth to Catholic school for the first ten years of her education, only allowing her to attend public school in the 11th and 12th grades after she begged and pleaded with them to let her do so. Like many lapsed Catholics of her generation, she developed a healthy dislike for the clergy—both priests and nuns—who were seen at best as restrictive and at worst as abusive.

---

6   Robert Temple, *Egyptian Dawn*, Arrow Books, London, 2011, p. 306.

She had taken courses at the University of Maryland, which included one on Gothic horror, where she devoured Bram Stoker's *Dracula* and Mary Shelley's *Frankenstein*. This contributed to her own "Typhonian" sensitivities, which—until she met Jeffrey Evans—had been restricted to the realm of the imagination.

In 1974, at the age of 21, she was in an auto accident. This seemed to signal the beginning of a long history of health issues, along with Jacksonian tremors (a type of seizure disorder she seemed to have been inherited from her father), Type-II diabetes (a condition possibly inherited from her mother), and by the time of her death in 2019 at the age of 65, she had been suffering glaucoma, clogged arteries, a deficiency of cartilage in her knees, a bad back, and other issues.

Yet, in spite of all of this, she managed a demanding schedule of rituals, both with the K'rla Cell as the "Agent" of the rite, and as a practitioner of Santeria, as well as volunteering at various organizations such as Narcotics Anonymous and often holding down a job as well.

She met Jeffrey Evans in 1977, shortly after Jeffrey had his momentous encounter with Karla on Key Bridge in Washington. He was 27, and she was 24. He was working in a bookstore known as the "M Street Newsstand" that sold adult magazines, and she had a job at a bank upstairs in the same building. She came in one day and saw Jeffrey studying a pile of papers that did not seem to have anything to do with pornography. She had come in to buy a joke present for someone's wedding, but when she saw Jeffrey's intense perusal of arcane texts she asked him what he was doing. He responded by explaining "Qabalah" and "gematria" to her, and she begged him to loan her a book that would introduce her to these topics. All he had at hand was a copy of *Liber AL*, which he was loathe to loan her, but she pressed him with such intensity that he relented. She promised to return it the next day, and she did, with tremendous excitement. It was, as they say, the beginning of a beautiful friendship.

Jeffrey had already been passed to the V° O.T.O. on the autumnal equinox, 1977, and was empowered to start his own circle. Ruth had her own circle of friends who called themselves the Fiendious [sic] Children. Many of these were childhood friends from Ruth's Catholic school days, and they were very possessive of Ruth whom they called the "goddess of truth" for her outspoken honesty. This moniker would become identified forever with Ruth when (as mentioned above) she chose the magickal name Maat—the Egyptian Goddess of Truth—but with the addition of a central, phallic "I" in the word, making it *Maiat*. This would take place in a few months once Ruth was admitted to the Order. Jeffrey thought that this group could become the nexus of his V° circle, but it was not to be.

The Fiendious Children objected by and large to Ruth's friendship with Jeffrey and in several instances actively tried to sabotage their relationship. After Jeffrey had returned from England after that first visit to Kenneth Grant in December of 1977, he and Ruth moved in together in 1978—a development that was resented by the Children. At a party held in November 1978, the Children—and one member in particular, nicknamed "Teeth" because as a child in grade school she bit Ruth on her arm since she looked "tasty"—attempted to freeze Jeffrey out of their charmed circle by conducting an impromptu ritual of dashing from one room of her apartment to another, and then back again, playing the piano at a frantic tempo (the "William Tell Overture"), and then simply rushing back and forth with the rest of the crowd following her. This bizarre scenario affected Jeffrey in some way and the emotional and psychological stress of the past four years took their toll and Jeffrey suffered his first seizure. From that time to the present, no physical cause of these recurring seizures has ever been identified.

According to what he later learned, he had fallen down a flight of stairs during his seizure. He had no memory of the event and woke up in the hospital. Gradually, it was becoming obvious that the Fiendious Children—despite their hostility to Christianity and their "magical mottos"—would not form the core of a new Power Zone. He and Ruth decided to leave Washington, D.C. and relocate to Miami, Florida, in January of 1979. Jeffrey had passed to the VI° O.T.O. at this time and started to assemble the Miami Power Zone with a core of 5 members.

Ruth had begun her Probation period the first week of September 1978, two months before the infamous party at "Teeth's" apartment, focusing on the Lesser Banishing Ritual of the Pentagram. Once in Miami, they connected with another Order member—known as Frater Ananael, 138—who had become involved with Santeria. Eventually Frater Ananael would dissociate from the Order to focus exclusively on Santeria. At the same time, Jeffrey and Ruth became involved in Afro-Caribbean religion as well, through Omi Ademi (Silo Crespo), a well-known Santero in Miami who had a botanica off Flagler Street.[7] Around the time of the vernal equinox, 1979, Jeffrey and Ruth became initiated into Santeria and by the fall of 1979 they had received their *ileke*[8] and their *Guerreros*. Ruth would remain faithful to the orishas for the rest of her life, as is Jeffrey to this day. They were told by Kenneth Grant, however, that the shedding of arterial blood was not allowed in the Order, so they never participated in animal sacrifice. This was a sticking point with Frater Ananael, who refused to abandon the ritual sacrifices as required by Grant and would leave the Order.

Ruth and Jeffrey went to England in 1980 to visit Kenneth Grant. This was Ruth's first visit, and Jeffrey's second. They discussed the proposed K'rla Cell Rite with Grant, who encouraged them to incorporate the Lovecraftian Old Ones in the ritual. Ruth, as Soror Maiat, would be the Agent of the ritual, which in this case meant the Priest or

---

7   Silo Crespo was later initiated into the Yoruba religion and Chief Araba of Lagos by Chief Fadunmoya Awontumba and by the famous Oba (King) of Lagos, Adeyinka Oyekan II.

8   *Ileke* is the name given to the beads appropriate to the different orishas or deities of Santeria and Palo Mayombe. Each deity has a different color or combination of colors. These beads are usually worn around the neck of the initiate. The Guerreros (or "Warriors") are a group of orishas that act as specific guardians of the initiate and must be propitiated weekly (usually on Monday). These Guerreros can be *Eleggua, Ogun, Ochosi*, etc.

the Entity of the "Old Ones" in charge of the "abduction" and mummification of the Priestess, in this case Frater Khephra-ma-Ast. (Also, during this year Soror Maiat was raised to the IV°.) During that visit, Grant suggested they contact another Order member who lived in Ithaca, New York. Known as Frater OTz PTN, 690, he ran a commune there with his partner—Soror Oma Ku, 137—and agreed to invite Jeffrey and Ruth there for what became a nine-month period involving a great deal of ritual magic and, at least for Frater OTz PTN, the consumption of magic mushrooms.[9]

They arrived in Ithaca late in 1980, having driven up from Miami. By the end of that year, Frater OTz PTN decided they would have a group ritual and that Jeffrey and Ruth should prepare their own.

The ritual was held over the New Year's holiday, from December 31, 1980 to January 1, 1981, beginning at midnight. In retrospect, this would mark the start of the K'rla Cell ritual series.

Jeffrey and Ruth opened the ritual, with Ruth performing the Lesser Banishing Ritual of the Pentagram from *Liber O vel Manus et Sagittae*. Jeffrey then performed the Lesser Ritual of the Hexagram and followed with *Liber V vel Reguli* "The Ritual of the Mark of the Beast," which begins with a spiral dance from the center of the circle to the circumference and back again, as Ruth beat rhythmically on a drum.

It then became their host's turn.

The temple was arranged with the four Enochian watchtowers in their appropriate quarters. Frater OTz PTN shone a light on each of the four watchtowers in turn, evidently highlighting a different square in each. But he was unable to finish the ritual.

Something had terrified him, and he raced out of the temple, breaking the circle. Several days later, Ruth was able to ask him what had happened.

---

9   This account is based on emails from Jeffrey Evans to Peter Levenda, dated Nov. 24, 2019 and subsequent.

He replied, "I never knew somebody else's ritual could be so powerful!"

One of the possible effects of taking psilocybin is panic, but everyone present had taken the drug prior to the start of the ritual. It is possible that some of that panic was due to the mushrooms, but it is also likely that the dramatic performance of the opening rites by Ruth and Jeffrey had created a "set and setting" to the effect that someone less prepared would react strongly.

On January 11, 1981, eleven days after the New Year's Eve ritual, the first K'rla Cell "mummification/abduction" rite was held as designed by Jeffrey with considerable input from Kenneth Grant. Jeffrey had been getting "into character" during his stay in Ithaca to that point, dressing and living as a female. The ritual required him to identify with a female—the Egyptian Priestess Makare[10]—being abducted and tightly bound and gagged before burial. During this first ritual, Ruth—as the Priest and Agent—began reciting sections from the Papyrus of Ani and, after about an hour and a half, the Agent stimulated the "clitoris" of the Priestess with a vibrator as the Priestess resisted all attempts to bring her to orgasm. The accumulated sexual energy was to be directed towards the goal of the Ritual which was to contact the Old Ones.

The use of the gag had the added benefit of training Evans in the yogic method of *keccarimudra*: this is a technique in which the tongue is brought back to touch the palate, or the back of the throat, in order to maintain a flow of *amrita*.

While the K'rla Cell created a temple space in Ithaca and lived there a total of nine months, the living arrangements became untenable. Their temple had been entered on occasion when they were not around, and things were moved. This is especially problematic since the Guerreros had been moved from their usual spot at the entrance, something

---

10   Makare was a name "heard" by Jeffrey Evans as a child that made a strong impression on him.

that strangers are not allowed to do. This led to arguments, and eventually Jeffrey and Ruth realized that it was time leave Ithaca and return to Miami, which they did on the summer solstice, 1981, after painting over the occult symbols and murals in their temple space.

In time, Ruth had attained the IV° which—in the Kenneth Grant OTO—was connected to the practice of Bhakti (Devotional) Yoga. (Jeffrey had performed Bhakti on Krishna by assuming the persona of the Indian goddess of Love, Radha, for his IV°.) She began a practice based on *Liber HHH* as her V° practice, being admitted to that degree by Grant. This well-known text consists of exercises in asana and pranayama, among other yogic techniques, and contains this quote from *Liber Lapidis Lazuli* at the beginning of section II AAA:

These loosen the swathings of the corpse; these unbind the feet of Osiris, so that the flaming God may rage through the firmament with his fantastic spear.

The reference to swathings of a corpse and to Osiris had (perhaps unintended) resonance to the mummification ritual of the K'rla Cell. Section II AAA of the *Liber* is a meditation on death and resurrection itself. Since she was struggling with the asanas and pranayamas of *Liber HHH* Ruth began to take care of the Guerreros as a substitute work of Bhakti. The state of her health probably affected her ability to perform the asanas as required. As mentioned previously, she had numerous health issues all her life which made her success at attaining the degrees of initiation (up to VIII° at the time of her death) all the more remarkable.

At the same time, Ruth had been requested to write up the K'rla Cell rituals and associated documents. Kenneth Grant wanted to include a detailed analysis of what the Cell was up to in one of his works as he was fascinated by the creativity of the Cell and their application of what he recognized as Austin Osman Spare's "Death Posture" and its innovative blend of Egyptian mummification, transgenderism, and Lovecraft's Cthulhu Mythos. She did not feel up to this task but set her mind to it, anyway, jotting down notes and scraps of information along the way. It is possible that her strict and overbearing Roman Catholic upbringing combined with the extreme counterweight of Thelema (both heavily involving ritual and a hierarchy) was causing a kind of psychological overload. Her devotion to Thelema was never in doubt, however, and she wanted to succeed so desperately that she chose a fateful path long before she was prepared to withstand its consequences. By that, we mean the Oath of the Abyss.

Anyone—according to the system created by Crowley—can take the Oath of the Abyss. Without going into too much detail (and it is assumed that whoever is reading this is already aware of most of it) it includes a commitment to annihilate completely one's contact with the Holy Guardian Angel until the Abyss is crossed. In the Qabalistic terms of the Golden Dawn, the Abyss is reflected in the sephirah of Da'ath, which for Grant is an entrance to the Dark Side of the Tree.[11]

Jeffrey and Ruth faithfully continued the K'rla Cell Ritual for the next few years, performing it sometimes weekly, "then at the lunar quarters; twice a month; and finally once a month (usually at the New Moon)."[12] The rituals were always in the same general format with additions and amendments as they saw fit over time. They incorporated chants that included the names of the Lovecraftian Old Ones; at one point Jeffrey realized that a human being abducted by aliens might not hear an Earth language, so Ruth was encouraged to perform a kind of glossolalia rather than a standard English, Hebrew, or Greek incantation, sprinkled with references to Cthulhu, Yog-Sothoth, etc.

This continued throughout the rest of 1981, and through 1982 and 1983, and in 1984 there was a breakthrough.

---

11 See chapter 7 of this work for more information on the "Dark Side" of the Tree, the *Sitra Ahra*.
12 Private communication, Evans to Levenda, email dated November 15, 2019.

By the spring of 1984, they did not seem to be making very much progress. But then on April 2, 1984—immediately after the Ritual was completed—Jeffrey started to write down what he had experienced during the "alien abduction" (which had as its focus the star Betelgeuse in the constellation Orion) and "fell into what the Beast would probably call 'a trance, or swoon'"[13] and realized that the verses in *Liber AL* could be construed as decimals. Specifically, *AL* I:25 could be understood as 1.25. That verse is "Divide, add, multiply, and understand." It is obviously a mathematical injunction, especially when the verse is extended to include the command, "Listen to the numbers and the words." 1.25 is a number, and "divide, add, multiply, and understand" are the words.

Jeffrey began to write down the formulas as specified by the verse:

Divide: $(1.25 \div \sqrt{1.25}$ $= 1.118033989\ldots$
Add: $+ \sqrt{0.25}$ $= 1.618033989\ldots$
Multiply: $1.618033989 \times 1.618033989$ $= 2.618033989\ldots$

This may not seem meaningful or relevant at first, depending on one's level of mathematical training, but $1.618033989\ldots$ is immediately identifiable to math scholars as the ratio known as Phi, or Φ: called variously the Golden Ratio, the Golden Section, or the Golden Mean. And, as Euclid presented it, the "extreme and mean ratio." It is to be found employed in the design of the Egyptian pyramids, in various artworks throughout the ages, and in the angles and triangles of the Pentagram.

The number 2.618033989 is the same as Φ^2, which is an indication of the strangeness of this number as the digits to the right of the decimal point in Φ^2 are identical to those in Φ itself (1.618033989). And Φ^{-1} (that's Φ to the minus 1 power) $= 0.618033989$. Φ is a number of

---

13   Private communication, Evans to Levenda, email dated November 25, 2019.

infinite decimal places, however, like Pi or Π (3.1415…) but when you work with powers of Φ they keep repeating the same (infinite) numerical sequence.

Jeffrey identifies Φ^{-1} as representing Nuit; Φ as Hadit; and Φ^2 as Ra-Hoor-Khuit, as we will see in the next chapter.

This is not as outlandish as it may seem to those not conversant with the various histories involved. First, the external focus of the Ritual was Betelgeuse, which is the star on the shoulder of Orion. In ancient Egypt, Orion was associated with Osiris and with themes of Resurrection. The placement and arrangement of the three great pyramids at Gizeh are believed by some to be oriented towards Orion and specifically to Orion's Belt. The Ritual of the K'rla Cell was a re-enactment of an Egyptian mummification ritual that would have had as its focus the resurrection of the Priestess: a resurrection that would have brought her to Orion (in this case, via Betelgeuse). In this context it also should be mentioned that the two large pyramids and temple at Teotihuacan in Mexico are also arranged in imitation of Orion's Belt and oriented precisely the same way as the Egyptian pyramids. The buildings were erected circa 2nd century BCE and were believed to have been created by a race of giants, the Quinametzin Giants. Coincidentally, the name "Betelgeuse" is believed to have come from the Arabic *yad al-jawza*, meaning "Hand of the Giant." The giant, in this case, meaning Orion itself. Thus, the K'rla Cell had picked a potent symbolic direction for their rites, one that recapitulated their occult intention.

Just as importantly, however, was the discovery of a kind of Qabalah of decimals and fractions, moreover one that included more advanced mathematical functions such as squares, cubes, powers, and negative quantities such as negative powers.

If one adds a whole number to another whole number, the result is a whole number. If one subtracts a whole number from another whole number, the result is a whole number (although it could be a negative whole number, such as 1 - 2 = negative 1). If one multiplies a whole number by another whole number, the result is always a whole number, etc. This primacy of whole numbers has dominated Qabalistic thinking for more than a thousand years and more likely two thousand years. However, when one divides a whole number by another whole number, the result may not be a whole number. For instance, 3 divided by 2 equals 1.5, or 1 and one-half: a whole number plus a fraction. Qabalistically speaking, what is the value of the one-half?

The act of division opens up a world beyond the simple, school-child system of placing whole blocks on top of other whole blocks to build a castle. Adding and multiplying are easy; subtracting not so much, and division is another story altogether. But the first mathematical function listed in *AL* I:25 is "Divide." When one starts dividing, one sees immediately that fractions enter the picture. But division can still be thought of as a form of multiplication, as in the example of cellular reproduction. It is when we approach the idea of endless decimal places that we touch the face of Infinity. That is when the actual digits in the flow of decimal places distract us from the essence of the number itself and what it represents: in our case Φ but also Π. What the K'rla Cell accomplished—if nothing else—was the discovery of a Qabalah of Irrational Numbers.

What is an "irrational" number?

First, there are *rational* numbers, and these are the whole numbers with which we are all familiar, but also fractions of whole numbers like one-half, three-fourths, etc. An *irrational* number is a number that cannot be expressed as either a whole number or a simple fraction of a whole number, but which would have to be expressed as a non-repeating decimal. In other words, a ratio like Pi which starts 3.1415 and then goes on forever without repeating and without end. Pi is an irrational number. The square root of 2 is also an irrational number, as it cannot be expressed with a repeating or ending decimal. (The square root of 2 begins as 1.4142135... and continues forever.)

The discovery of irrational numbers is said to have begun with a student of Pythagoras who came upon the concept during an analysis of the sides of the Pentagram. Thus, the idea of irrational numbers has its origin in that most famous icon of esotericism and occultism (and Thelema): the five-pointed star.[14] In fact, this discovery was considered somewhat blasphemous, and resulted—according to legend—in its discoverer being thrown overboard to drown! Therefore, one may suggest that the realm of irrational numbers is to number what the Tunnels of Set are to the Tree of Life.

The problem was in the explanation of this discovery. Jeffrey had no mathematical background and had failed math in high school (possibly due more to his missing school in his early years than to any natural antipathy). He was able to identify the number as Φ after much research, but that seemed to be the extent of it. He kept calculating various formulas to see where Φ would lead him—Φ squared, cubed, etc., or in combination with other numbers, rational, irrational, and transcendent—but was not able to demonstrate the importance of the discovery. Even after sending the results of his findings to Kenneth Grant—who wrote to him "Your numbers overwhelm me!"—he could not get enough traction there, either.

Grant did write up the K'rla Cell as an entire chapter in his *Beyond the Mauve Zone* and did reference Φ but concentrated on its isopsephy rather than on the prevalence of the number in other esoteric traditions. He focused on the ritual itself, its assumption of Spare's "Death Posture" and some of Evans's research concerning astronomical phenomena: for shortly after the discovery of Φ Evans began to incorporate what he had learned concerning a collection of stars known (in the northern hemisphere) as the Winter Hexagon, an asterism composed of the stars Rigel, Sirius, Procyon, Castor & Pollux, Capella, and Aldebaran, with

---

14　See chapter 11 of this volume for more detail.

Betelgeuse in the space encircled by these stars. This discovery led to the identification of three other asterisms, known as the Spring Triangle (composed of the stars Arcturus, Spica, Regulus, and Denebola); the Summer Triangle (Altair, Deneb, and Vega) and the Northern Cross (Deneb, Sadr, Gienah, Delta Cygni, and Albireo). As Deneb appears twice in the list, there are seventeen stars in all in the four asterisms and these Evans associated with the four hexagrams in what the Golden Dawn called "The Lesser Ritual of the Hexagram" or, in Thelemic recension, *Liber O vel Manus et Sagittae sub figura VI.*[15] This became part of Kenneth Grant's chapter on the K'rla Cell in *Beyond the Mauve Zone.*

Grant was constructing this volume of his Typhonian Trilogies with the idea that there would be three chapters from the K'rla Cell, and three each from two other sources: one in Chicago and one in a European country. Evans and Keenan worked on compiling the information he would need for these chapters, but the problem was the incomprehensibility of the Cell's mathematical discoveries. Evans had a difficult enough time explaining the relevance of Φ to the non-mathematicians in the UK who felt it was somehow "not occult" even though it is plain to anyone who has studied sacred geometry that Φ is a central concept to esotericism and Hermeticism. Those schooled in Hebrew gematria and Greek isopsephy would fail to see the relevance in an irrational number: it's not something one could look up in *777*. Yet, it has a tremendous pedigree in Hermeticism dating back to Pythagoras.

In a biography of the alchemist R. A. Schwaller de Lubicz, it is reported he said:

> The secret of genesis, a spontaneous existence out of a state of equilibrium, out of a homogeneous causal state that separates into the heterogeneity of above and below ... the becoming of number-form through the function *phi*, that is a path totally missed by analysis.[16]

---

15 See the section entitled "Seventeen Stars" in the Grimoire section of this book for more details.
16 Andre Vandenbroeck, *Al-Kemi: A Memoir*, Lindisfarne Press, Hudson (NY), 1987, p.180.

Here Φ is identified with the *process* and the *function* of *becoming*, the "secret of genesis." And, indeed, it is the secret of alchemy and of all the arts of transformation and resurrection. This simple yet noble function is the Genius that arranges the numerologies of Hebrew and Greek—and Coptic, and Sanskrit, etc.—and lies at the heart of the materialization of Spirit. Through its cognate, the Fibonacci Series, it manifests in the "real" world as the spirals of nature. And it is, indeed, "totally missed by analysis," that is, the analysis of information in patterns predetermined by custom and culture. Qabalists miss it in their analysis; Thelemites miss it in theirs. At least, until now.

The date that Jeffrey Evans received the inspiration to recognize Φ in *Liber AL* was—according to Kenneth Grant—the day Evans was "impregnated." As the abducted Priestess who was transported to the "Beyond the Mauve Zone," he had been subject to the rapacious ministrations of the Agent of the Old Ones in the catacomb that was the spacecraft that was the sarcophagus of R'lyeh. Used as a sexual battery whose energy was directed and controlled by the Agent, the Priestess caught sight of the infernal machinery that exists beneath or beyond the visible spectrum of humans and there found the heart of all mathematical systems. Φ is an irrational number in our wake world; but in the Mauve Zone and beyond, it is the base numeral, the primal 1 or, perhaps, the primal $0 = 2$. The *mathemagical* system—as Jeffrey Evans coined the phrase—flips the script on our measurements and calculations and quantifications, making all our numbers "irrational." It is what Qabalah tends towards, by associating numbers with letters and therefore words with formulas: the tendency is always towards the ineffable, and numbers are used as a language to describe what cannot be spoken and therefore what is ineffable and beyond language.

So, on that day, on April 2, 1984, the date of his "impregnation" by the Old Ones, Jeffrey Evans took the Oath of the Abyss.

And Ruth Keenan, despite Jeffrey's advice, took the same Oath shortly thereafter.

Ruth Keenan's determination to demonstrate her devotion to Thelema and to the Work was unparalleled. She maintained the Guerreros faithfully every day, performing the required rituals, and tried her best to document the operations of the Cell. In addition, as she was passed to the V° she was expected to administer the Miami Power Zone as Jeffrey was passed to higher degrees and eventually to X° as head of the Order in the United States.

They married in 1984, and then eventually moved into a large apartment in Miami that would house their more than 900 books and documents. Their occult practices continued steadily, through the years that became decades. But there was a parallel consideration that was operative at the same time, and that was a particular task that was given to only three people in the world by Kenneth Grant: the LAM Cult.

As many already know, Grant was the owner of the original LAM drawing made by Aleister Crowley and which served as the frontispiece to a work by H. P. Blavatsky, *The Voice of the Silence*, in 1919. The LAM figure looks remarkably like the figure of the "alien" on the cover of *Communion*, an account of alien abduction by Whitley Strieber, which has given rise to a great deal of speculation that the two may be related: Crowley's vision of a kind of Tibetan avatar named LAM and the alien entity encountered by Strieber in December of 1985, less than two years after Evans's discovery of the Golden Section code in *AL*. Strieber characterized the "alien" in the cover drawing as female and associated it with the Sumerian goddess Inanna/Ishtar. Crowley told Grant that the Lam portrait was drawn from life.

The announcement of the LAM Cult was made on the Spring Equinox, 1987—coincidentally only a month after the publication of Strieber's *Communion* in February 1987. Grant believed that something important was about to transpire, as *Liber AL* had stressed "I am the warrior Lord of the Forties: the Eighties cower before me, & are abased" (*AL* III:46). This put the decade of the 1980s at the same level of importance as the decade of the 1940s, when the world was torn apart by war and the first atomic bombs were dropped.

It was Grant's idea to form a network of LAM cultists to make contact with non-terrestrial forces and "praeter-human" intelligences. This manifesto is enshrined in a document entitled *Dikpala of the Way of Silence* (sometimes referred to as the Lam Manifesto) and it details a ritual method and a mantra that should be used by qualified initiates to make contact—through Lam—with those very forces. The initiates were to work independently and were not to communicate with each other but only with Grant. Jeffrey Evans was one of those three individuals chosen by Grant for this task and, indeed, as Evans pointed out the *Manifesto* is issued from "London and Miami"—whose initials spell "LAM."

As Evans and Levenda were communicating the details of the K'rla Cell for this book in 2019, Evans had a sudden breakthrough. He had discovered the inner mantra of the Lam Cult, and it was a model of occult symmetry on several different levels. The details are too complex to go into in this summary, but they are included in the "Grimoire" section of the book, in Evans's own words.

This would be followed by another discovery, that of the code embedded in *Liber AL* II:76.

All of this was taking place at a critical juncture in the life of Jeffrey Evans, for in March 2019, his wife and partner of more than forty years—Ruth Keenan Evans—died at the age of 65. She had attained the VIII° by then but was becoming increasingly debilitated and was no longer ambulatory. Jeffrey stayed at her side to the end. This took place shortly after he and Levenda had begun corresponding on the subject of the K'rla Cell. Jeffrey Evans has maintained a heavy schedule of correspondence since then—emails between Evans and Levenda come easily to over a thousand pages—and continues to make new discoveries, not only in the "mathemagic" of the complex formulas and functions involving irrational and transcendental numbers but also in the Typhonian magic of his mentor, Kenneth Grant. It is hoped that this volume—composed of introductory and explanatory material as well as Evans's own writings and records—will go some way towards honoring Ruth's contribution as well as Jeffrey's own.

N.B.: Readers who are familiar with the website of Peter Koenig and in particular the web page[17] that addresses the Typhonian Order will be aware of some gossip and innuendo that appeared there concerning Jeffrey Evans. It is well to address those remarks now, so that any possible misunderstanding may be put to rest.

The article in question—"Plan 93 from Outer Space"—notes that Jeffrey Evans took over as X° (Head of the Order in America) after Janice Ayers resigned from that position. So far, so good. But then the article states that Jeffrey Evans was expelled from the O.T.O., which is *not* correct. Evans surrendered all his Order documents to Grant at Grant's request, who then raised him to the XI°. Evans and Ruth Keenan were by this time heavily involved in the K'rla Cell ritual process and not able to administer the American branch of the Order at the same time.

The footnotes that accompany the article require attention, as well. Evans never contemplated gender reassignment surgery, for instance; he did not trash the temple in upstate New York, as claimed; Grant was more than supportive of Evans's exploration of transgenderism (specifically cross-dressing) as a magickal technique and never interfered in any way with that aspect of the Cell except to request that Evans only incorporate transvestism as a part of the ritual and not in everyday life, a request with which Evans immediately complied. There was considerable animosity towards Evans from the complainant in this footnote, and Evans feels that it is due to Grant's expelling the complainant from the Order and placing Evans in charge. Had Grant really objected to

---

17   *www.parareligion.ch*

all the things listed in the footnotes there was no way he would have praised the work of Evans and the Cell in his *Beyond the Mauve Zone* and devote an entire chapter to its magical experimentations.

We have discussed this episode briefly already, so interested readers can put two and two together and make up their own minds as to what really transpired.

BOOK TWO

The Discovery

CHAPTER FOUR

The Discovery of the K'rla Cell

A t this point, it would be beneficial to quote from Jeffrey Evans's own account of the discovery. Later on, we will try to explain it and amplify it further, but for now the details are as follows:[18]

I'm so glad you wrote that detailed letter to me, because it opened the door for telling you about the following incident. Ruth and I kept Working, at first once a week, then at the lunar quarters; twice a month; and finally once a month (usually at the New Moon). I also started dressing as a Priestess only when we planned to Work.[19]

Since she couldn't write a Ritual, I finally realized that a girl abducted by an Agent of the Old Ones would probably not even understand what was going on around her, or what was being said!! So, I told Ruth to at least start using the Names of Old Ones in her improvisational ritual-work, and I—as the abducted Earth-girl—wouldn't know what the hell was going on around me!! We began Working more and more this way, and on April 2nd, 1984 (which Kenneth marks as "the date of my impregnation") there was an astounding revelation.

---

18   This is from an email from Evans to Levenda, dated November 25, 2019.
19   The cross-dressing aspect of the Ritual will be covered in a separate chapter.

There is an *equation for the Golden Mean* in *Liber AL*, given to us by Nuit! The reason I asked you for "what you know" about the Golden Mean and its significance to Thelema, is because I know that if you'd realized this you would have told me about it. I've been watching online information about it, and its relation to Thelema, for 35 years, and have seen no hint from anyone that they're aware of it. It may be the next step in the development of the 93 Current; I hope you'll agree. On that day I suddenly fell into what the Beast would probably call "a trance, or swoon," and saw in *AL* I:25, "Divide, add, multiply, and understand," the Decimal Number 1.25. *AL* also tells us, "Listen to the numbers and the words," and 1.25 is a number! For the first time in my life I was motivated to go buy a calculator and begin experimenting with the number.

Do you know that applying those functions, in that order, produces the Golden Mean? Witness:

Divide: $(1.25 \div \sqrt{1.25}) = 1.118033989....$

Add: $(+\sqrt{0.25})\quad = 1.618033989....$

Multiply (times itself) = *The Powers of the Golden Mean!*

Of course, any number raised to the power of zero equals One, but here we have

$\Phi^{-1} = 0.618033989.... =$ Nuit

$\Phi^{1} = 1.618033989.... =$ Hadit

$\Phi^{2} = 2.618033989.... =$ Ra-Hoor-Khuit

...plus the fact that the geometry of the Golden Mean produces a Geometry of the square root of five, and 5 is the number of the Old Ones, and of Their mathematics!!

We can see here Brahma/Atman and Their field of interplay (Maya), Zos/Kia and Their field of interplay in the neither-neither, etc.—all the so-called "dualities" of so many occult systems around the world!

My seizure-problem[20] began to become very intense at this point, so I decided to try to "get them under control" by taking the Oath of the Abyss and simply remaining as calm as possible. Its culmination was (I suspect) the destruction of my 900-book library in the 2012 house fire, because despite it, I kept on going. Thus, it was a nearly 27 or 28-year "crossing." (If, indeed, that ever "ends"!). That's about one "lunar cycle."

I also suspect that since $\Phi^1 + \Phi^{-1} = \sqrt{5} = \Phi^2 - \Phi^{-2}$, and 5 is the traditional number not only of the Old Ones and of Mars, Horus, etc; but also of the werewolf (*vir*-wolf, or man-wolf of folklore), we have here a mathematics suggesting the principle of atavistic resurgence.

I began to feel as if we'd accomplished the goal Kenneth set us on. We have a mathematics of Thelema, the mathematics of the Old Ones, and of the occult systems of humanity in general. But, everyone is running scared from it. Kenneth said it "overwhelmed" him, and gave me the names and addresses of about 8 people to send it to ... Most occultists think it's over their heads, and every mathematician I've tried to deal with wants nothing to do with it, since it involves mysticism and Magick. As I told you when you were here, it seems to have "perched me on a fence." I had to spend 35 years teaching myself (a NON-mathematician) Fibonacci mathematics, which I'd never heard of before that discovery on April 2nd, 1984.

I'm sure you know that the Qabalistic value of Φ is 500, and that it replaced the old digamma (F) in sound-value. When that happened, the Greeks gave the combined sigma-tau, or *stau*, the value of 6, and:

$$500 + 6 = 506 = (8 + 80 + 418).$$

20   Jeffrey Evans began suffering from epileptic-type seizures. The onset of these seizures is discussed separately, but they seem to have been brought on by psycho-somatic rituals involving music, fast movement, and psychological tension focused on Jeffrey.

RITES OF THE MUMMY

I have many notebooks verifying a lot of this material (although much of the original stuff was destroyed in that fire), plus more, so it's convinced me that it's on-track. ...

You know, historical records tell us that Leonardo de Pisa (Fibonacci) possibly learned this number-system from either Indian astronomers, or Arabic astronomers.

Perhaps he learned it from a mad Arab named Abdul al-Hazred --??[21]

This is the direction this Work has gone. With Ruth, I seem to have caused "change to occur in conformity with Will" by turning myself into a Magickal mathematician, and by overcoming my compulsion to cross-dress by using it strictly magically.

I'm sure you can see why I've kept the lid on this equation for so long (for one thing, in order to make sure I could verify it), and have kept my eyes open over the years to see if anyone else has noticed that equation in *AL* I.25. Even you! Thank you again for being patient with me.

• • •

A few remarks for the sake of the Thelemites reading these lines who found the foregoing confusing, if not somehow heretical:

In the first place, we all know that numbers were not attached to individual verses until after the Book had already been received. An examination of the holographic manuscript shows no verse numbers for Chapter I, so the assignment of verse number 25 to this particular line occurred after the Book was received in Cairo in April of 1904. What does this mean?

Quite possibly, it indicates that there was an unconscious motivation for Crowley to assign the numbers that he did to the verses that

---

21   Jeffrey is being ironic here, alluding to the Typhonian Order's fascination with all things Lovecraft and in particular the *Necronomicon* whose putative author is the Mad Arab, Abdul al-Hazred (or, perhaps more correctly, Abdul Hazred).

he did. Or, just as possibly, the verses were in that particular order for a particular purpose. No matter how it happened, the proof is in the decryption itself.

The previous verse is the misdirection:

"I am Nuit, and my word is six and fifty," which is followed immediately by "Divide, add, multiply, and understand." One would be justified in believing that verse 25 thus referred back to verse 24, which is why (understandably) most people connect the two. As we shall see later, however, I:24 is decrypted as well, and the results do not disappoint.

What Evans did was focus on the line itself, with its specific numeration: I:25 (i.e., Chapter 1, verse 25) as if it were 1.25. A decimal number. "Divide": how to divide a number by itself and not get simply "1"? Realizing there were three arithmetical commands given—divide, add, multiply—he realized that one solution presented itself immediately: the square root of 1.25.

When one multiplies a square root of a number times itself, one gets the original number. The square root of 4 is 2; 2 x 2 = 4. Evans realized that the square root of 1.25 was the missing factor in the equation. 1.25 divided by the square root of 1.25 should give an interesting result. Just as 4 divided by the square root of 4 (which is 2) results in 2 as the solution, Evans intuited that 1.25 divided by the square root of 1.25 (which is 1.1180339) would give the same solution: 1.1180339.

So far, so good. Basic arithmetic. Now take the square root of the verse itself, .25, which gives us 0.5. Add it to 1.1180339 and you get 1.6180339.

1.6180339 is, seemingly impossibly but nevertheless inevitably, the Golden Mean. The Golden Mean is buried within the very verse that exhorts "Divide, add, multiply and understand."

Finish the command by multiplying 1.*6180339* by itself, and you get 2.*6180339*. How does that happen?

Take Pi, for instance. We know from secondary school that the value of Pi is 3.14159265 ... in an unending trail of decimal places. If we multiply Pi by itself, we get 9.869604... Nothing particularly interesting about that. But multiply the Golden Mean by itself and you get a whole number followed by the original decimal value of the Golden Mean. Thus, the square of the Golden Mean 1.6180339 gives you 2.6180339, and so forth. This is a rather unique quality for a number to have, especially one with so many places after the decimal!

Evans's interpretation concludes that 0.6180339 refers to Nuit; 1.6180339 is Hadit; and 2.6180339 is Ra-Hoor-Khuit. The symmetry of these numbers is plain.

But that is not all. The ancients had a way of calculating the Golden Mean using the simple formula of $(1 + \sqrt{5})/2$. The square root of 5 is 2.2360679. That number, plus 1= 3.2360679. Divided by 2 = 1.6180339, or the Golden Mean. That is what Evans is saying when he says that his discovery "produces a Geometry of the square root of five, and 5 is the number of the Old Ones, and of Their mathematics." The number 5 as the number of the Old Ones is a direct reference to Lovecraft, and it appears again in the writings of Kenneth Grant.

Now we realize that many readers will be suffering from MEGO ("My Eyes Glaze Over") syndrome. The innumeracy of occultists and of people whose degrees are in the humanities is well-known, even as it hamstrings their ability to make sense of the classics in their fields. Number, and the manipulation of number—whether for philosophical reasons, or astrology, or architecture, or Qabalah—was a central concern to the sages of the past. As the bifurcation between science and religion began to take hold, the language of mathematics was all but lost to the esoterically minded. There was Qabalah, but that is a relatively simple system when compared to the multi-dimensional systems of geometry, trigonometry, calculus, and the like. Thus, there is a tendency to ignore the higher forms of mathematics not because they are not relevant—they most certainly are!—but because it's a lot easier to deal with gematria and with isopsephy (provided one is reasonably conversant in either Hebrew or Greek which, well, need we clarify *that* point?).

In order to provide some relief, we will not expound at length on the Golden Mean or Golden Section (as it is also known) at this point. We will, however, append more discussion where relevant. At this time, we should demonstrate the relevance of this formula to Thelema outside of the analysis of the verses *in Liber AL*. For that, we need to refer to the Stele of Revealing.

CHAPTER FIVE

The Golden Section and the Stele of Revealing

What could be more Thelemic than the Stele of Revealing? It was this stele that attracted the attention of Rose Kelley while she and Aleister Crowley were on their honeymoon in Cairo. She happened to see it in a museum there and pointed it out to her husband. With astonishment, he realized that the Stele was numbered 666: his personal number as the Beast of the Apocalypse (as his mother used to call him).

We point out several things at once. First, it was the *number* that shocked him, not the details of the stele itself. Second, it was a *woman*—his wife—who pointed it out, not realizing the significance of the number, and it was another *woman*—his mother—who had designated him as the Beast of the Apocalypse, or 666, when he was a child.

It was a verse in the chapter of *The Book of the Law* that is written in the voice of Nuit (another "woman") that contains the mysterious encoded reference to the Golden Section. In fact, it is the goddess Nuit *who introduces number to the entire text*, and thus to the system of Thelema based on that text.

But what of the Stele of Revealing itself? What can that show us?

The Stele of Revealing

We would like to draw the reader's attention to two elements of the Stele. The first is the throne upon which the god, Horus, is seated. One should note the unusual design (which nonetheless is one we find on many such steles depicting Egyptian gods seated on thrones).

While noting the design of the throne, you may recognize the Fibonacci Spiral, a demonstration in geometry of the Golden Section.[22] Simply turn that illustration on its side:

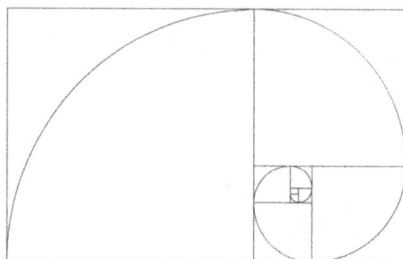

According to Robert Lawlor—a student of R. A. Schwaller de Lubicz—the throne as depicted in a similar stele of Osiris "is clearly depicted as the square of 4, as it transforms into the square of 5 through the principle of 5 on which all the Φ proportions rest. It is therefore shown as the seat of the world of transformation through death and rebirth, represented by Osiris."[23] While Lawlor is making these associations with a throne of Osiris, it is clear that the thrones of various Egyptian deities are all depicted in the same way. There is a rectangle within the rectangle, emphasized with a different color as if to draw attention to the relative dimensions of each rectangle: the smaller one within the larger one, and always in the same proportions. In the Stele of Revealing, the throne is of Horus but still reflects—in our view—an attempt to show a design similar to that of the diagram above: which is the traditional, if not iconic, depiction of the Golden Section and its resulting Fibonacci spiral.

This type of throne is called *ḥwt* (possibly pronounced "hut") in Egyptian and was used only for the thrones of the gods or for the pharaoh when he was shown in a religious context. Thus, the design was

---

22   See Chapter 11 for more information on the Fibonacci Series.
23   Robert Lawlor, *Sacred Geometry: Philosophy and practice*, Thames & Hudson, London, 1982, p. 72

considered sacred.[24] Called a "block throne" by Egyptologists, there is no further explanation for its singular design, except the proposal that it was meant to represent a house, and thus that the god was sitting *on* the house, thereby establishing sovereignty over it.[25] The term *ḥwt* was also used to denote "palace" or "temple," thus emphasizing its sacred nature. The same word is also found in the name of the goddess Hathor—*ḥwt-ḥr*—meaning "Palace of Horus" or "Mansion of Horus," or even just "House of Horus."

The second element under discussion is that of the two banners hanging behind the throne. This is the symbol for Amenta: the Egyptian Land of the Dead. It depicts the sun setting in the West, which for the Egyptians was the place of Death. On closer inspection, we find the two banners—integral to the sign for "Amenta"—but with different color bands. The ratio between the lengths of the two banners is 3 to 5; in addition, the number of red bands on the smallest is 3, and on the largest is 5. (As Evans notes, "5 is the essential Fibonacci number.")[26] This ratio is consistent with the Fibonacci series (which is also a reflex of the Golden Section). In fact, the overall dimensions of the Stele are 31 centimeters by 51.5 centimeters, repeating the 3:5 ratio.

As Evans discovered—and detailed in an email dated June 11, 2019—if we divide 51.5 by 31, and then 31 by 51.5, and add their results together, we get a number roughly equal to the square root of 5:

51.5/31	= 1.6612903
31/51.5	= 0.6019417
1.6612903 + 0.6019417	= 2.263232

The square root of 5 equals 2.2360679, showing a difference of only 0.0271641.

---

24 See Klaus P. Kuhlmann, "Throne" in *UCLA Encyclopedia of Egyptology*, 2011.
25 Why the god was on top of the house rather than inside the house is anyone's guess.
26 Evans email to Levenda, June 11, 2019.

We are not suggesting that the design of the throne was a deliberate representation of the Golden Section by the ancient Egyptians. We have no way of knowing that, and scholars are divided as to whether the Egyptians had that degree of mathematical knowledge. Some, like Schwaller de Lubicz, Robert Lawlor, and Stephen Skinner are of the opinion that they did and that they deliberately referenced these proportions not only in their steles but also in the Great Pyramid of Gizeh itself. It is also possible that the Egyptians were aware of proportion in general but had not codified it in a system of mathematics. The impressive statuary and other iconographic evidence of ancient Egypt shows a sophisticated appreciation of proportion in human form as well as in physical structures, and it is possible that the Golden Section made its appearance in Egyptian architecture merely as a result of attention to proportion and not as a specific reference to a mathematical formula: a kind of side effect.

That, however, cannot be said of the verse in *AL* I:25. The verse and its associated number is too specific, and seemingly too deliberate, to be coincidence. And, as we will see, other numerical phenomena abound in *Liber AL*.

Another aspect of the Stele that should be remembered is that it is a *funerary* stele, that is, it was used to commemorate the death of the individual mentioned, in this case Ankh-f-n-Khonsu. Its association with Death is, therefore, absolute. By applying a ritual steeped in the mummification process, with the Priestess wrapped tightly as a mummy and the Priest reciting incantations over her, we are approaching the state in which the Stele of Revealing was first created. The Stele was part of the Death process, a memorializing of the Death of Ankh-f-n-Khonsu, and the ritual of the K'rla Cell we are calling a form of the Death Posture took the message of the Stele as its starting point and traveled to a moment *prior* to the creation of the Stele when the Body was in the process of being mummified.

Death is the great mystery of humanity. It is Death, the fear of Death, and the inaccessibility of the Dead, that inspires the religious impulse all over the world to the extent that ritual initiations involve enactments of Death. We know that the Masonic initiation ritual of the Third Degree involves a ritual murder, death, and resurrection. At the heart of Christianity is the idea that a murdered man was resurrected. The Rites of Eleusis involve death and rebirth, as do the Rites of Mithra. Even the term *goetia* comes from a Greek word that has its roots in funerary rites, a word that references the wailing of mourners and which was used to refer to incantations and the summoning of the dead. Death and magic, like Death and religion, are inextricably bound together.[27]

In Asia, mystical practices from the Chinese to the Indian and the Tibetan were designed to enable practitioners to transcend Death, to create or strengthen their spiritual identities to survive the moment of Death. The Dalai Lama, for instance, as of this writing is preparing for a practice known as *mahāsamādhi,* which is designed to enable his spirit to survive, intact, after Death and consciously reincarnate in his successor. Chinese forms of Daoist alchemy involve creating a spiritual identity, strengthening it, and preparing it to survive the death of the alchemist. As we know, there are many cultures that cling to a belief in reincarnation: that some essential aspect of ourselves survives death and returns to life in this world as another being. The *Bardo Thodol*, or the "Tibetan Book of the Dead" as it is popularly known, prepares the soul for its sojourn in the *Bardo*—the intermediate state between life and death—and its eventual reincarnation.

The Death Posture ritual of the K'rla Cell enabled the Priestess to pierce the Veil between the Living and the Dead, which is one way of describing entering the Tunnels of Set. What is experienced after death but before rebirth is an encounter with various spiritual forces and includes visions of the gods copulating (as symbolic of the soul's

---

27   To which we can include philosophy as a "training for death," per Plato (*Phaedo* 67cd).

re-entry into the sphere of the Living). These visions are karmically-induced, that is; they are images provided by the degree to which one's spiritual evolution has taken place, and the negative as well as the positive consequences of one's life and accumulated deeds. (This is similar to the point of view expressed by certain pop occultists that the demons one confronts during rituals of ceremonial magic are "nothing more" than entities from one's own unconscious mind, as if they were somehow "less real" than the magicians themselves.)

This ritually induced experience of Death enabled Evans to make contact with forces from the dark side of the Tree of Life, specifically within the Tunnel of Niantiel. According to Kenneth Grant, they "had established contact with the Old Ones in the specific form of KRLA-MKR. This formula has the numerical index of 511, or 93 plus 418, thereby revealing at its heart the 93 Current—Aiwass."[28]

Niantiel is the Qliphotic presence behind the path on the Tree of Life that leads from Netzach to Tiphareth, and which is represented by the Tarot trump *Death*. The Netzach/Tiphareth path connects Venus (Netzach) with the Sun (Tiphareth) but since it is a Qliphotic Tunnel we are discussing, the reversal of normative gender polarity (Sun = Male, Venus = Female) to Sun = Female and Venus = Male was reprised in the K'rla Cell ritual where Jeffrey Evans became the Priestess and the passive member of the ritual, and Ruth Keenan became the Priest and the active member.

Tiphareth is also the station on the Golden Dawn's initiatory system that represents the crucifixion of the initiate: the Adeptus Minor

---

28 Kenneth Grant, *Beyond the Mauve Zone*, p. 95. This is by way of gematria, in Hebrew. One could also point out that 511 = 500 + 11, or the value of the Greek letter *Phi* plus the number of magic, 11. The Greek valuation (isopsephy) of KRLAMKR would be 311, which is the value of words like σομα (soma, "body" and "life") as well as αλιος ("the Sun," "the East") and λαιος ("left" and "left hand"). It is also the number for the word for "unity" in Greek, ομονοια. It should be noted that the term "soma" is a synonym for the Sanskrit *amrita*: the nectar of immortality. The combination of these ideas provides a provocative analysis of the mantra KRLAMKR specifically, but also of the K'rla Cell's method generally.

ritual, enacting the Death and subsequent Resurrection of the initiate. It may be considered odd—in retrospect, at least—that the Golden Dawn, with its heavy emphasis on Egyptian themes and religion, did not choose to employ an ancient Egyptian ritual of mummification here which is, after all, a death-and-resurrection scenario. However, aside from occasional use of the formula INRI using Egyptian deities there are no Egyptian references in the ritual, being more concerned with Christian iconography and its connection to the Rosicrucians.

The Adeptus Minor ritual also involves an introduction to the Vault of Christian Rosenkreutz once the initiate is led down from the cross. This is fertile ground for analysis—as presumably it was meant to be— and a study of the ceiling and the floor of the Vault is educational. There is a seven-pointed star within a septagon on both the ceiling and the floor, and an equilateral triangle in the center of each. Taking note of what we will discuss concerning triangles, angles, polygons, and number, this should provide enough data for an "initiated" understanding. Unfortunately, this is not the space to go into that now for we must concentrate on the K'rla Cell and its utilization of the formula of the Stele of Revealing.

We would like now to call the reader's attention to another geometric proof that is familiar to Freemasons as a depiction of their philosophy and which has resonance for our own.

The illustration on page 50 is taken from Euclid's *Elements* and is widely known as Proposition 47.

As the reader can see, it is "held by us as a memorial of Pythagoras." That is because it is a demonstration of the Pythagorean Theorem for computing the sides of a right triangle, which every high schooler recognizes as the formula $a^2 + b^2 = c^2$.

In the above proof, the nature of "squares" is represented by actual squares around the triangle in the middle. Thus, the length of the line represented by the letters AC is one side of the square ACKH; the next side is represented by the line BA, which is one side of the square

THEOREM.

" In any right-angled triangle, the fquare
" which is defcribed upon the fide fubtending the
" right angle, is equal to the fquares defcribed
" upon the fides which contain the right angle."

The DEMONSTRATION.

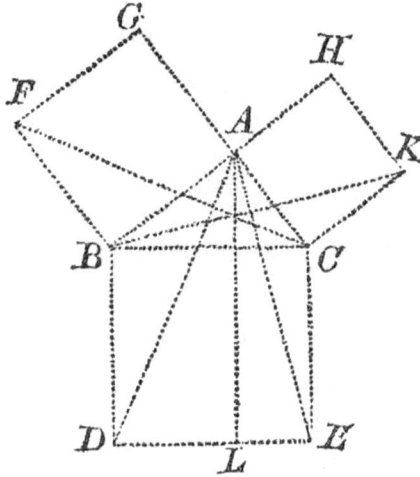

In geometrical folutions, and demonftrations of
quantities, this propofition is of excellent ufe,
and the example is held by us as a memorial of
Pythagoras.

Proposition 47

BAGF. The hypotenuse of the triangle—the side of the triangle opposite the right angle—is BC and the resulting square is BCED.

The lengths of the sides are 3 (ACKH), 4 (BAGF) and 5 (BCED), making the smallest of what are known as the Pythagorean Triplets: whole numbers that satisfy the equation $a^2 + b^2 = c^2$. This means that $3^2 + 4^2 = 5^2$. (Which is another way of saying $9 + 16 = 25$; since $25 = 5^2$, the length of line BC, the hypotenuse, is 5.)

This particular image of the famous Pythagorean Theorem, however, incorporates actual squares on each of the three sides of the triangle. Astute readers will realize that the square of 3 could be understood as the *kame'a* or magic Square of Saturn from the grimoires. The square of 4 then is the Square of Jupiter, and the square of 5 is the Square of Mars. Could a magic triangle designed with these—or similar—squares in mind be adapted for use in the evocation of spirits to visible appearance?

For the purposes of this study, however, let us realize that the very image above from Euclid's *Elements* illustrating the Pythagorean Theorem is known familiarly as "the Bride's Chair." In other words, it is a throne, moreover a throne for a goddess.

In Qabalistic parlance, the "Bride" is the Shekinah: the spiritual presence of God among the people who desires to be brought back into God's embrace. In Gnostic terms, she is Sophia—Wisdom—the goddess who descended into the world of forms and who was called the divine (female) twin of Jesus. In Tantra, she is Śakti or Parvati: the consort of Shiva who helped call this world into being. In Thelema, she is Babalon; in the Gnostic Mass, she is the Priestess who rouses the Priest from his slumber in the Tomb.

In Egyptian terminology, she is Nuit, the mother of Isis and of Nephthys, represented in the first chapter of *The Book of the Law*.

This arcane diagram even makes its way into Freemason Albert Pike's famous *Morals and Dogma*. There are several pages devoted to its description, and to Pike's contention that the three squares represent Osiris (3), Isis (4) and Horus (5).[29]

But ... there is yet another wrinkle.

No one is certain where the term "Bride's Chair" comes from where this form of the Pythagorean Theorem is concerned. In fact, some believe it was a mistranslation of the Greek word νύμφη (nymph) which *does* mean "bride" or "nymph," but which can also mean "winged insect" or "pupa." This seems like a coy allusion to Typhonian iconography and perhaps even to the Tunnel of Niantiel itself which symbols include the scorpion and the beetle, but the isopsephy for νύμφη is 998, which also equals Κορη Κοσμου (Kore Kosmou) or "The Virgin of the World." This is the title of a famous Hermetic text in which Isis has a conversation with her son Horus about the creation of the world. One of the more popular translations of this text was by Anna Kingsford and Edward Maitland: two early members of the Theosophical Society who founded their own Hermetic Society in the late nineteenth century and who were also influential in the early days of the Golden Dawn.

The opening lines of *The Virgin of the World* read:

"Having thus spoken, Isis first pours out for Horos the sweet draught of immortality which souls receive from the Gods ..."

This, then, is a reference to soma or amrita, and thereby to the formula of the K'rla Cell KRLAMKR ... and thus this brief description of the deeper significance and "codes" embedded in the Stele of Revealing comes full circle and to an end.

29   Albert Pike, *Morals and Dogma of the Ancient and Accepted Scottish Rite of Freemasonry*, Charleston, 1871 (1947), pp. 86-88.

BOOK THREE

The Ritual

CHAPTER SIX

The K'rla Cell and the Death Posture

Sleep?-This sexual excitement still obtains. Procreation is with more things than women. The function of the sexuality is not entirely procreation: stranger experiences are promised than ever imagination conceived! One must retain-to give birth to will.[30]

I t is best at this time to briefly describe the salient points of the ritual as performed by the K'rla Cell and which opened the gateways to new sources of information for the Cell (which were mostly of a purely mathematical nature).

The ritual had an Egyptian theme—consistent with that running through *Liber AL*—but with a focus on mummification. The "priestess"—in this case, Jeffrey Evans—was bound completely so that he could not move his arms or legs; he also was gagged and blindfolded. The role of "priest" was assumed by Ruth Keenan Evans. The gender switching was a key element in the ritual, for the purpose was to "gate crash" the Tunnels of Set and pursuing a gender-normative approach might have taken too long and required a much greater conscious expenditure of energy.

---

30   Austin Osman Spare, *The Focus of Life*, London, 1921.

RITES OF THE MUMMY

The "mummy" had the tip of his penis exposed. This was manipulated by the priest almost to the point of orgasm but not quite allowing ejaculation or orgasm. A similar technique is "karezza" which was employed by the quasi-Thelemic group in Chicago led by Louis T. Culling (the GBG or "Great Brotherhood of God" or "Gnostic Body of God" depending on the source), which had its origins in the Choronzon Club founded by Crowley disciple Cecil Frederick Russell. Culling later went on to join the O.T.O. In this case, the glans penis took the place of the clitoris.[31] Of course, as Evans has noted in correspondence on this point, the clitoris does not ejaculate and therefore to maintain ritual verisimilitude it was necessary that no ejaculation take place.

The inclusion of a sexual element to the ritual was deliberate as well. It represented a fusion of the Egyptian mummification theme with the "alien abduction" theme. This referenced an attempt to link Lovecraftian ideas about ancient religions with a "starry wisdom" concept.

In Mr. Evans's own words:

Ruth wrapped me from head-to-toe with latex bandages and duct-tape, even gagging me with cloth, and duct-tape over my mouth. The only visible parts of my body to an onlooker would have been my nostrils, and the glans penis (the "clitoris" of the Priestess

---

31   The role of the clitoris had resonance as well. Evans's K&C of HGA took place on Key Bridge over the Potomac. In Evans's words: "The first thing I noticed was that "Key" in Greek can be κλειτορις (clitoris), and the formula I was given reveals KR (=220) plus LA (=31), hence 251. The reflex, 152, is comprised of the same three digits although in a different sequence. The chapter and verse number in *AL* (discovered by our priestess) that reveals the Golden Mean (1.25) are again the same three digits, and so is the value of the mantra used by the Cell to invoke the Old Ones: KR-LAMA-KR = 512. This was comprised by the adjoining of the two names K'RLA + MAKR, which Kenneth goes into in his Chapter on the K'rla Cell." Personal communication, dated April 6, 2019. The Greek κλειτορις may be related to the word κλειδί for "key"; there are also etymologists who believe it is related to words for "shut," and "closed" (κλείνω) as well as an archaic Greek term for "small hill." It is believed that "potomac" is an Algonquian word meaning "river of swans," which suggests another category of meaning pertaining to death and the afterlife.

Makare,[32] which is why that formula figures into Kenneth's chapter so heavily). She tied me down to a board we'd set up for the purpose. Then, she began to act the part of an Egyptian Priest preparing to bury the bound-and-gagged Priestess of Isis for the Pharaoh. About an hour-and-a-half into the Rite, she put a vibrator on the clitoris of the Priestess, and continued chanting sections of the Papyrus of Ani, with the doomed Priestess listening, and trying to calm her breath as best she could.

I need to point out that the technique of the gag helped me to learn keccarimudra easily, while the bondage helped me remain still. Later, in a letter to me, Kenneth wrote "This is a tantric form of the Death Posture!!"[33]

The Death Posture referred to is described by Austin Osman Spare in his *The Book of Pleasure (Self Love)* and referenced by Grant in *The Magical Revival*. We will examine it more closely in the pages that follow.

• • •

Ancient Egypt—and ideas about Ancient Egypt—has exerted extraordinary influence over the evolution of Western occultism. Much of what we know about the *Corpus Hermeticum*, for instance, tends to locate its origin in Egypt. Gnosticism either had its birth in Egypt or was so prevalent in Egypt that some of its most important texts survived in

---

32 *Makare* was a word that Evans had "heard" in 1960, without realizing its relevance. The *makara* is a sea dragon or water monster familiar from Indian religion and culture and found carved at the entrances to temples as guardians. It is also a term used to refer to the pancamakaras or "Five M's" or taboos that are part of some Tantric practices. These include Madya (wine), Mangsa (meat), Matsya (fish), Mudra (parched grain), and Maithuna (sexual intercourse). The Makara as a sea monster is the vehicle for a number of Indian goddesses as well as for Varuna: the male god of the Sea who rides a Makara as his vehicle. See also Levenda, Peter *Tantric Temples: Eros and Magic in Java*, Ibis Press, Lake Worth (FL), 2011 for descriptions and photos of Makaras found in Indonesia.
33 Private correspondence dated November 24, 2019; email entitled "The Ritual." The keccarimudra—sometimes spelled kecharimudra or other variants—is the mudra of bending the tongue backward in the mouth so that it touches the palate during meditation. It is believed that this mudra enables one to collect the amrita and to experience altered states of consciousness. For some practitioners, it is the ultimate mudra.

the Nag Hammadi Library which was discovered in Egypt in 1945. In 1784, an "Egyptian Rite" of Freemasonry was created by the Italian adventurer Cagliostro (Joseph Balsamo), which eventually became the Rite of Misraim (a word which means "The Two Egypts," i.e., Upper and Lower Egypt) and which was joined to the Rite of Memphis (indicating the ancient town of Memphis in Egypt) and which is known today as the Rites of Memphis and Misraim, an "irregular" Masonic organization. Prominent members included the Italian politician and general Garibaldi, and the occultists John Yarker and Theodor Reuss: the latter, of course, famous to us all in his role as head of the original Ordo Templi Orientis. The Hermetic Order of the Golden Dawn used Egyptian imagery and god-forms extensively in its rituals, and these were picked up and expanded in turn by Aleister Crowley in his own *Argenteum Astrum*. Even the broad term "alchemy" has been translated as a form of *al-khemia*, or "the Egyptian matter."

The latest influence from Egypt, however, is clearly in Thelema and particularly in Crowley's reception of *The Book of the Law* in Cairo, Egypt, in 1904. The *Book of the Law* is divided into three chapters, each of which is in the voice of a different Egyptian deity. Crowley identified the modern age as the Age of Horus, thus further imprinting Egyptological themes and essences upon Western occultism.

This is not the place to critique the use of old, romanticized ideas about Egypt as containers for Western and European projections of mystery and magic. As I have said elsewhere, one does not use Crowley as an academic source for Egyptology. However, that was never the point anyway. Egypt was a prism through which to view the multi-hued rays of light of esoteric thought and practice: a way in, and not a destination itself. In fact, the more we know today about the religion and culture of ancient Egypt the more we can review the texts and rituals of Thelema with a more intense, more revealing gaze. This was accomplished by Kenneth Grant who saw relationships and correspondences between

Egyptian religion and magic on the one hand, and more modern paradigms such as those involving H. P. Lovecraft, the Tunnels of Set, and East Asian and African (and Afro-Caribbean) forms of esoteric practice and perception.

So it should come as no surprise that the K'rla Cell actively employed a deliberately Egyptian framework in their rites; further, it should be acknowledged that their discovery was nothing less than a confirmation of the mysterious origins of *The Book of the Law* in the very fact of the mathematical formula concealed within it: a formula that was used in the design and construction of the Great Pyramid of Gizeh itself. A monument, by the way, that is only about 15 km from very spot where *The Book of the Law* was received.

In this section we will examine the actual K'rla Cell ritual itself, a ritual involving the iconic Egyptian practice of mummification, but from a distinctly Tantric perspective. This ritual is an analogue—as Kenneth Grant himself observed to Mr. Evans—of the "Death Posture" described and illustrated by Austin Osman Spare in his *The Book of Pleasure (Self Love)*. It was an astute observation, as we shall see.

In the first place, the Stele of Revealing is the burial stele of the priest Ankh-f-n-Khonsu. Khonsu is the Egyptian god of the Moon. His iconography is revealing, as he is often depicted as a mummy himself. He is also shown with the forelock on his head indicating he is a child. Thus, we have multiple images to work with in just this simple icon.

The mummy is perhaps the most obvious one, at least as refers to the Ritual of the K'rla Cell in which Jeffrey Evans was wrapped as a mummy. The second instance is that of the child. A prepubescent child is a gender-ambiguous image, and in the case of the Ritual Jeffrey Evans—biologically male—assumed the role of the Priestess. The Child is also the key figure of the Aeon of Horus, that is, of the Crowned and Conquering Child. The possibility that this refers to an Age in which gender specificity and traditional gender roles are challenged is a theory that goes beyond the scope of this work, but in the case of the K'rla Cell it is an approach that worked.

Khonsu is also, and most importantly, a god of the Moon: the traditional symbol of change as it goes through its phases every month. But it is also a symbol of the *kalas*: the fifteen or sixteen subtle fluid secretions that Kenneth Grant identifies as most important to the work of opening the Gate to the Tunnels of Set.

To go a step deeper, the Creation Epic as depicted on the wall of the temple of Karnak shows Khonsu as a serpent fertilizing the Cosmic Egg. In fact, at this late period in ancient Egyptian history—the Ptolemaic era which saw considerable Hellenic influence—there was an effort to raise the worship of Khonsu to the same height as the other Gods by giving him a role in the creation of the universe. In the hieroglyphics from Karnak concerning Khonsu we read of a king making offerings to three deities: Khonsu, Thoth, and Osiris. Khonsu in these wall panels is identified as an aspect of Ptah, the Egyptian creator god who made the world from his own semen and who fertilized the Egg from which all existence came forth, including first of all the Ogdoad: the eight principal Egyptian deities. There is a lot of discussion of serpents and eggs in these panels and the role they played in the Creation, but what is most compelling here are references to Khonsu's identification with an untranslated Egyptian word which is usually rendered as *Bnnt*. This term is used as referring both to a place (or perhaps a state of being) and an object, as well as to Khonsu himself. From its usage in the texts, it seems this term references the *prima materia*: the base matter from which all Creation emerged. Khonsu is "the ancient being" in *Bnnt* (or "of" *Bnnt*) and is also a play on words which historians assume refers to the seed of Ptah.[34]

---

34 See for instance R.A. Parker & I. H. Lesko, "The Khonsu Cosmogony," in *Pyramid Studies and Other Essays Presented to I.E.S. Edwards*, The Egyptian Exploration Society, London, 1988, pp. 168-175; and Eve A.E. Reymond, *The Mythical Origin of the Egyptian Temple*, Manchester University Press, New York, 1969, pp. 64-65.

Khonsu is also said to "go forth on the lotus like Shu, the son of Amun, and he says to the king that he causes that the moon go around in accordance with Ma'at to the place where the king is."[35] Here we have references to the lotus, to the moon, and to Ma'at. The lotus immediately conjures the image of Harpocrates (Hoor-paar-kraat): the Child god who sits on a lotus. We have not been able to find any other reference to Khonsu (or to Shu for that matter) sitting on a lotus.

The Moon, of course, is Khonsu's icon, and the association with Ma'at—which is ubiquitous at Karnak—may presage the fascination with the Aeon of Ma'at in later Thelemic circles including, of course, those of the Typhonian Order. As the priest of Khonsu, Ankh-f-n-Khonsu would have been aware of all of these associations including the Egg—which plays such an important role in the Amalantrah Working (1918)—and the Serpent which fertilizes the Egg. That, and all the many references to semen and to sexual activity that we find on the walls at Karnak in the area dedicated to Khonsu would seem to reprise the eighth and ninth degrees of the O.T.O. quite nicely, if not also the tenth (the role of the King) and the eleventh degrees.

Recourse to the records of the Amalantrah Working show that it does, indeed, concern Egypt, a King, a pylon, and other iconography suggesting the Karnak cosmogony:

> The wizard's function with me is to get the truth. He knows the truth for me and is a guide to me. He expects me to go to Egypt to get the egg. He expects T. to go. (*Amalantrah Working*, February 12, 1918)[36]

And:

> The egg is a work which must be done—the great work. By doing the work we get to the key.

---

35   Parker & Lesko, op. cit., p. 175.
36   "T." = Therion, i.e., Crowley.

And:

> T. knows his work, his special work and this is only the means of doing it, like speaking of the cosmos, but the egg is the special work.

And:

> I see the path and something forming out of indefinite material like in the egg of the first vision.

The references go on and on, but the idea is clear, even to the "indefinite material" of the egg, because that is as good a description as any of the *Bnnt*. On February 3, 1918 we read the following:

> We are to go to Egypt for the key. The key might be in center of egg when it is broken. It is a small golden key.

The "small golden key"—in light of what we have been discussing so far—could be construed as a reference to the Golden Section. We admit that might be straining at the correspondence, but the Golden Section was discovered hidden within the "center of the egg" that was found in Egypt: *The Book of the Law.*

As the wizard in the *Amalantrah Working* informs us (January 14, 1918), "It's all in the egg."[37]

But as this chapter refers to the Death Posture it may be well to quote from the same Working regarding Death and consciousness since it pertains to the K'rla Ritual just as easily:

---

37 As this book was being completed, Levenda came across a mysterious entry regarding the Amalantrah Working on a Thelemic website, dated October 30, 2011. It reads, simply:
LAM + Der Goldene Schnitt im Ei (= The Golden Section in the egg) =
The Golden Section in the LAM zoom detail IT'S ALL IN THE EGG
There is no further clarification or explanation of this posting, and the poster was anonymous. Why the phrase "The Golden Section in the egg" appears first in German is also mysterious. From a forum on *www.lashtal.com,* last accessed June 27, 2020.

10:30 Reached stage where you can breathe ether through nose and mouth. Fear of death simply fear of loss of consciousness. Cowardly to speak so much of fear. Stage of having killed subconsciousness.

10:31 Death superfluous. Now understands why Achitha[38] laughed when taking too much. Also understands how absurd it is to say this. Important note. Change of consciousness = change of rapidity of vibration. Understand true point between sub-consciousness and unconsciousness. (*Amalantrah Working*, March 17, 1918)

Jeffrey Evans's "Death Posture" was just that: a change of consciousness that was at the "true point between sub-consciousness and unconsciousness" as he was still conscious, but in a dramatically altered state that could not be confused with ordinary consciousness. In the above example, ether was being taken; but in the K'rla Cell Ritual there were no drugs of any kind being consumed. The altered states of consciousness obtained were due to the Ritual itself: to the mummification of the Priestess and to the lengthy, droning incantations of the Priest.

Austin Osman Spare was the inspiration for Kenneth Grant's discovery of the Death Posture as the mode in which the K'rla Cell made contact with the Old Ones. This was a method that did not use drugs, but which relied more on a neurological technique. Grant first discusses the Death Posture in the first book of his Typhonian Trilogies, *The Magical Revival* (1972). Austin Osman Spare is discussed at length in Chapter 11 and then the Death Posture specifically in Chapter 12, entitled "The Death Posture and the New Sexuality." This is a reference to Spare's *The Book of Pleasure (Self-Love): The Psychology of Ecstasy* (1913). In the chapter on the Death Posture, Spare specifically connects it to "the restoration of the new sexuality."[39]

---

38   Achitha refers to Roddie Minor who was a major participant in the Working.
39   Austin Osman Spare, *The Book of Pleasure (Self-Love): The Psychology of Ecstasy*, self-published, London, 1913, pp.17-19.

It is a difficult chapter to understand, due largely to Spare's rather awkward phrasing. He specifies that one should stare at oneself in a mirror until one's image becomes blurred. Then, one must stand on tip-toe, "with arms rigid, bound behind by the hands, clasped and straining the utmost, neck stretched—breathing deeply and spasmodically , till giddy and sensation comes in gusts, gives exhaustion and capacity for the former." Then one lays on one's back, motionless, "forgetting time."[40]

These are all methods for accomplishing a degree of dissociation. The staring in the mirror is a familiar and common technique for achieving a kind of hypnotic state. The stress of standing on tip-toe with arms rigid and bound, breathing deeply, further taxes the physical organism to the point of collapse, which then results in the subject lying flat on the ground in what is known as the "corpse pose" or *savasana*. In the ritual of the K'rla Cell, this same goal was accomplished by the subject being wrapped as a mummy—completely restrained—and in total darkness. It was the equivalent of a sensory deprivation tank, except for the chanting of the Priest that provided a channel for the consciousness of the mummified Priestess to travel deeper within the sub-conscious. The Death Posture of Austin Osman Spare is connected to what he called the "new sexuality" although that is not defined. The Death Posture of the K'rla Cell had a sexual component, however, in that the glans penis of the Priestess (Jeffrey Evans in this case) was exposed and subject to the ministrations of the Priest (Ruth Keenan).

In *The Focus of Life*, Spare writes:

> By the "death posture" (A simulation of death by the utter negation of thought, i.e. the prevention of desire from belief and the functioning of all consciousness through the sexuality) [not for subjection of mind, body or longevity nor any thing as such] the Body is

---

40   Ibid., p. 18.

allowed to manifest spontaneously and is arbitrary and impervious to reaction.[41]

Thus, we see that the Death Posture is a theme which reappears in Spare's work and with which sexuality is intimately associated and the channel through which the simulation of death is achieved. Consciousness, according to Spare, is shifted from the rational, thinking brain to the "serpent brain" at the base of the skull. What Grant suggests in *The Magical Revival* is what the K'rla Cell achieved in reality: the application of Spare's Death Posture to a ritual of pure Thelemic intention, a ritual that employed the "new sexuality" within a framework of Egyptian religion, Thelemic ritual, and even alien abduction.

Communion

> In the union of electro-chemical and stellar vibrations represented by Babalon and the Beast, lies the key to the next stage in the advancement of evolution upon this planet. It will be achieved by a willed congress with extra-terrestrial entities of which, in a sense, Aiwaz is the immediate messenger to humanity. ... Aiwaz is therefore the *type* of extra-terrestrial Intelligence such as we may expect to come into conscious contact with, as the aeon develops.[42]

If one can make any generalization about the Typhonian perspective on magic and on Thelema, it is the deliberate involvement of extra-terrestrial, ultra-mundane entities in the Work. Kenneth Grant is all about contacting forces from off-planet, and he views magic as a technology of human contact with aliens; whether this contact was deliberate or accidental, ancient or modern, it doesn't matter to the core concept of human-alien communion.

---

41 Austin Osman Spare, *The Focus of Life*, London, 1921.
42 Kenneth Grant, *The Magical Revival*, Samuel Weiser, New York, 1972, p. 210 (emphasis in original).

In various places in the Trilogies he speaks of the UFO phenomenon as being inextricably linked to magic and to ritual. He cites references from Lovecraft and Lovecraftian literature to expand upon this idea and, indeed, incorporated Lovecraftian elements in the rituals his Nu-Isis Lodge performed in the 1950s. Lovecraft worked with the same equation as Grant: there are cults that exist in the world that use ritual magic to contact alien forces. These forces are located either on distant planets or lurk in dimensions parallel to our own. It is a blending of science-fiction with gothic horror from a literary point of view, but it is also an empowerment of literature as a framing of occult possibilities.

That there are occult aspects to the UFO Phenomenon has not gone unnoticed by journalists and researchers in the field. But while sightings of unidentified flying objects can be verified with video tape and radar traces, the effect of these sightings on the human psyche has yet to be studied in a thorough manner. In addition, there is the ancillary phenomenon of alien abduction: an area in which commentators are divided. Is the alien abduction phenomenon really part of the UFO/UAP Phenomenon or is it something else entirely, some kind of psychological disorder or hallucinatory experience that is linked—rightly or wrongly—with "flying saucers"? Unfortunately, the US government muddied the waters even further with their famous press conference in Washington D.C. in July of 1952. In addressing the widespread sightings of flying saucers over the nation's capital that month, the Air Force generals holding the conference started referencing psychic phenomena and Biblical precedents!

This set the stage for a spate of "close encounter" experiencers who claimed that the aliens were benign beings—angels, advanced souls of some sort—who were here to guide the planet. Later that same year, George Adamski claimed he had been visited by an alien from Venus with the name Orthon who communicated via telepathy and who was worried about the Earth's use of atomic weapons. The idea that aliens were concerned about life on Earth self-destructing already had been introduced in the 1951 film *The Day the Earth Stood Still*, starring Michael Rennie as the alien Klaatu who warns the Earth that the rest of the universe will not tolerate an out-of-control military with atomic bombs. Klaatu was not entirely angelic, however. He brought with him a robot, Gort, member of a race of robots who punish violent offender planets. In Klaatu's words: "Your choice is simple: join us and live in peace or pursue your present course and face obliteration."

Thus, as early as 1951 the popular sentiment concerning the possibility of non-terrestrial beings with enormous power was that they were alarmed at the Earth's technological prowess because it came with a kind of prepubescent spirituality. Virtually every popular representation of aliens depicts them as alarmed at humanity's irresponsibility and immaturity. They never seem to arrive and compliment humans on their wisdom and self-restraint! Having enormous power, the aliens are seen as a potential threat but in terms of a stern parent who wishes to raise their child properly.

By 1954, Kenneth Grant was running his Nu-Isis Lodge of the O.T.O. and incorporating alien-based themes from the work of H. P. Lovecraft. Rather than the viewpoint that space was the field of benevolent beings interested in saving humans from themselves, Lovecraft saw space as the realm of monstrous creatures who were either indifferent to humans or actively hostile. Lovecraft also posited the existence of human cults on planet Earth who were in contact with those alien beings and for whatever pernicious reasoning they were intent on bringing them back to Earth, through a hypothetical "Gate" between their world and ours. A central figure in what would become known as the "Cthulhu Mythos" was Cthulhu itself: a High Priest of the Old Ones who lay "dead but dreaming" in a sarcophagus in the sunken city of R'lyeh.

The body of a creature somewhere between alive and dead, in a sarcophagus, and in telepathic contact with its human followers on Earth ... the images bleed over into the Joan Grant mummy-as-battery vision and the ritual that eventually would be developed on that basis by the K'rla Cell. The charged emotional and psychological state of Frater Kephra-ma-Ast in a state of bondage and near-total sensory deprivation except for the weird chants and other sounds emitted by Soror Maiat mimicked not only the human abductee of alien forces, but the state of Cthulhu itself in his deep entombment. Just as Cthulhu remained in contact with his worshippers through dreams, so did Frater Kephra-ma-Ast wend his way—blindly, but aware—through the Tunnel of Niantiel on his way to sunken R'lyeh.

The Death Posture is an attempt to jump out of normal human waking consciousness and arrive at a place that cannot be found on any map, not even maps of the mind. It is a state of pure perception, without conscious editing of the experience or the process. One abandons the five senses entirely. One is dead to the world, but not in the way we stand around the body of a corpse that does not react to our speech, but the experience of death *by the dead*: a seeing, a perceiving that takes place in the absence of the usual external stimuli. It is a brain falling back into itself, a mind confronted with its own contents unmixed with the conflicting messages coming through from the wide world. Slowly, form and function are separated from each other; purpose becomes a quaint idea of the first humans to walk erect. In the Death Posture one is in the moment completely, without external referents, without memories for comparison, and there is a moment of complete terror when one realizes that one's identity has evaporated until there is only Nothing left.

That is the moment when the Big Bang implodes rather than explodes, and the entire universe comes rushing back to its primary form, the *materia prima* becoming the *prima materia*. The *Bnnt* of ancient Egypt. And you see the Origin.

And when you see the Origin, everything that comes after is simply shadow.

CHAPTER SEVEN

In the Tunnels of Set

While the concept of the Tunnels had been anticipated to some extent in Qabalistic writings (primarily those of Isaac Luria as interpreted by Hayim Vital) and in Crowley's own *libri*,[43] it was Kenneth Grant who fleshed them out in his *Nightside of Eden* (1977). They were not referred to as such before Grant, but their existence was implied in studies of the *Qlippot* (תּוֹפִיְלֹק),[44] the "shells" or "husks" of Lurianic Qabalah that were broken pieces of one of the original sephiroth, specifically the sephirah Geburah, the fifth sephirah on the Tree of Life. That specificity is one explanation given for why the Pentagram is such a powerful symbol for use against the Dark forces of the Tree, as the *Qlippot* were pieces of the fifth sphere that was shattered in a catastrophic event prior to the Creation as we know it. However, they are not evil in the sense that one says that demons are "evil" but rather are the shards of an ancient Creation that still remain at the boundaries of this one and which, paradoxically, contain sparks of the Divine within them.

There is another possibility for the reason why the Pentagram is a potent symbol for counteracting qlippotic forces, however, and that is the relationship between the Golden Mean, the five triangles that make

---

43   See for instance *Liber CCXXXI*, in *Equinox* I, vii.
44   Singular הָפָּלְק or *qlippa.*

up the Pentagram, and the square root of 5: a relationship that further can be divined from the writings of H. P. Lovecraft which speak of an alien geometry of 5 dimensions. This is especially evident in his novella, *At The Mountains of Madness*, where he mentions the number 5 fifty-two times in different contexts (number of planes, number of men, number of tentacles, etc.), such as in the following:

> According to the carvings from which we had made our map, the desired tunnel-mouth could not be much more than a quarter-mile from where we stood; the intervening space shewing solid-looking buildings quite likely to be penetrable still at a sub-glacial level. The opening itself would be in the basement—on the angle nearest the foothills—of a vast five-pointed structure of evidently public and perhaps ceremonial nature, which we tried to identify from our aërial survey of the ruins. No such structure came to our minds as we recalled our flight, hence we concluded that its upper parts had been greatly damaged, or that it had been totally shattered in an ice-rift we had noticed. In the latter case the tunnel would probably turn out to be choked, so that we would have to try the next nearest one—the one less than a mile to the north. The intervening river-course prevented our trying any of the more southerly tunnels on this trip; and indeed, if both of the neighbouring ones were choked it was doubtful whether our batteries would warrant an attempt on the next northerly one—about a mile beyond our second choice.

And:

> He has on rare occasions whispered disjointed and irresponsible things about "the black pit," "the carven rim," "the proto-shog-goths," "the windowless solids with five dimensions," "the name-less cylinder," "the elder pharos," "Yog-Sothoth," "the primal white jelly," "the colour out of space," "the wings," "the eyes in darkness," "the moon-ladder," "the original, the eternal, the undy-ing," and other bizarre conceptions; but when he is fully himself he repudiates all this and attributes it to his curious and macabre

reading of earlier years. Danforth, indeed, is known to be among the few who have ever dared go completely through that worm-riddled copy of the *Necronomicon* kept under lock and key in the college library.

The idea that the Pentagram is a potent symbol for protection is confirmed by Aleister Crowley's reworking of the Golden Dawn's Lesser Banishing Ritual of the Pentagram as the *Star Ruby* ritual, with its opening line in Greek: "*Apo pantos kakodaimonos!*" or "Away every demon!" (or "evil spirit"). The connection between the *Star Ruby* ritual and the K'rla Cell ritual will be amplified below but suffice it to say now that the number of the Liber is *XXV* or 25, which—as Crowley himself points out—is 5 x 5, or 5^2. It is the *square root of 5* that becomes an essential element of the equation that gives us the Golden Mean, as we have seen.

There is also the traditional Qabalistic concept of the *Sitra Ahra* (ארחא ארטס), the "dark side" of the Tree of Life, which is considered to be the domain of a "Negative" or even demonic Tree: the opposite of the more familiar Tree of Life. According to Grant, he became aware of this possibility when reading the works of Frater Achad (Charles Stansfeld Jones) and realizing that the flat, two-dimensional Tree could be represented as a three-dimensional construction. Once that was realized, it was a short step from there to the understanding that the paths that linked one "sphere" (*sephirah*) to the other were also three-dimensional: they were tunnels rather than paths, and the tunnels on the reverse side of the Tree formed a structure that was totally unlike the obverse although connected to it in ways that could not be ascertained if all one did was "walk" the Tree in its daylight form. To walk the Tree in its Nightside form was to walk the Tunnels of Set: the Egyptian deity of opposition, darkness, and night.

What Grant had not expressed in his published work was that a three-dimensional Tree implied a three-dimensional Qabalah, although

71

he was open to the suggestion that new approaches to Qabalah were absolutely necessary in the New Age:

> Unless occultism becomes creative in the sense of opening up new approaches, modifying and developing traditional concepts and generally revealing a little more of that Supreme Goddess whose identity is hidden behind the veil of Isis, Kali, Nuit, or Sothis, there will be stagnation in the swamp of beliefs rendered inert by the recent swift acceleration of humanity's consciousness, which is little short of miraculous. If the science of the unmanifest is not to remain grounded at a prepubescent stage, while the manifested sciences soar into space, the mature occultist must put aside the toys of superstition and face fearlessly the Trees of Eternity whose trunks and branches glow with solar fire, but whose roots are nourished in the dark.[45]

In this way, Grant had thrown down the gauntlet. He could see where science was heading, and this was way before the advent of the personal computer and the Internet, before advances in Artificial Intelligence and the smartphone. Occultism was in danger of being abandoned as a quaint reminder of a pre-technological age as science seemed every day more and more like magic. As Arthur C. Clarke famously observed: "Any sufficiently advanced form of technology is indistinguishable from magic."[46] Grant understood that and was concerned lest we throw the baby out with the bathwater. Magic is about much more than technological advances or scientific discoveries; it is a spiritual process that involves the whole being—the mind as well as the body, the world as well as the temple—but it deals with *every aspect* of experience, including those we normally would avoid or suppress. It is not opposed to science, but on the contrary welcomes each new development and discovery as further points of illumination on

45 Kenneth Grant, *Nightside of Eden*, Skoob Books, London, 1994 (1977), p.4.
46 Arthur C. Clarke, "Hazards of Prophecy: The Failure of Imagination" in *Profiles of the Future: An Inquiry into the Limits of the Possible,* Harper & Row, New York, 1962.

the path. In fact, the old, artificial and cultural divisions between science and magic—or alchemy and chemistry, Tantra and neurobiology, etc.—no longer obtain. Humanity is on the threshold of discovery of a "grand unified theory" of consciousness and physics, and it is entirely possible that the occult disciplines either hold a key to that discovery or will be irrevocably changed by it.

This is all a necessary preamble to what follows. It was the extension of traditional forms of Qabalah into multiple dimensions that inspired Grant to focus more clearly on the forms of magic that had been abandoned or cordoned off as "evil" or "demonic" or even "satanic." There is no "evil" science; there is only the application of science to unwholesome ends. The same is true of occultism. Concepts like "black magic" serve only as placeholders to differentiate traditional, "acceptable" forms of magic from forms that society feels are scarier, more sinister, even deadly. When one goes to a psychiatrist it is to uncover the unconscious, darker elements of one's personality and not to obtain friendly confirmation of one's conscious biases. Magic should be the same, and for Typhonians it *is* the same. Hence, the concentration on Tantra—which has always had an ambiguous relationship with traditional religion, whether Buddhist or Hindu—and on Afro-Caribbean forms (such as Vodun, Santeria, Palo Mayombe, Candomble, etc.), which traditionally have been proscribed or suppressed by colonial authorities.[47] What the occult historian James Webb called "rejected knowledge" in describing occultism itself[48] could also be interpreted as "rejected forms of consciousness," along with psychotropic drugs and "deviant" sexuality.

---

47   Ironically, the act of suppressing another culture's religion, gods, rituals, and artifacts gives them greater power in the collective unconscious of the suppressor. The persecution of Christians during the religion's first three hundred years gave it an emotional energy—made of Christianity a neurosis if not a psychosis—that exploded in religious wars, the Inquisition, and the murder of "witches." This was exacerbated by Christianity's own eventual suppression of the sex instinct, and their suppression of the gods of Europe. Thus, the old adage is proven true with time: the god of one religion becomes the devil of the next.

48   James Webb, *The Occult Establishment*, Open Court, LaSalle (IL), (1976) 1991, p.15.

The Tunnels of Set are pathways on the Dark side of the Tree, and therefore they represent forces that medieval occultists would have termed demons. They are more than that, however. Think of the sewer systems in any city; think of subterranean cable and water systems; steam tunnels; all necessary, but all below street level, below conscious awareness. The difference is this: these systems are built as the city is being built. In our context, however, the Tunnels pre-exist the City and are integral to it. The City is an outgrowth of the Tunnel system: it is the phenomenal world as a manifestation of the noumenal world.

Grant approached this idea by referencing scientific discoveries pertaining to "dark matter" and even black holes as a way of explaining or clarifying what he intended by the Tree of Death/Da'ath, the Night-side or Dark Side of the Tree of Life. One could argue that even such phenomena as dark matter and black holes are discoverable through instruments and machines and as such may be part of the phenomenal and not the noumenal world which is the domain of the Nightside Tree, but as most of us do not understand the math or the science behind either dark matter or black holes it is probably a moot point!

What we can take away, however, is the undeniable fact that the current state of Qabalistic training is inadequate to a full understand-ing of the phenomenal world and thereby puts Qabalists at risk of a lopsided or imperfect perception of their field. This does not mean that previous Qabalistic knowledge is incorrect, only that it does not go far enough to accommodate all the data concerning the mathematics of multi-dimensional existence. It also implies that those magicians with a deeper grasp of multi-dimensional Qabalah will be empowered in ways that Old Aeon occultists can not imagine.

Grant was fully aware of the Qabalistic antecedents to his own sys-tem, as well as the Tantric and other Indian ideas about the structure of the universe. His approach was not to parrot these ideas without having explored them himself first. The expedition comes first—to those realms marked "here there be monsters"—and then come the maps. One could say that Grant was recruiting explorers who would discover new lands beyond (or behind) the Tree of Life, and those explorers would return with new topologies and new maps. He availed himself completely of the parallel research of Michael Bertiaux and his novel approach to the Tree and to the Mauve Zone: an area that has been linked to Lovecraft's ideas concerning the Rub al-Khali, the "Empty Quarter" of the Saudi desert. The Tunnels of Set are pathways that exist on the reverse side of the Tree, sometimes called the Tree of Death or the Tree of *Da'ath*, in the realm of the *qlippot*, and they are analogous to those pathways through the desert that Bedouin tribesmen know and travel even though they do not appear on the maps with which City people are familiar.

Grant acknowledged[49] that the K'rla Cell traveled in the specific Tunnel known as Niantiel. This is the Tunnel that connects the Darkside Netzach (known to some as *Harab Serapel*) to the Darkside Tiphareth (known as *Thagirion*), the path represented by the Tarot trump *Death* (and the Hebrew letter *Nun*) on the Tree of Life. In Grant's understanding, the sphere known as Tiphareth to the Qabalists is one of the portals to the Darkside of the Tree, another being the "non-sephirah" Da'ath. Recourse to *Liber DCCCLXVIII* (*Viarvm Viae*) will show that the path of Niantiel is described as "The Preparation of the Corpse for the Tomb" which obviously is what the Egyptian mummification process represents. It is also connected to *Liber XXV*, otherwise known as *Star Ruby*. This is an echo of the novel by Bram Stoker, *Jewel of the Seven Stars*, in which the cross-dressing Queen Tera possesses a ruby ring engraved with seven stars. This novel was unknown to Jeffrey and Ruth at the time, but possibly was known to Crowley.[50]

The Egyptian priestess-as-mummy-as-sexual battery episode mentioned by Grant in *Cults of the Shadow*—which gave Evans the idea for the K'rla Cell ritual after being inspired to do so by Karla herself—is

---

49   Kenneth Grant, *Beyond the Mauve Zone*, p. 95.
50   This novel will be discussed at length in the following chapter.

taken from the autobiography *Gate of Dreams* by Charles Beatty. Beatty was the husband of novelist Joan Grant—author of the best-seller *Winged Pharaoh*—and the episode was actually an experience of one of Beatty's former lives. Beatty had been "haunted" in a sense by several of his past incarnations who turned out to be women. The Egyptian priestess was experienced by Joan Grant when she tried to understand the core of the problem, and she turned out to be one of Beatty's earlier incarnations. Thus, it is no stretch to understand how a man, dressing as a woman, would be able to recreate that episode so faithfully.

It is worth pointing out that Joan Grant (as a teenager) had met Aleister Crowley on at least one occasion; and that she and her husband Charles Beatty were close personal friends of occult novelist Dennis Wheatley.[51] In fact, if it had not been for Wheatley's heavy promotion of *Winged Pharaoh,* it is doubtful she ever would have become the well-known novelist and "reincarnationist" she did. Beatty had also met Hans Holzer and famous "pop" witch Sybil Leek, which also reveals connections to the Wicca movement that was heavily influenced by Crowley's friend and O.T.O. initiate Gerald Gardner. The more one investigates and researches these connections, the tighter they seem.

These connections, however, are often the trace evidence of a deeper system at work. Like coincidence and synchronicity, they operate below the level of conscious awareness. This is one of the reasons why so many "conspiracy theories" fall apart upon inspection. The "conspiracy" is often not of a group of men in a back room, smoking cigars and plotting murder and mayhem; rather the conspiracy is a result of interlocking forces, perhaps at a psycho-spiritual "quantum" level: the level of dreams, of nightmares, of hallucinations and visions and hauntings; non-local; entangled. Of the death posture, mummies bound alive, and alien abductions.

---

51   These references and more are to be found in Charles Beatty's book, *Gate of Dreams*, Geoffrey Chapman, London, 1972.

The Typhonian magician in this context is a lot like Captain Willard in *Apocalypse Now!*, going up-river to find Colonel Kurtz in the jungles, past the bridge, on the other side of the wire, in hostile territory. Those jungles contain invisible enemies, throwing spears and firing automatic weapons into your fragile PBR. And when you find Colonel Kurtz, and pick up the manuscript—the *liber*, the word of the Magus—you realize that Colonel Kurtz, the man you just killed, is you.

And you reverse that old adage: The devil of one religion becomes the god of the next.

This is what the K'rla Cell was about. They dove in, struggling at first with the structure of the Ritual, its components and moving parts, finding their rhythm, but the core idea was there, fully formed, and eventually they got it right. There was no suppression of ideas or of action. What they were doing was dangerous for any level of initiate. There are UFO carnival barkers out there who promise their fans that they can contact UFOs at will; they bring them out to the desert—for a considerable fee—and spend the night watching the sky and "summoning" the aliens. What the Cell did was far more serious and potentially far more dangerous: they were recreating the circumstances of an alien *abduction*.

Moreover, they were doing so within the context of the Cthulhu Mythos, and in a ritual structure based on both Thelema and Santeria, not to mention Tantra. It was a celebration of the Typhonian system, with all its infamous components working together: invocations of the orishas; Thelemic banishings; incoherent mumblings of unintelligible chants mixed with the names of the Lovecraftian gods; prolonged sexual stimulation nearly to the point of ejaculation; tight bonds, blindness, gags. Darkness. Silence. An atmosphere of imminent threat, and of sinister alien presence. Dislocation. Disorientation.

Dissociation.

The Tunnel was dark and perilous, as one might expect, but they were after Gold. There was no way to know ahead of time where that

Gold might be, or what it might look like. They were looking for trea-sure without a map. They knew where they were coming from and had a general idea of where they were going, but no way to know how long the journey would take—how many iterations of the ritual would be required—or what they would find when they reached the end.

When they finally reached their goal—saw "light at the end of the Tunnel" so to speak—Evans found himself awash in *numbers*. Num-bers, for a man who was generally innumerate (like most of us). These were numbers within numbers: proportions; ratios; a sea of flowing digits, decimals, square roots, sine, cosine, all going off on tangents. How could he explain what he saw? How could he communicate the enormity of the discovery? He was like the saint who saw the ineffable and found herself unable to describe what she saw because it was, well, ineffable. That's the point.

Like Jim Carrey in *The Number 23*, Evans started to see the Golden Mean everywhere, tantalizing him, beckoning him, and shin-ing through the verses of *Liber AL*; he was like a safecracker listening to all the tumblers click into place. He had found the Gold, a Gold somewhere between figurative and literal like any good Qabalah. The Golden Mean was everywhere; *Phi* was everywhere. Multiples of it, squares and cubes of it, reciprocals of it. The Fibonacci Series flowed around him like a halo spun of fractals and vibes or swinging like a pendulum on either side of *Phi*. It was the root of all the sacred architecture in the world, from Egypt to India, from Templar castles to Gothic cathedrals, and the architecture was forming crystalline struc-tures in his brain, re-forming him, *impregnating* him.

That is what Kenneth Grant called it, anyway, when informed of what had happened that fateful day in April 1984. He said Jeffrey Evans had been *impregnated* by the Old Ones. Well, it *was* consistent with the theme of the ritual, the alien abduction, for that is what many abductees have always claimed: that they had been impregnated by the aliens and their fetuses removed and cultivated like plants in test-tubes aboard a sterile spacecraft. And now Evans himself—Frater Kephra-Ma-Ast—had become a hybrid creation, his own nervous system fighting him all the way, the seizures increasing in number and strength; but the calculations and the formulas were implacable in their demands and like a character in a Lovecraft story Evans was being driven mad by the fifth-dimensional non-Euclidean geometry of the sunken cities he saw glittering with an unholy glamour in the eldritch Tunnel of Niantiel on the Other side of the Tree of Life.

He wrote about this to Kenneth Grant. He told him what he had discovered in long, complicated letters adorned with mathematical symbols and dripping with decimals and orishas and alien ichor, and Grant plucked "Phi" out of the stream of consciousness arithmetic and divined its meaning and published his meditation on it. The rest—the stunning realization that a mathematical code had been embedded in the very verse that demands "Divide, add, multiply, and understand"—remained misunderstood. Unfathomable. Grant's associate, charged with reading and summarizing the correspondence, did not communicate the revelation to his superior, either through incomprehension or disinterest—and Evans wondered why there was no acknowledgment of what he had seen sparkling in the Tunnel like a vein of ore in the hideous, Qliphotic darkness.

Evans wrote, and there was silence. Or, worse, complaints that he was *not* writing! Something was amiss, but that did not stop the K'rla Cell from working its Ritual, week after week, month after month. The architecture of Phi was being revealed and deconstructed, but like any ineffable secret it could not be communicated easily. It was as if the vision was purely internal, a figment of Evans's imagination or a by-product of the seizures and could not be shared with mortal humans. But this was not the case, as the following will attest.

When Levenda began a tentative correspondence with Evans in early 2019, and Evans began to share bits and pieces of the 1984 revelation with him, he thought the guy must be insane. He knew the K'rla Cell story from *Beyond the Mauve Zone*, of course, and knew this was the same Jeffrey Evans who had a whole chapter devoted to him in that book, and anyway they were both in South Florida, so he gave him the benefit of the doubt, took out his calculator and tried to reproduce the results.

They came out exactly as Evans had explained, every time. The Golden Mean *was* encoded in *Liber AL*, I:25, just where he said it would be.

Levenda had been familiar with the Golden Mean from previous research, especially where sacred geometry was concerned. He is a fan of the work of Louis Charpentier's book on the Gothic cathedral at Chartres[52], with all the discussion of the architecture serving as a kind of initiatory machine for those who understood the *mathematical* code. There was, however, no precedent for a study of sacred geometry in the written record of Thelema. It was treated, if at all, as a completely separate issue with no connection to Crowley's writings, to the Qabalah, to Tantra or anything else. This was suspicious, in a way, since the primary mover of Thelema in the public sphere is a secret society named after the Knights Templar, who arguably brought the concept of sacred geometry to Europe from the Middle East nearly a thousand years ago. And it was Dr John Dee, of Enochian magic fame so dear to Thelemites, who introduced the first translation of Euclid's *Elements* to an English-speaking audience and who was Euclid but the Father of Geometry? And Dee's partner in Enochian or Angelic magic was Edward Kelley, whom Aleister Crowley claimed as a previous incarnation. So ... why no sacred geometry in Thelema?

Was it again a question of innumeracy, of the lack of any kind of advanced education in mathematics beyond the more trivial arithmetic

---

52   Louis Charpentier, *The Mysteries of Chartres Cathedral*, Research Into Lost Knowledge Organisation, Hammersmith (UK),1972.

that informs basic Qabalah? Or was it, perhaps, due to the fact that Thelema has no actual buildings to call its own, no sacred temple space that can be arranged according to the principles of sacred geometry? That sounds a little harsh, but even Kenneth Grant conceived of a system of Order lodges that were independent power zones with no need of elaborate ritual initiations in the Masonic style, so basically no need for elaborate buildings, either. So that raises the question: is sacred architecture a "thing" if there are no buildings to materialize it?

The answer is a most emphatic "yes." Sacred architecture reveals the intricate relationship between human beings and their environment: both the terrestrial environment and the larger cosmic environment of which the Earth is a part. All one has to do is study the subject for a short time and one comes away with the understanding that each element of the human body—a major concern for Thelema, especially in the upper degrees—is represented by astral correspondences as demonstrated in works on yoga, Tantra, and the like. The medieval European occultists depicted the human body in exactly that way, as a glyph of the cosmos written in miniature, otherwise astrology—for instance—has no relevance to magic at all.

Buildings—sacred buildings, like churches and temples—are ways of representing this intimate correspondence and are also a means of heightening the experience of microcosm-macrocosm, of "as above, so below," and all the other ways in which magic serves to reinforce that connection, to "cause change to occur in conformity with Will." A temple is a way of enclosing space in such a way as to stimulate the senses and direct consciousness towards the inner workings of the physical world which is the gateway to the spiritual world. That is why the Lovecraftian emphasis on weird architecture is so revealing: it suggests other ways of seeing reality, of experiencing our relationship to a cosmos that is largely unknown to us, and mostly misunderstood. A temple built according to Lovecraftian principles of architecture would surely stimulate experiences of an otherworldly, even frightening nature. A temple built according to the principles of sacred architecture—notably based on permutations of the Golden Mean—would stimulate experiences of a different nature, one that would integrate the soul with its physical counterpart.

Kenneth Grant, however, saw a little further than most in this regard. He understood that even the temple has a basement where all the broken things are kept. The Tree of Life has a dark side, a suppressed or repressed dimension, replete with crawling, amphibious creatures from earlier stages of human evolution. Thus, even the sacred architecture of our ancestors—the Gothic cathedrals, the mosques, the round Templar churches—conceal deeper, darker truths as well.

Charpentier alluded to as much when he wrote about the "Black Virgin" found in a kind of grotto in the mound over which Chartres Cathedral was built: a pagan survival which made the land on which Chartres Cathedral was built so holy in the first place. The Black Virgin predated the arrival of Christianity to Chartres—according to Charpentier—and was a place of pilgrimage for centuries. There is a well in the crypt said to have curative properties and the statue of a woman with a child on her knee had been at one time carved into the trunk of a tree above the well. The statue was blackened with age and bore an inscription in Latin: *Virgini pariturae*: "the Virgin who will give birth."[53] Charpentier claims this was erected by the Druids, before the Romans came and possibly added the inscription. A statue of a woman with a child could as easily represent Isis with Horus as Mary with Jesus, of course.

And the official name of Chartres Cathedral is *Cathédrale Notre-Dame de Chartres,* which means "Cathedral of Our Lady of Chartres," so it is anyone's guess which specific "Our Lady" is intended. But the point to be made is that the cathedral was built over a spot sacred to pagan faith, a spot that had nothing at all to do with the religion or

---

53   Louis Charpentier, op. cit., pp 17-19.

the rituals of the Catholic Church but was still considered—somewhat superstitiously, perhaps?—a source of supernatural power and energy. It was repressed, in a way, located deep within the bowels of the church, and its ancient message reinterpreted for the incoming foreign religion. The 33-meter-deep well was called *Puits des Saints-Forts* or "Well of the Strong Saints" and is said to refer to a legend that Christian martyrs were thrown into the well to die.

Deep wells, tunnels, death, a labyrinth, conversion by sword, a temple of light built (with the Golden Mean) over a temple of darkness. A Black Virgin:

"I am black but lovely, O daughters of Jerusalem..."
Song of Solomon, I:5.
"My color is black to the blind..." *Liber AL* I:60
"Behold! the rituals of the old time are black." *Liber AL* II:5
Indeed.

The *Song of Solomon* was a main focus of the father of the First Crusade, Saint Bernard of Clairvaux. He wrote extensively on it. Spoke sermons about it. He also chartered the Knights Templar and sent them to the site of Solomon's Temple in Jerusalem and the rest is history. That first group of Templars—who had taken vows of poverty, chastity, and obedience—had returned to France and started building Gothic cathedrals all over the country. It was from the idol the Templars were accused of worshipping—Baphomet—that Aleister Crowley took his motto as the head of the British section of the O.T.O.

So why don't Thelemites the world over take a closer look at the tradition they hail from?

Because the Germans who created the O.T.O. focused on the sexual and the Middle Eastern aspect of the Order and, to a certain extent, their reputation as Satanists. The Templars were accused of all sorts of heresy and of sexual "deviance"—homosexuality in this case—believed to have been adopted from their contacts with various Middle Eastern sects. Add to that their supposed worship of an idol called Baphomet and you had all the ingredients necessary for a really edgy cult.

As we now know, however, the Templars were recently exonerated from these charges. No weird sex. No idol of Baphomet. No devil worship. Just a lot of money—they more or less invented the modern international banking system and the letter of credit—and a lot of real estate. Neither of which are exactly hallmarks of Thelema today.

But to ignore the Templar contribution to the development of the Gothic cathedral just because you can't build one yourself is to miss the most important elements: the sacred architecture; the application of mathematical principles to consciousness; and the integration of the Crypt with the Nave, the Dark Tree with the Tree of Life.

Jeffrey Evans, Ruth Keenan, and the K'rla Cell made that connection, unaware at the time what was happening or where they would eventually wind up. This is what made their accomplishment all the more impressive: there was no preconceived idea of what they would find. No one could have predicted it. A code buried in *Liber AL*, moreover one with definite links to an ancient mystery tradition? A code that not even Crowley himself had discovered (although he always suspected it was there)? A code you would need a scientific calculator to discover, but once you did you couldn't forget it?

And, as if to reinforce that discovery, once Jeffrey Evans began to look at other verses, he found further verification. In fact, a simple calculation involving the infamous verse *AL* III:76 would reinforce the connection between Thelema's most sacred document and the very depths of the Tunnels of Set, thus confirming that Kenneth Grant had been on the right track all along.

CHAPTER EIGHT

The Body Mandala

The *bissu* are imagined to be hermaphroditic beings who embody female and male elements. While it is enough that one's body is imagined hermaphroditic, while often being anatomically male, *bissu* consciously dress in ways that highlight male and female characteristics. ... It is essential that *bissu* have good connections with the spirit world in order to make contact with the gods.[54]

W hile the discovery of the Golden Section lurking like a Minotaur in the Labyrinth of *Liber AL* is the focus of this volume, we would be remiss if we did not address one of the most critical elements of the ritual itself, which involved the biologically-male Jeffrey Evans functioning as a Priestess and the biologically-female Ruth Keenan as a Priest. There has been some controversy in Thelemic circles of late over the issue of gender fluidity and gender normativity—particularly with reference to the Gnostic Mass—and the reader will be grateful, presumably, that we will not dip into those dangerous waters specifically, but nonetheless several of the issues we discuss in the pages that follow are relevant to that discussion as well.

---

54   Sharyn Graham, "Sex, Gender , and Priests in South Sulawesi, Indonesia," in *IIAS Newsletter*, #29, November 2004, p. 27.

There are two categories of gender identity that the rite of the K'rla Cell introduces, and these are what we may call "performative" categories, i.e., the actual experience of gender non-conformity within the context of the ritual and the application of that non-conformity to the performance of the ritual.

One of these categories involves the Egyptian "motif" or element of mummification, which—deliberately or accidentally—reprises many of the *fin-de-siècle* attitudes and understandings of ancient Egyptian views of sexuality. We will find that they have an interesting context from the point of view of Typhonian magic.

The next category is that of the history—in religious studies circles—of the role that intersexed individuals have played in the magical rituals of their respective cultures and times, from the most ancient records available to us (those of Sumer and Egypt) to the Corybantes and other religious sects of the ancient Middle East and the Mediterranean, to the hijra of India and to related shamanistic societies of South East Asia. (We can also add to that list the indigenous North American concept of the "Two Spirits" or "Double Spirits": the idea that two genders [spirits] can live in one body.)

We will examine each of these in turn, but we also will expand the current level of discourse to include two seemingly unrelated ideas: the "body mandala" as depicted in Tibetan and South Asian sources, and the idealization of the Body of God in Qabalistic sources. As we will see, these have relevance not only to the specific ritual of the K'rla Cell but also to Typhonian practices generally. They represent an amplification of the psycho-biology as illustrated in the Trilogies, but also returns the focus from an external Other—the Tunnels of Set, traversed by the K'rla Cell and other Typhonian groups—to the internal Other represented by locations in the physical body of the initiates.

It may seem somewhat odd that a philosophy that embraces Tantra and "sex magic" has focused so little on the human body and its esoteric correlates and correspondences, and has not addressed any of the deeper implications of gender. Any aspect of the human experience that has been socially constructed rather than science-based is vulnerable to a New Aeon re-evaluation and re-interpretation, for Thelema claims to be the new dispensation with its resultant rejection of old systems of belief and practice. There is a danger that the desire to create a rigid hierarchical system of belief in imitation of older forms of lodge, church, and temple will inadvertently enshrine old ideas about social organization and social roles with only a minimum of difference between the previous Aeon and the present one. Thus, it would seem that a full-on attempt at a reconstruction of gender would have the added benefit of realigning Thelemic organizations generally in such a manner as to take advantage of New Aeon systems of belief and practice in ways that were not imagined before. Indeed, if Thelemites are correct, the New Aeon eventually will abandon the old forms anyway—so it would be better to find oneself ahead of the curve.

However, that does not mean that New Aeon perspectives on gender, human anatomy, and sexuality are without precedent. As we will demonstrate in our chapter "The Golden Section and the Fibonacci Series," the human body has been a focus of occult attention for millennia and is seen as a copy of the cosmos (or, at least, the solar system) in miniature. The famous illustrations of the man in the pentagram by Agrippa, for instance, are excellent examples of this but there are much older texts that relate the human body to non-human exemplars. At the very least, we can consider the body of Nuit, the Star Goddess, who arches over the world from horizon to horizon and whose body is filled with stars. She is obviously not a human being, but human form is attributed to her. The same is true for the other Egyptian deities who are depicted either in human form, or in animal form, or some hybrid of the two. There has been very little analysis of this type of representation in terms of the selection of humans and/or animals as placeholders for gods. There seems to be an assumption that the qualities of humans and animals—occupation of space, freedom of movement, other potential powers, and capabilities—are as close as the ancient artists can come to reflecting the attributes of gods.

In Sumer, arguably the oldest human civilization for which we have a written record, the gods are also depicted in human form but with the addition of the "star" sign to indicate their divine (i.e., non-human) status. And in Genesis we read that humans were "created in the image and likeness of God." (Genesis 1:27)

This equation finds itself referenced again in Asia. In Tibet, we learn that in the seventh century CE, the King of Tibet—inspired by his wife, the Chinese princess Wencheng—identified the topography of Tibet as the body of a demoness. Presumably, Princess Wencheng was introducing him to the practice of feng shui, or geomancy as it is sometimes called in the West, and he began to erect temples at various points on the body of the demoness, that is, at landmarks considered to represent her anatomical features. In this way was born the concept of "body mandala." It later expanded to include ideas about the human body as a mandala, and the location of various deities at specific points on the body or areas of the body.

The following is a typical illustration of the "demoness"—also called the "Earth Goddess"—as defined by Tibetan tradition, with temples located at specific points on the "Body" of Tibet:

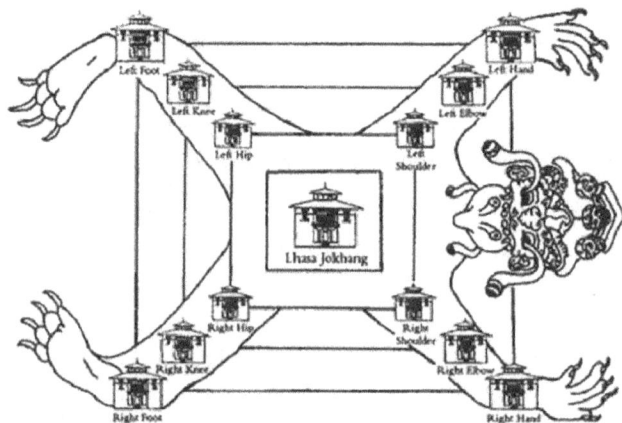

Kenneth Grant wrote about specific points on the Body using the Ayurvedic term *marmas*. For instance, in *Beyond the Mauve Zone*, he defines them as follows:

> The stellar anatomy of the subtle body in man consists in *marmas* or cross-currents of energy which appear to clairvoyant perception as a network of magnetic vectors, star-waves and lunar lattices common to cosmic power zones throughout the solar system.[55]

The identification of the *marmas* of the human subtle anatomy with cosmic power zones is important as it reinforces the idea that the human body has an equivalent to terrestrial topography, which is itself equivalent to an astral or extra-terrestrial topography or anatomy. It is common to see the Qabalistic Tree of Life, for instance, overlaid on a diagram of the human body to reinforce the "microcosm-macro-cosm" equivalence. Indeed, Qabalistic ideas about the Divine or Primordial Man—Adam Kadmon—reprise this equivalence, and so does the concept known as *Shi'ur Komah*, translated as the "Body" or the "Height" or "Measure" of God. If we consult Gershom Scholem, we find that discussions of the *Shi'ur Komah* segue into discussions of the *tselem*, a Hebrew word that is difficult to translate but which seems to mean—according to Scholem—the "astral body" of the mystic. In fact, Scholem goes even further by citing authorities who claim that this "astral body" is in reality their own higher selves[56]: the closest Qabalistic equivalent we have to the Golden Dawn and A∴A∴ concept of the "Holy Guardian Angel," a term taken from *The Book of the Sacred Magic of Abramelin the Mage* in its translation by Golden Dawn co-founder MacGregor Mathers.[57] However, we can see that the

---

55   Kenneth Grant, *Beyond the Mauve Zone*, Starfire Publishing, London, (1999) 2016, pp.111-112.
56   This startling claim is made in Gershom Scholem, *On the Mystical Shape of the Godhead*, Schocken Books, New York, (1962) 1991, pp 251-273.
57   See, however, the excellent new translation by Georg Dehn, *The Book of Abramelin: A new translation*, Ibis Press, Lake Worth (FL), 2015 which provides much-needed context and amplification of this important text.

concept of a "higher self," who may appear at times to particularly enlightened and accomplished mystics and magicians, is much older than the *Abramelin* example. In fact, Scholem references the infamous volume of the tenth-eleventh century work *Picatrix* (original title *Ghayat al-Hakim*) as another source for descriptions of this "higher self" or "angel" and, indeed, we find in Book Three, Chapter Six of the *Picatrix* the following statement:

> So Hermes asked the spirit, who are you? And he answered him;
> I'm your perfect nature. If you desire to see me you have to call me
> by my name.[58]

The entirety of Chapter Six in the *Picatrix* describes this "perfected being" with references and proof texts from Aristotle, Hermes, and Socrates. It is important to point out that in all of these examples the spirit or angel appears in human—or humanoid—form. Thus, the concept is put forward that magicians are not complete without union with their Angel: that face-to-face confrontation with the Angel is a necessary stage in the process of initiation. This is evidence that the idea of the Holy Guardian Angel was not merely a conceit of the Golden Dawn or the *Book of the Sacred Magic of Abramelin the Mage,* but has been acknowledged in traditions going back a thousand years or more.

This idea of a human Body that is sacralized—reinforced with images of deities and supernatural essences, including an "astral body" or a "Holy Guardian Angel"—is an optimistic approach to theology: the understanding that the Body is either perfectible or that its perfection is merely a question of accurately perceiving it as what it is: the image and likeness of God. The sacralized human Body then becomes an image of the land in which it finds itself, the planet on which it lives, and the cosmic system in which its planet finds its place.

---

58   Hashem Atallah & Geylan Holmquest, trans. *Picatrix: Ghayat al-Hakim: The Goal of the Wise,* Volume II, Ouroboros Press, Seattle, 2008, p. 56.

This sacralized Body is not, however, gendered. It is the same for every human being, no matter what race or gender it was born into or adopted later in life. It is as much part of a human being as breath, heart rate, and growth. The same is true, of course, for kundalini: the Serpent Power said to reside at the base of the spine (or a spot in the subtle body analogous to the base of the spine) and, with proper training by the adept, to rise along the chakras until it reaches the head. Again, there is no question of gender here, neither male nor female nor any form of gender identity. The existence of kundalini is a given for everyone.

Thus, when Jeffrey Evans decided to assume his female persona as Priestess in the K'rla Cell Ritual he was not defying accepted magical practice but, in reality, acting in accordance with an ancient tradition of cross-dressing priests, priestesses, and shamans going back thousands of years and found in every corner of the world.

We know that Aleister Crowley himself was—as would be said today—"gender fluid," especially when it came to magical rituals. His female persona, Alys Cusack, was used as a *nom-de-plume* for various literary works as well as to indicate his level of sexual availability at his Abbey of Thelema at Cefalu.[59] The male assumption of a female persona does not always mean the person is homosexual and, in cases of transvestism or cross-dressing, the male is often heterosexual: the female clothing and female imagery are not intended to attract men for sexual purposes but provide psychological relief in other ways. Crowley was famously bisexual or, one might say, omnisexual, but he made a point to incorporate many (if not all) of his sexual encounters within the framework of magical ritual. In this, he sensed a current running through occultism that is otherwise unspeakable in the sense that there is no standard vocabulary to express what it is or how it works except through symbols and allusions.

---

59 As we all know, he would post a sign over his bed at the Abbey that said "Alys Cusack is Hot at Home" with the letter "H" in "Hot" that could be replaced with "N" to read "Not at Home." Crowley was usually the passive partner in homosexual acts.

To get a better grasp of what this is, we can remember that transvestism is a sign of occult ability in many cultures. This does not necessarily include homosexuality, by the way, although it can and has done
so throughout history.

A good introduction to the field can be found in "Priests of the
Goddess: Gender Transgression in Ancient Religions" by Will Roscoe.
In this paper,[60] published by the University of Chicago in its *History
of Religions* series, we find many citations involving cross-dressing
priests and priestesses in ancient Egypt, Sumer, Anatolia, the Roman
Empire, and elsewhere in the ancient world. The most famous, of
course, were the *galli* who were priests of the mystery religions of
Cybele and Attis who were despised by the early Christians more for
their cross-dressing than for their devotion to mysterious gods. Roscoe
goes further, relating the *galli* (some of whom castrated themselves) to
the transvestite priests of Inanna and Ishtar (known as *kalû, kurgarrû,*
or *assinnu*) and all the way to the *hijra* of India. It is relevant to this
study to point out that the rituals of the transvestite priests of Sumer,
Akkad, and Anatolia involved ecstatic trances, often to the accompani-
ment of flutes and drums. This was not the careful, measured, English
drawing-room magic of the Golden Dawn but the energetic "derange-
ment of the senses" (a "divine madness") we have witnessed among
the Afro-Caribbean rites of Santeria and Vodun (or referenced in the
writings of Austin Osman Spare and Kenneth Grant). However, even
in the latter examples, these rituals are never simply ad hoc affairs of
wild music and orgiastic expression but are carefully designed ahead
of time, albeit with sufficient room for whatever improvisation might
prove necessary as the trances continue.

---

60   Will Roscoe, "Priests of the Goddess: Gender Transgression in Ancient Religion," in *History of
Religions*, Vol. 35, No. 3 (Feb., 1996), 195-230. See also Voula Lambropoulou, "Reversal of Gender
Roles in Ancient Greece and Venezuela," in B. Berggreen & N. Marinatos, eds., *Greece & Gender*,
Bergen, 1995: ISBN 82-91626-00-6, pp. 149-154, for a discussion of transvestism in rituals designed
for initiation or other specific purposes rather than reflecting a total transformation or lifestyle where
transvestism is purely performative.

In India, the hijra are in a similar, liminal state as regards their position in society. They are considered devotees of the mother goddess Bahuchārā Mātā, and while they are considered neither male nor female but some "other" gender, their blessings are sought after for fertility and childbirth. However, crossing a hijra for any reason might mean becoming the target of a curse or spell. They also perform music with drums, flutes, and other instruments just like their counterparts in the Mediterranean and the Near East. We have witnessed the same presence of transvestite musicians in Indonesia, in particular in Yogyakarta on the predominantly Muslim island of Java. In fact, Indonesia has a long history of transvestite and gender-transgressive shamans and performers that predates Islamic influence and may be attributable to their prior history as an extension of the South Asian subcontinent and known as "Far India."

Gender nonconformity is seen as contributing to an altered perception of reality such that the transgendered individual is believed to be in contact with supernatural forces. Jeffrey Evans was aware of his cross-dressing nature since a very young age and in South or Southeast Asia he would have been allowed to indulge that nature, albeit in such a way as to isolate him from gender-normative society and relegate him to a life in a hijra community under the leadership of a guru. As it was, in the United States he was able to change his name so that he could drive and otherwise function legally as a female. Kenneth Grant was aware of Evans's status as a cross-dresser from their first meeting in December 1977, and his reaction was interested and curious and without judgment. He had no problem with it nor did he have a problem with Evans functioning as a Priestess during the K'rla Cell rituals.

The interesting aspect of this case is the selection of the Egyptian motif for the ritual. While inspired by the episode in Grant's *Cults of the Shadow*, which was itself referencing a vision of the author Joan Grant (no relation to Kenneth), it nonetheless has elements of a specific theme that has been popular in English and American fiction for a century.

Eleanor Dobson[61] provides an interesting context for our study of the K'rla Cell. Her article explores how fantasies about ancient Egypt (some of them created by amateur archaeologists themselves) influenced a generation of artists and writers who focused on the sexualization of certain aspects of what was seen as Egyptian culture and religion. These fantasies can be traced to a handful of very influential novels of the late nineteenth and early twentieth centuries, including one by Bram Stoker, the author of *Dracula*.

This was *The Jewel of Seven Stars*, published in 1903. It concerns the discovery of a female mummy—called Tera—by an Egyptologist who has a daughter nearly identical in appearance to the mummy, who then becomes psychically connected to the dead Egyptian queen. The novel was published in 1903, the same year that Howard Carter discovered the tomb of Queen Hatshepsut, the only female pharaoh in history. In the novel, the body of Queen Tera has been remarkably well-preserved to the point that her beauty is obvious to all who see her and her resemblance to the archaeologist's own daughter is undeniable. The daughter was born on the same day that her father discovered Queen Tera's tomb.

The real Queen Hatshepsut was known to dress as a man in order to emphasize her rulership in a country and an era where a female monarch was an incredible anomaly. Her cross-dressing extended to a fake beard as well as masculine attire. In the novel, we read about the fictitious Queen Tera:

> In the Chamber of the sarcophagus were pictures and writings to show that she had achieved victory over Sleep. Indeed, there was everywhere a symbolism, wonderful even in a land and an age of

---

61   Eleanor Dobson, "Cross-Dressing Scholars and Mummies in Drag: Egyptology and Queer Identity," in *Aegyptiaca* 4 (2019) pp. 33-54.

symbolism. Prominence was given to the fact that she, though a Queen, claimed all the privileges of kingship and masculinity. In one place she was pictured in man's dress, and wearing the White and Red Crowns. In the following picture she was in female dress, but still wearing the Crowns of Upper and Lower Egypt, while the discarded male raiment lay at her feet. In every picture where hope, or aim, of resurrection was expressed there was the added symbol of the North; and in many places—always in representations of important events, past, present, or future—was a grouping of the stars of the Plough. She evidently regarded this constellation as in some way peculiarly associated with herself.

Perhaps the most remarkable statement in the records, both on the Stele and in the mural writings, was that Queen Tera had power to compel the Gods. This, by the way, was not an isolated belief in Egyptian history; but was different in its cause. She had engraved on a ruby, carved like a scarab, and having seven stars of seven points, Master Words to compel all the Gods, both of the Upper and the Under Worlds.[62]

There is a great deal to unpack here. The reference to Queen Tera wearing male attire is germane to this discussion and mimics exactly what is known about the historical Queen Hatshepsut, but the reference to the Plough constellation of seven stars is also remarkable as it is the theme on which the entire novel is based and entitled, and this constellation—or asterism—is known to us as the Big Dipper part of the Ursa Major, or Great Bear, a constellation which has an important role in the Typhonian Trilogies.[63] It is also prominent in Chinese alchemy and in Daoist practices where it goes by different names but where it is identified with specific functions in the human body, particularly

---

62   Bram Stoker, *The Jewel of Seven Stars*, William Heinemann, London, 1903 edition.

63   This identification is made many times in the Trilogies, but one can start with the first book of the Trilogies, *The Magical Revival*, pages 44 and 64. In the latter, the seven stars of Ursa Major are specifically identified with Typhon and with Nuit. This theme is continued through the nine books and is reprised in the final volume of the Trilogies, *The Ninth Arch*.

those related to longevity and immortality. In Wang Jie's fourteenth century work, *Commentary on the Mirror for Compounding the Medicine* (*Ruyao jing zhujie*), we read that the spinal column is linked to the Milky Way galaxy and that breath control (in India *pranayama*) is connected to the circuit of the Big Dipper around the Pole Star.[64]

In addition, Queen Tera has a ruby, carved like a scarab, with "Master Words to compel all the Gods, both of the Upper and the Under Worlds"—in other words, both the Dayside and the Nightside of the Tree of Life.

One should also point out that this novel was published the year before Crowley went to Cairo where he would receive his life-altering contact with Aiwass; indeed, the American edition of *The Jewel of Seven Stars* was published in 1904. Thus, these ideas about Egypt, sexuality, reanimation, mummification, and Ursa Major were abroad in the world at the time Crowley found himself staring at the Stele of Revealing in the museum in Cairo with his wife Rose Kelley informing him "They are waiting."

The Joan Grant vision recounted in *Cults of the Shadow* depicted her as a woman wrapped like a mummy during a ritual in which she was being used "as a battery." The Egyptian context was obvious, and the sexual aspect implied. The elements of being helplessly bound, at the mercy of the Priests, and being sexually excited/exploited for the purposes of a ritual over which the "mummy" had no control were all present in the Joan Grant vision and were employed in the K'rla Cell version with the addition of the cross-dressing, gender transgressive element that we find in the Bram Stoker novel as well as in the history of Queen Hatshepsut.

---

64   Fabrizio Pregadio, trans. *Commentary On the Mirror for Compounding the Medicine: A Fourteenth-Century Work on Taoist Internal Alchemy*, Golden Elixir Press, Mountain View (CA), 2013, pp.17-18. Also see Levenda's *Stairway to Heaven*, Continuum, New York, 2008 where this theme is elaborated upon at length.

The mechanics of the cross-dressing Priest/ess is considered one of the mysteries, not only of the ancient cults of Attis and Cybele but also of the Siberian shamans. In one old text we learn of the biologically male Yakut shamans of what is now known as the Sakha Republic of the Russian Federation. These individuals dress in a coat with "two iron circles representing the breasts" and part their hair in the middle after the fashion of local women.[65] Among the Chukchee (another Siberian people), the same source informs us that there are various degrees of gender transformation, such as wearing women's clothes:

> In his youth he had been afflicted by an illness and had been greatly benefited by the change of dress.[66]

Another degree of transformation is described as:

> The change in the habits of one sex is shown when the man "throws away the rifle and the lance, and the lasso of the reindeer herdman … and takes to the needle and the skin-scraper. … Even his pronunciation changes from masculine to feminine. His body loses its masculine appearance, and he becomes shy.[67]

A further generalization is made as to the peculiar status of the shaman in the Siberian communities:

> Socially, the shaman does not belong either to the class of males or to that of females, but to a third class, that of shamans. Sexually, he may be sexless, or ascetic, or have inclinations of homosexualistic character, but he may also be quite normal. [68]

---

65   M. A. Czaplicka, "Shamanism and Sex" in *Aboriginal Siberia: A Study in Social Anthropology*, Oxford: Clarendon Press, 1914.

66   Ibid.

67   Ibid.

68   Ibid.

The above gives us some entrée into this complex subject, but for another perspective we refer to the Southeast Asian phenomenon known as *bissu*.

Found throughout Indonesia in one form or another, the *bissu* proper are indigenous to South Sulawesi. They constitute the "fifth gender," the other four being cisgendered men and women, and "effeminate" men and "masculine" women. The *bissu* are believed to dwell simultaneously in two worlds: the world of normal human consciousness and the spirit world. Identified as such in their twenties, young men become *bissu* and are expected to function as shamans.

The *bissu* were honored in Indonesia in the days before the arrival of Islam and even during the Islamic period and under Dutch control. But with independence came the brutal suppression of any type of perceived sexual transgression, and *bissu* were hunted down and killed.

Today, the *bissu* are once again valued for their spiritual abilities and are known as healers. Their ability to walk between two worlds is prized by the community and is not considered contrary to Islamic teachings.

In Malaysia, the *manang bali* occupied the same field in the nineteenth century as the *bissu* do today in Indonesia. They were (usually) biologically male and presented as female. They were also shamans, members of the Iban people of Borneo. Like the *bissu*, they were believed to be in direct contact with the spirit world and were considered the highest rank of shamans.

$$\bullet \; \bullet \; \bullet$$

We have taken all this time to describe various incarnations of cross-dressing shamans and priests around the world to provide a context for the K'rla Cell ritual. It is entirely possible that some readers will consider this aspect as either irrelevant or of less importance than the actual formula of the ritual itself, but that would be a mistake. There is virtually no discussion of transvestite or transgendered ritual specialists in modern esoteric or occult circles, but in many areas around the world—and in many ages—such were ubiquitous, especially in the mystery religions. Jeffrey Evans, functioning as the Priestess in the ritual, merely reprised this long-forgotten phenomenon within the parameters of Thelemic magic. In this ritual, the body itself became the focus of the operation: a body that was simultaneously male and female, set up as a battery with two poles. In so many cultures around the world, cross-dressing shamans are believed to be in contact with spiritual forces by their very nature, and in the K'rla Cell this belief was put to the test. Not only was Jeffrey Evans functioning as the Priestess, but his partner (and, later, wife) Ruth Keenan was functioning as the Priest. Thus, the incorporation/utilization of trans-gender roles was complete.

Keenan actually performed the ritual incantations and other gestures necessary for the fulfillment of the rite, driving Evans further and further into the Mauve Zone. Keenan was the female priest in male raiment (as per Hatshepsut and the fictitious Queen Tera) in charge of the ceremony, and Evans was the dipole "battery" whose charge was conducted by Keenan. In this sense, Evans was the "Joan Grant" character and Ruth Keenan was the abducting Alien.

(Please compare the two illustrations on page 100 with that of Nema in *Beyond the Mauve Zone* in which she perfectly encapsulates the mystery of the K'rla Cell.)[69]

In all of these examples, the body itself is the subject of ritual, mysticism, sexual fantasies, ideas about life-after-death, and the presence of a spirit or soul. The fears of Western observers that the dead Egyptian may rise up and take vengeance on the tomb raiders became expressed in horror fiction and horror film, while at the same time exhibiting various degrees of sexual fascination. If we look at the image of six men and one woman standing over a mummy on an examination table,

---

69   Kenneth Grant, *Beyond the Mauve Zone*, Starfire, London, (1999) 2016, Plate 8.

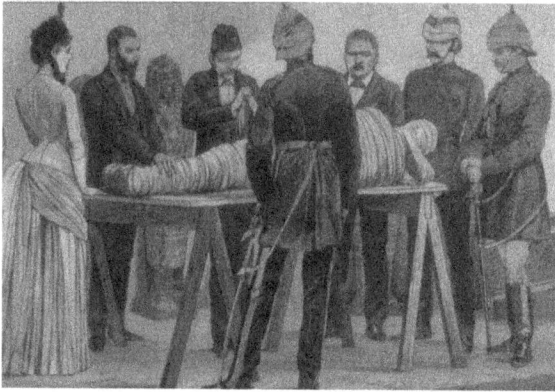

though, we also have the alien abduction scenario. Simply replace the mummy with a "human" body—a live body—restrained and helpless on a table and surrounded by uncaring individuals, lacking empathy, whose only interest is in the scientific prodding of the body, and we pass effortlessly from the mummy fantasy to the alien abduction fantasy and both are a means of piercing the veil that separates the "normal" world of average consciousness from the "other" world that is the domain of death and life after death—the bardo state. The bardo state is the liminal state not only between consciousness and unconsciousness but between the Old Aeon and the New. We have moved the focus of *external* symbols—the Cross, the Star of David, the Star and Crescent, and all the signs and signifiers of the past millennia—to an *internal* landscape of chakras, marmas, nadis; of fear and terror; of the rising kundalini and the falling amrita. We have moved our magic from the external forms of a linear Qabalah to an internal ceremony of nervous system and involuntary processes. This is what we mean by the sacralization of the Body.

But this sacralization is not complete without understanding that there are locations within the Body and the processes it enacts that are in the darkness. Inasmuch as there are vast distances of empty space between planets and stars, and that these distances are utterly dark and cold and without air, there are places within the subtle body of the magician that are similarly constructed and which are known to Typhonians as the Mauve Zone.

Let us use a mind experiment to illustrate what we mean, using the ancient concept of astrological charts to explain the power zones in relation to the Body Mandala.

The power zone occupied by the K'rla Cell was topographical to the Earth both in time and in space. In other words, it could be found in New York one year and in Florida the next. The movement of the power zones relative to fixed positions on the planet (and therefore to the solar system) is an integral feature. Think of a natal horoscope chart that reflects the positions of the planets and stars over a specific geographical spot on the Earth at a specific time; then that person moves across the face of the Earth and can be found at different places at different times. The combination of the natal chart with the transit chart over the new geographical location gives a different set of values for that same individual. Then imagine that person traveling through space, leaving the Earth with its astrological coordinates based on the perceived positions of the stars to another planet or another star or simply another set of coordinates in deep space. The natal horoscope chart would seem to lose relevance with each celestial mile, but the person for whom the chart was erected is the same person. There would seem to have been nothing in that natal chart to suggest that the native would be found in another solar system altogether, and no terrestrial system of astrology would obtain in the new destination, the new solar system, with its different zodiacal belt and its different planets.

However, the fact that the native is traveling through space is a biological fact and a physical fact that can not be denied simply because terrestrial astrological systems can not account for it. In fact, there would have to be a refinement or adjustment to traditional astrological knowledge and practice to accommodate the new data of a human being now on the other side of the solar system, perhaps vulnerable to transits of the moons of Saturn or to the "Sun" of another star in another system. How would one erect a transit chart for someone born on the Earth who is now orbiting Betelgeuse?

All of this can be accommodated if one transposes the cosmic Body onto the terrestrial, Earthly Body. Such a transposition was always intended because the "Body Mandala" presupposes that the vast darkness of space—and the peculiarities of a time subject to general and special relativity—as well as the countless numbers of stars and their associated planets, are already present in some form not only in the natal chart of the subject but in the subtle body of the subject as well, and therefore in the Mandala, which represents the entire cosmos. If the ancient hermetic maxim "that which is above is like that which is below" is correct, then all of the immensity of space—including other galaxies, black holes, and all manner of astronomical phenomena—can be represented in some way in the human body. Otherwise, we would be forced to accept that the Tree of Life with its ten sephiroth represent the reality of our local solar system only and not the infinite contents of all of Creation.

Ironically, this is indeed how the Tree of Life is presented and explained to most new initiates. We assign planetary significance to the sephiroth without realizing that in the New Aeon dispensation the

Tree cannot be contained within our local system but must represent a different perspective altogether. Of course, the sephirah Tiphareth (for example) is not really the Sun as know it, but a collection of ideas—cultural, religious, etc.—that we associate loosely with the Sun. But even that is too limiting. As we have explained already, the New Aeon requires a New Qabalah and therefore a new understanding of the Tree. This is merely a suggestion at this time, as there is not enough space here to go into sufficient detail, but a truly comprehensive Qabalah of the New Age would include the vast diversity of cultural, scientific, mathematical, psychological, and neurological data that humanity has accumulated in the centuries since the structure of the Tree of Life was first proposed. Kenneth Grant understood this and realized that this new Tree would have to include ideas and concepts borrowed from artists and writers as well as from scientists and occultists. The horror fantasies of H. P. Lovecraft would have to be accommodated in this new structure as well, as the recent "secular religion" of the UFO.

The "alien abduction" scenario was Kenneth Grant's inspired choice for retooling the Joan Grant "Egyptian mummy" vision for a purely Typhonian purpose. Evans wanted to traverse the Tunnels of Set and had to locate those Tunnels using magic that had not yet been invented. In O.T.O. terminology, this would involve technologies of the VIII and IX degrees but redesigned for a transgendered apparatus. While the O.T.O. degrees as popularly understood presuppose a heterosexual, gender normative context, the K'rla Cell broke new ground by exploring the possibilities of these degrees within a transgressive context, thus reinventing the system for application to the Night Side of the Tree: the realm of the trans-Plutonian planets, the domain of the Old Ones, and the Elder Gods. This was done by exploring the Body Mandala in ways that had not been imagined before, at least not in a traditional Western esoteric tradition. This meant that not only were the genders "swapped" but that the OTO's sexual degrees would be interpreted within a bondage context as well, with Evans-as-Priestess restrained completely during the ritual. We might say, with Lovecraft, that the ritual was in the "space between" the VIII and IX degrees.

To those unfamiliar with the alien abduction scenario we can do no better than to quote from Dr. John E. Mack's ground-breaking book on the phenomenon:

> To be paralyzed and taken against one's will by strange beings into a foreign enclosure and subjected to intrusive, rapelike procedures, some of which are especially humiliating to human dignity ...[70]

And:

> The most common, and evidently most important procedures, involve the reproductive system. Instruments that penetrate the abdomen or involve the genital organs themselves are used to take sperm samples from men and to remove or fertilize eggs of the female.[71]

The taking of sperm samples was reenacted in the K'rla Cell ritual under conditions that mimicked both the alien abduction scenario and the Egyptian mummy scenario in a single ritual.

To those unfamiliar with the technologies under discussion, recourse should be had to the very first volume of Grant's Typhonian Trilogies where all of this is laid out quite clearly:

> The mental exaltation generated by a magically controlled orgasm forms a lucent lense-like window past which stream the vivid astral imagery of the subconscious mind. ... These images are dynamic links with the deeper centres of consciousness and act as keys to the experience or revelations which form the object of the Operation.[72]

---

70   John E. Mack, *Abduction: Human Encounters with Aliens*, Ballantine Books, New York, 1995, p. 29

71   Ibid., p. 24.

72   Kenneth Grant, *The Magical Revival*, Samuel Weiser, 1972, p. 27.

This unique combination of ideas, symbols, and practices contributed to a great degree of psychological and neurological stress and was not without its blowback in the form of seizures experienced by Evans in succeeding years for which he had, on occasion, to be hospitalized. But the success of the series of rituals was not to be denied. Areas of Evans's consciousness were stimulated in wholly unimaginable ways and he began to function as a kind of mathematical savant as new neural pathways were opened, triggered by the intensity of the psychobiological experience that had, as its purpose, contact with those Forces that exist in the Tunnels.

He and Ruth Keenan also became initiated into the Afro-Caribbean cultus and devoted themselves to "the obeah and the wanga" as prescribed in the first Chapter of *Liber AL*, (I:37). This expansion of Thelemic study into Afro-Caribbean practices energized the couple and sent them along deeper pathways, armed with the perspective that the Old Ones had been worshipped with strange, orgiastic rites in the darkness and in haunts remote from the dwellings of modern society, such as the rites of Cthulhu in the Louisiana bayous as described in "The Call of Cthulhu" by H. P. Lovecraft. The ritual as set forth in that seminal work was celebrated by individuals of various races and ethnicities—Asian, African, Latin, Caucasian—and accompanied by sexual acts at which the author only hints but which are nevertheless present, as if the O.T.O.—liberated, finally, from historical and intellectual restraints forged from purely European steel—conducted a Gnostic Mass in all its passionate, energized, and enthusiastic glory: a Mass intended not for spectators but for participants only, where the sacrament of Communion is between the non-human, non-terrestrial Old Ones and their human subjects.

The lack of a body-centered theory and practice in Western ceremonial magic is more than compensated by the extensive literature on the Body-as-Map in Asian tantras that form a centerpiece for Kenneth Grant's work on Thelema. This is picked up by the Afro-Caribbean researches of Michael Bertiaux and the theory of the *points-chauds*. While a complete discussion of this is beyond the scope of this work, interested readers are urged to consult the texts of these two individuals for further clarification. In short, however, we can say that the Body is a map of the Earth; and that the Earth is a map of the Body. Both are iterations of the Map of the Cosmos. This is the heart of the Doctrine of Correspondences on which such works as *Sepher Sephiroth* and *777* are based. Knowing this, the keys that unlock the Gates to the Tunnels are readily available.

BOOK FOUR

The Golden Section

CHAPTER NINE

The Golden Section Explained

R ather than indulge in an orgy of mystification and suspense, let us look at how Jeffrey Evans himself describes the Golden Mean in his own words:

The Golden Mean was discovered by an Italian mathematician named Leonardo de Pisa, of the Dark Ages, commonly known by his nickname of "Fibonacci." For this reason, the mathematician Edouard Lucas (1842—1891) gave this system the name "Fibonacci mathematics." Fibonacci travelled all about with his Father (a merchant) when he was a young child, studying the numerical systems of every country he was in, and was the most brilliant mathematician of his time. He revolutionized economics with his 1202 book *Liber Abaci*, which converted all of Europe from Roman Numerals (which had been in vogue since the time of Julius Caesar) to the Hindu-Arabic numerals that we use today. He saw that Roman numerals were impossible to use for problems of multiplication and division, and you can barely even subtract with them.

He learned the Golden Mean from either Indian Mathematicians or Arabian Astronomers. Most mathematicians today obtain it with the equation

$$(\sqrt{5} + 1) \div 2 = \Phi$$

...or, sometimes $\qquad$ $\tfrac{1}{2}\sqrt{5} + \tfrac{1}{2} = \Phi$

where $\qquad$ $\Phi^{-1} = 0.61803398875....$

$\Phi^{1} = 1.61803398875....$

and $\qquad$ $\Phi^{2} = 2.61803398875....$

This means that: $\qquad$ $\Phi^{1} - \Phi^{-1} = \Phi^{2} - \Phi^{1} = 1$

...and also: $\qquad$ $\Phi^{-1} + \Phi^{-2} = 1; \ \ \Phi^{2} - \Phi^{-1} = 2; \ \text{and} \ \Phi^{2} + \Phi^{-2} = 3$

Surprisingly, it also forms the basis of a geometry of 5 and of the square root of 5, since

$$\Phi^{1} + \Phi^{-1} = \Phi^{2} - \Phi^{-2} = \sqrt{5} = 2.2360679775....$$

...and, since $\Phi^{3} = 4.2360679775....$

$$\Phi^{3} - \sqrt{4} = \sqrt{5} = 2.2360679775....$$

Also, $36 = 6^{2}$; and $2\cos(36^{0}) = \Phi$; and $\Phi^{5} - \Phi^{-5} = 11$

...just like $\qquad$ $6 + 5 \qquad = 11$

and $\qquad$ $2\Phi^{1} - \sqrt{5} = 1$

It's actually a ratio found in a number-sequence called "The Fibonacci Sequence," in which every number in the sequence is the sum of the two numbers preceding it:

1 2 3 5 8 13 21 34 55 89 144 233 377 610 987....

....are the first sixteen Fibonacci Numbers (Fn),

and $\qquad$ $(1 \div 1) \qquad = 1$

$(2 \div 1) \qquad = 2$

$(3 \div 2) \qquad = 1.5$

$(5 \div 3) \qquad = 1.666...$

$(8 \div 5) \qquad = 1.6$

$(13 \div 8) \qquad = 1.625$

$$(21 \div 13) \qquad = 1.615384615....$$

$$(34 \div 21) \qquad = 1.619047619....$$

$$(55 \div 34) \qquad = 1.617647059....$$

$$(89 \div 55) \qquad = 1.618181818....$$

$$(144 \div 89) \qquad = 1.617977528....$$

$$(233 \div 144) \qquad = 1.618055556....$$

$$(377 \div 233) \qquad = 1.618025751....$$

$$(610 \div 377) \qquad = 1.618037135....$$

$$(987 \div 610) \qquad = 1.618032787....$$

....Notice how it swings back and forth, on either side of the Golden Mean, like a pendulum? It approaches the Golden Mean, closer and closer, on to infinity, and mathematicians take the ratio $(121,393 \div 75,025)$ or $(Fn_{26} \div Fn_{25})$ ---the 26th Fibonacci Number divided by the 25th --- as the "most exact" for practical purposes. This ratio finally equals $1.61803398875....$ which has all the properties I demonstrated above. It is very interesting that the 26th Fn divided by the 25th Fn gives the Golden Mean, since 25 is the Square of 5.

In the Fibonacci Sequence, the ratio $(8 \div 5) = 1.6$ is seen as a perfect representation of the Golden Mean, since it is the closest ratio to it in the first decad.

A unique property of the Golden Mean ratio itself, is that every odd power minus its reciprocal, equals a whole number; and every even power plus its reciprocal, equals a whole number.

It is also the only number the multiples of which, equal its sums: i.e.,

$$(\Phi \cdot \Phi) \quad = \Phi^2 \quad = (\Phi^0 + \Phi^1)$$

$$(\Phi^2 \cdot \Phi) \quad = \Phi^3 \quad = (\Phi^1 + \Phi^2)$$

$$(\Phi^3 \cdot \Phi) \quad = \Phi^4 \quad = (\Phi^2 + \Phi^3)$$

....etc.

Compare the numbers of the Fibonacci Sequence to the numbers of the Decimal Sequence, and you will find:

1 1 2 3 5 8 13 21 34 55 89 144 233 377 610

| |

1 2 3 4 5 6 7 8 9 10 11 12 13 14 15

The number 1 is both the first and the second Fibonacci Number; and the only place where the two sequences match, is at the numbers 1 and 5.

Some contemporary progressive physicists are even using the Golden Mean in order to depict a universe of eleven dimensions, in which the ones we normally perceive (one through four; or light, space, time, and gravity) have a dependent fifth through which only can we access the other six dimensions, which are microcosmic. Recall that $\Phi^5 - \Phi^{-5} = 11$.

Michio Kaku thinks that way, with his M-Theory. He even proposed using a model of the Tree of Life to depict his ideas of the concepts of other dimensions.[73]

And further:

Is the Fibonacci system the mathematical undercurrent in *Liber AL* that Crowley sought all his life, but could never find? He even consulted with such renowned mathematicians as J.W.N. Sullivan (1886—1937) who first explained the Theory of Relativity to the public in a non-technical way.

Fibonacci geometry is a spiral geometry, and apparent even in DNA. And, I did the full spiral dance both deosil and widdershins in Liber V, which made me giddy. But I also know the dangers of working this way. For one thing, the seizures certainly showed me that …

---

73   Private communication from Evans to Levenda, dated November 26, 2019.

DNA = 55 = (Shekinah) =Σ [1-----10] = the Tenth Fibonacci Number,

and the Fibonacci numbers intertwine with the Lucas numbers, named after 19th century mathematician Edouard Lucas, who studied Fibonacci Numbers and gave them their name.

...

sin (666) +cos(6^3) = $-\Phi$, and 2cos (36) = Φ; thirty-six is the number of the Hexagram, the Ritual of which we did over New-year's night in 1980-81. Also, 2sin (18) = Φ^{-1} ; and 18 = $\Phi^6+\Phi^{-6}$. It's also the geometry of the Pentagram, and of a 5-dimensional universe (leading on to multi-dimensions?); and the central Ritual in Ithaca was "Liber V vel Reguli: the Ritual of the Mark of the Beast."

This would be a non-Euclidean Universe and the number 4 is not in the Fibonacci Numbers. Also, Φ^3 = $\sqrt{4}$ _plus_ $\sqrt{5}$.

The geometry of the Golden Mean unites the Five and the Six, and the addition of those equals 11, which is Phi to the fifth power minus it's reciprocal.

It could be fiction. It could be _"technical,"_ for Thelemites, but wouldn't have a wide appeal.

I once thought about writing something called "The Book of Fibs."

The Greek word for "cut," or "section," τομη, has the numerical value of 418, and the Greek tau is frequently used to stand for the Golden Mean.[74]

• • •

While the above commentary by Evans is a succinct explanation of the relevance of the Golden Mean or Golden Section to esotericism in general and to Thelema in particular, other authors in this field have

---

74   Further communication from Evans to Levenda, November 26, 2019.

identified the importance of the Golden Mean with particular concentration on its application in Egyptian architecture: an area that has resonance for Thelemites as much of their iconography and practice derives from Egyptian culture, beginning with the receiving of *The Book of the Law*—with its Egyptian deities—in Cairo but extending to the Egyptian themes in the Golden Dawn rituals in which Crowley was initiated.

R. A. Schwaller de Lubicz—the controversial Egyptologist who was also an alchemist—pointed out the extreme importance of the Golden Section in his works on temple architecture, not only as a computation device for angles and lines but as a mystical function of *process*, of growth and reproduction, so essential to an understanding not only of sacred geometry in general but also of alchemy. Schwaller de Lubicz was a contemporary and associate—and sometime colleague— of the famous twentieth century alchemist Fulcanelli. His wife, Isha, wrote the famous series of *Her-Bak* novels. De Lubicz has been quoted in this volume already, and he helps to tie together the mathematics of the Golden Section and the spiritual processes of initiation and transformation of which the mummification procedure is an excellent metaphor.

Robert Temple, whose ground-breaking volume *The Sirius Mystery* captivated an entire generation of occultists in the West, has also focused on the importance of the Golden Section, not only in architecture but as emblematic of a deeper mystery. He goes into some length to expound on this in his *The Sphinx Mystery*, and has a chapter entitled "The Golden Angle of Resurrection" that is based on a function of the Golden Section known as the Golden Angle. As he writes:

> The ancient Egyptians weren't just a lot of idle nerds doing all of this for fun. To them, it was a matter of life and death.[75]

---

75 Robert Temple, with Olivia Temple, *The Sphinx Mystery*, Inner Traditions, Rochester (VT), 2009, p. 380.

Temple traces the prevalence of the Golden Section in areas as seemingly disparate as the paintings of Leonardo da Vinci, and the music of J.S. Bach and W.A. Mozart as well as the architecture of ancient Egypt, and offers the opinion that the reverence for the Golden Section originated in ancient Babylon.

Stephen Skinner devotes a chapter to the Golden Section in his *Sacred Geometry: Deciphering the Code*,[76] where he demonstrates how it appears in the geometry of the Pentagram and goes on to show its relationship to the Fibonacci Series (mentioned above by Evans).

> Yet, for all that, it remains an elusive subject in the library of works devoted to Thelema. Should Thelemites be concerned with it at all?

In the first place, it can be found in many places in nature and was formalized to the extent that it appears as well in architecture: in particular, sacred architecture. *The Book of the Law* was received in Cairo, which is a city that borders on the Pyramids of Gizeh. If we are to believe authors such as R.A. Schwaller de Lubicz, Stephen Skinner, and others the Pyramids (and other ancient Egyptian buildings) were created with the Golden Mean in mind (as well as a concern for astronomical orientation). As mentioned previously, it is curious that for a movement so imbued with the doctrines of occultism—particularly Western occultism and ceremonial magic, inherited from the Golden Dawn among other groups—that modern Thelemites pay so little attention to sacred architecture and astronomical orientation.

But the discovery of the K'rla Cell—combined with Crowley's own written musings on the possible mathematical mysteries encoded in *Liber AL* specifically—demonstrates beyond reasonable doubt that the Golden Mean is an essential element of this core text of Thelema. In fact, the entire document—all three chapters—can be analyzed mathematically and treasures will thereby be revealed. In other words,

---

76 Stephen Skinner, *Sacred Geometry: Deciphering the Code*, Sterling, NY, 2006, pp. 34-39.

there is a text buried within the text, and moreover it is a text written in numbers rather than letters. In Qabalah, this is to be expected: for instance, the calculation of the number for each Hebrew word in the Torah. In the case of *AL*, however, there is a layer of numerological significance that is buried a level deeper than even gematria, notarikon, or temurah. That Crowley had no more than a suspicion that this was the case confirms that the text of *AL* was transmitted unconsciously, i.e., by an intelligence other than Crowley's own.

The Golden Mean—also known as the Golden Section, the Golden Ratio, and other terms—is a simple ratio of line segments to each other, as we shall see. But it was considered so important that it was regarded with something akin to awe, both by Euclid and by the Pythagoreans. In fact, the most famous depiction of the geometry of the Pythagorean Theorem (Euclid's Theorem 47) is known as "The Bride's Chair," which certainly has significance and resonance for Thelemites (as it had for Freemasons of earlier generations) as we have seen.

The Golden Mean, especially through its correlate the Fibonacci Series, represents the phenomena of growth and evolution. It can be found in the famous example of the spiral of the nautilus shell. It is present in the human body, and in the numbers of the leaves of plants. As growth and evolution, the Golden Mean represents motion, movement, and progression. The gematria of Hebrew words and the isopsephy of Greek words are static representations of individual values, i.e., one word equals one whole number. There are no fractions, no decimal places, no considerations of space, of volume, or of time in gematria. The Golden Mean, on the other hand, offers all this once its mysteries have been plumbed.

The Pyramids and the great Gothic cathedrals of Europe are impressive because of the value of their architecture. They are machines for measuring, dividing, and crafting space. Further, they are oriented towards the stars and thus they also allude to a relationship with time. One archaeologist characterized the Great Pyramid of Gizeh as a "resurrection machine."[77] Chartres Cathedral has been called a machine for "setting mankind in movement."[78] This is due to the application of geometry—a word which means "measurement of earth"—to the contours of the land and of the sky: a point of tangency between ourselves and the stars. This is a mystical concept only insofar as we insist on an arbitrary division between our bodies and our consciousness, and only if we insist that our mind is imprisoned in our flesh.

The presence of the Golden Mean buried within the text of *AL* implies two things:

In the first place, it confirms and endorses the view that the text was not consciously crafted by Aleister Crowley or anyone else, any human being. If it was inspired, then it was a mighty inspiration that would have planted all the clues to its discovery so openly and yet manage to escape everyone who read it, including Crowley himself.

In the second place, it is proof that the relatively recent Thelemic tradition is part of a much older one: an ancient tradition that has its roots in the earliest recorded civilizations. As we have seen, it has been suggested that the Knights Templar were responsible for having introduced sacred geometry to Europe from the Middle East, thus providing yet another link in the Thelemic chain. And the Freemasons trace their origins to the same builders of both the Pyramids and the Gothic cathedrals. Thus, Thelema traces its roots to ancient Egypt—as evidenced by the Egyptian deities of the three chapters of *AL* and to the rituals of the Golden Dawn, based as they were on Egyptian motifs—and from them to the Templars and the Masons. What all of these traditions have in common is their connection to sacred geometry: a discipline that the Orders have so far ignored.

---

77   Toby Wilkinson, "Before the Pyramids: Early Developments in Egyptian Royal Funerary Ideology," *Egypt at its Origins, Studies in Memory of Barbara Adams*, S. Hendricks, Friedman, Ciałowicz, Chłodniki, eds. (Leuven: Peeters, 2004) p. 1141.

78   Louis Charpentier, *The Mysteries of Chartres Cathedral*, Research Into Lost Knowledge Organization, London, 1972, p. 180.

...

What the discovery by the K'rla Cell accomplishes is to move Thelema from the linear, static forms of Old Aeon Qabalah—not to ignore or abandon them at all, far from it—but to expand upon them, extend them into multiple dimensions, and in so doing prove its universality when united with the very basic yet profound equations of life, growth, and evolution that can be found everywhere on the planet, from ancient Egypt and Israel all the way to China and India, and to "obeah and wanga." It pulls Thelema out of a purely Western, Greco-Roman or Hebrew-Arabic context (limited by the vocabularies and gematrias of their respective languages) to the realm of pure number, of science, of mathematics: the universal language, and hence the universal Qabalah.

It demonstrates, once and for all, that "our method is science, our aim is religion."

CHAPTER TEN

The Golden Section and Western Esotericism

To the Freemasons, God is a Geometer. The symbol of Freemasonry is composed of two measuring instruments of the geometer and the builder: the compass and the square. If we realize that the foremost modern Western esoteric groups—the SRIA, the Golden Dawn, and the O.T.O.—all had Masonic origins and claims to Masonic pedigrees, one would expect that the ideas of esoteric geometry (and its manifestation as sacred architecture) would form an important element of their philosophy, their initiatory systems, and their rituals.

Nothing, however, could be further from the truth.

Much of what Crowley (and later Grant) wrote about magick was underpinned by Qabalah. Qabalah, at least the way it is understood by most, is mathematics and is based on simple arithmetic. It is a coding system where a number equals a letter, and combinations of letters can be reinterpreted as combinations of numbers. Words having the same numerical equivalent are believed to be equivalent in other ways as well.

Geometry is rarely included in any discussion of Qabalah or specifically Qabalistic number systems such as gematria. But what if more advanced forms of mathematics—geometry, algebra, trigonometry, calculus, etc.—also had Qabalistic significance? What if all those discussions of the Body of God (for instance) involved much more than arithmetic but also included numbers expanded into other dimensions, such as the three dimensions of space as well as the dimension of time?

What if geometric shapes that were similar could be shown to be equivalent in other ways, just as words having the same numerical equivalents are believed to be equivalent?

The Golden Ratio, as an example, is a simple formula but it expresses a phenomenon that is observable in two dimensions (such as I have suggested can be discovered in the depictions of the thrones of the Egyptian deities) and which can be applied to three dimensions (such as the design of a pyramid).

The *Sepher Yetzirah* teaches us that the ten emanations of God formed the created world. It is a description of divine force—of energy at different vibrational levels—that coalesced into matter, and not only the matter we can see and feel with our biological senses but matter at different levels of accessibility. (It may be that consciousness itself has a material analogue or is "an emergent property of the brain" as has been suggested by philosophers such as David Chambers; I prefer to say that "the brain is an emergent property of consciousness," however.) But those ten forces eventually (and perhaps simultaneously) expanded into at least the three dimensions we know (height, width, length) and the dimension of time, but quite possibly into multiple other dimensions as science now suggests (the multiverse concept, for instance, or the idea of a parallel universe or universes).

What all this suggests—or even requires—is a Qabalah that takes into consideration the properties of dimension as well as (or in addition to) the linear nature of simple arithmetic. There needs to be a Qabalah of geometry, and the perfect place to start may be the Golden Ratio.

The Golden Ratio implies a relationship between the whole of a figure and its component parts. What relevance does that have, for instance, to Tantra or even to Thelema?

Johannes Kepler, the great astronomer (and astrologer) is quoted as having said:

> The image of man and woman stems from the divine proportion. In my opinion, the propagation of plants and the progenitive acts of animals are in the same ratio.[79]

One could say, therefore, that the rite of *maithuna*—or the sexual union mimed in the Gnostic Mass—is a demonstration or manifestation of the Golden Ratio in biological terms.

Mario Livio, who wrote an entire book devoted to the subject of the Golden Ratio, observed:

> The sine of 666 degrees plus the cosine of six cubed (six times six times six) is a good approximation of negative phi.[80]

This would indicate a hidden presence of the Beast (as negative Φ) lurking within the tunnels of the trigonometric functions, like a Minotaur within the Labyrinth. 666 is an equivalent of the Greek phrase *To mega therion* ("the Great Beast") but when we apply sine and cosine to this number we are bringing the basic arithmetic of isopsephy (the Greek form of gematria) into two and then three dimensions.

Sine is the trigonometric function that refers to the ratio of the length of the side opposite a given acute angle in a right triangle to the length of the hypotenuse (which is always opposite the right angle). Thus, it is a function of the same geometric shape—the right triangle—that gave us the Pythagorean Theorem and the Egyptian pyramids. The word "sine" is cognate with the Spanish word for "breast" or "bosom"—*seno*—and is believed to have derived from the Arabic *jaib* which means the same thing, and most specifically to the *curve* of the upper part of a toga.

---

79 See the letter from Johannes Kepler to Joachim Tanckius in Leipzig, May 12, 1608, in *Johannes Kelpius Gesammelte Werke*, Band XVI, Briefe 1607-1611, Herausgegeben von Max Caspar, C. H. Beck'sche Verlagsbuchhandlung, Munich, MCMLIV, p. 154.
80 Mario Livio, *The Golden Ratio*, Broadway Books, NY2002, p.23.G

The word *cosine* is short for the longer term "complementary sine" and means the ratio of the length of the side *adjacent* to the acute angle to the length of the hypotenuse.

Thus, in a right triangle—and therefore in the very design of the Great Pyramid of Gizeh—there is a formula whereby sacred entities may be discovered hidden within the geometries of the architecture. This is an extension of Qabalah into the third dimensional world: an entire field of occult investigation waiting to be discovered.

While the mathematics of the Qabalah is primarily static and linear—*this* word equals *that* number which equals *another* word—the application of geometry and trigonometry to the same mystical problems reveals a dynamic energy at work. "A god," as Crowley famously offered, "is one who goes." The Golden Ratio is a link between the static and the dynamic, between Old Aeon Qabalah and New Aeon Qabalah.

There is, however, another advantage to this "New Aeon" Qabalah: it is universal and not ethnically or culturally loaded. Qabalah based on the Hebrew language is necessarily and inextricably linked to Abrahamic religions and cultures. A Qabalah based on geometric and trigonometric principles is not linked to any specific language, alphabet, or culture. Imagine a Qabalah based on pure math. That is what the Golden Ratio offers us: a way towards a multi-dimensional and multi-cultural mystical language.

Take, for instance, a paper recently published in a Chinese journal devoted to an integration of traditional Chinese and Western medicine, published by Springer-Verlag in 2013. Entitled "The Golden Ratio and Loshu-Fibonacci Diagram: Novel Research View on Relationship of Chinese Medicine and Modern Biology," it explores the traditional Chinese yin-yang symbol, the trigrams of the *I Jing*, and the Loshu diagram as a template for understanding (and applying) the Golden Ratio and the Fibonacci Series to Chinese medicine and biology. This illustrates the universality of the importance of the Golden Ratio and recognizes that it can, in fact, be applied to Asian esoteric systems.

One faction of the Western esoteric community that *did* understand the importance of geometry to the application of magical formulae was formed by initiates in Southern California, notably of the
Thelema Lodge of the Caliphate in Oakland, California and a working
group within that lodge mentored by David Richard Jones circa 1990.
The interest began with an exploration of the works of Dr John Dee
with special attention to the Enochian (or Angelic) system that was
foundational to the Golden Dawn and which had made such a profound impression on Crowley. It was Jones who pointed out the value
of studying the *Elements* of Euclid, as Dee himself had written the
introduction to the first-ever English translation, and he suggested that
it was impossible to understand the Enochian system without first grap-
pling with Euclid.[81]

Unfortunately, we do not know to what extent the geometrical
theorems introduced and explained by Euclid informed the Enochian
workings of the Thelema Lodge initiates, but we do know that this
group aggressively pursued the work. This is the only instance of
which we are aware of a study and an application of geometric principles (rather than simply gematria or notariqon) to occult working that
was undertaken in modern times in the west. The use of the concept
of "power zones" by Thelemites such as Michael Bertiaux and Kenneth Grant imply a topographical perspective which, when wedded to
astronomical calculations, provides a rough basis for a geometric interpretation of Thelema. We need, however, look no further for a "soft"
introduction to this concept than the Golden Ratio and the (related)
Fibonacci Series.

---

81 For a detailed account of these events, see Satyr. "The Black Lodge of Santa Cruz." In: Biroco,
Joel, (ed.). *KAOS* 14: *Supplement* [PDF Edition] London: The Kaos-Babalon Press, 2002.

CHAPTER ELEVEN

The Golden Section and the Fibonacci Series

> The Golden Number does not act solely as a function of an ideal proportion, but serves as the basis for a philosophy that makes the connection between the metaphysical state and the physical state. It is in this connection that the Golden Number's "sacred" character consists. Furthermore, the human body develops in terms of this number.—R. A. Schwaller de Lubicz, *The Temple in Man*

There is a lot of mystification surrounding the Golden Mean—also referred to, as in the citation above, the Golden Number—in studies of ancient Egyptian architecture, Greek architecture, the Pythagoreans, and so forth, and most especially in studies of what is known as "sacred geometry." Crowley used both gematria and notariqon in his writings but began to show a significant tendency to employ isopsephy. Terms like *Thelema*, *To Mega Therion*, *Agape* and the like are Greek, of course, and *Liber AL* uses Greek terms (*Hadit*, for instance, instead of the Egyptian *Heru-Behdeti*) interspersed with Egyptian references to the extent that the Book could be interpreted as a Greco-Egyptian text in the Gnostic tradition.

The Greek letter Phi (Φ) is used today to represent the Golden Section, but previously it had been represented by the Greek letter Tau (τ), as the initial of the word τομη or "cut" or "section."[82] For Thelemites, this has relevance, for the word is pronounced *tomi*—or "to me"—which could be a reference to *AL* I: 53 and *AL* I:65, "To me! To me!," and which in isopsephy adds to 418, the number mentioned in *AL* I: 46. Even further, if the word τομη is divided into two separate words—το μη—you have the Greek for "The Not" or "The Nothing," and the isopsephy is still 418: a number of tremendous significance for Thelemites.

Consider *AL* I:21 "With the God & the Adorer I am nothing …" or *AL* I:27-30:

"… O Nuit, continuous one of Heaven, let it be ever thus; that men speak not of Thee as One but as None; and let them speak not of thee at all, since thou art continuous!

"None, breathed the light, faint & faery, of the stars, and two.

"For I am divided for love's sake, for the chance of union.

"This is the creation of the world, that the pain of division is as nothing, and the joy of dissolution all."

In these verses, Nuit is understood as None, as divided, and quite specifically as division equaling nothing. These are all reprised in the Greek τομη as "cut, section" and το μη as "The Nothing" and, of course, as "To me."

The division represented by Nuit is a reflection of the division between what Schwaller de Lubicz, above, refers to as the connection between the metaphysical state and the physical state: the connection represented by the Golden Section. The yearning of the physical being—represented by the Priest—for the metaphysical state is the

---

82 Another correspondence is that of the Latin word *templum* and the Greek *temenos*, both of which mean "temple" and which come from the same root: *tem*, "to cut" or τέμνω "I cut," from the Proto Indo-European **tem-* or **temh₂-* "to cut." It signifies a space divided from the surrounding area, demarcated, "cut off" from normal activity. Consider the expanded relevance for Thelemites in the term "Knights Templar" or more specifically "Ordo Templi Orientis." There is also the connection to the Proto-Indo-European root **di-mon-* which comes from **da-* also meaning "to cut up," or "to divide" and is the root of the English word "time." Thus the Latin *tempus*—"time"—and *"templum"*—temple—can be seen as related, and both to τομη and thus to the Golden Section. The temple is "cut off" both from time and from space to create a liminality, a sacred area that transcends its physical coordinates.

iconic dimension of Chapter I of *Liber AL*. Nuit is the goddess of the heavens and specifically of the Night Sky, studded with stars, which is the domain of the gods and of the souls of the Dead.

Then consider the following verses, also from Chapter I:

45. The Perfect and the Perfect are one Perfect and not two; nay, are none!

46. Nothing is a secret key of this law. Sixty-one the Jews call it; I call it eight, eighty, four hundred & eighteen.

Once again, the emphasis on "none" as a combination of two ideas, in this case of the idea of "Perfect."

And, of course, the statement that "Nothing" is a secret key. In Hebrew, it is *Ain*, spelled Aleph-Yod-Nun, which adds to sixty-one. And then, *immediately*, the reference to 418: τομη or το μη. To me.

We feel that this convergence of explicit references to identical ideas, supported by the numbers, is too overwhelming to ignore. A great degree of focus on the gematria of *Ain* as "Nothing" has ignored the Greek alternatives which, in this case, are far more promising as a way to "decode" the mathematical references as well as draw attention to the underlying theme of the Golden Section, which very well may be the "secret key" to *Liber AL*.

So, what, exactly, *is* the Golden Section?

Simply stated, it is a ratio or a calculation of proportion, as in this illustration:

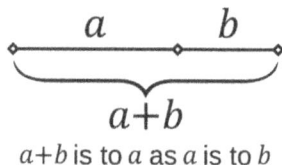

$$\underbrace{\overset{a \qquad b}{\rule{6cm}{0.4pt}}}_{a+b}$$

$a+b$ is to a as a is to b

In other words, the longest length $a+b$ is to the shorter length a, as the shorter length a is to the shortest length b. When that occurs, then the lengths are in the Golden Section ratio or Golden Section proportion. Divide the longest length differently, and the lengths are no longer in the right proportion and there is no Golden Section. So, we have "cut" the length $a+b$ in the right proportion.

This applies also to geometric shapes:

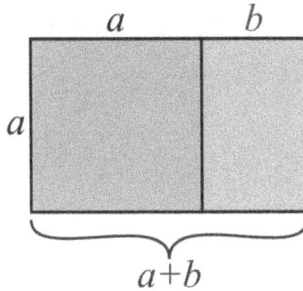

In this case, the lengths marked "a" form a perfect square as all its sides are equal. The length marked "b" appears on the top and bottom of the diagram on the right side, while the length on the right is the same as "a." Since its overall length $a+b$ is to length a as a is to length b, the above rectangle is also a demonstration of the Golden Section.

What if we start adding more rectangles to the above illustration?

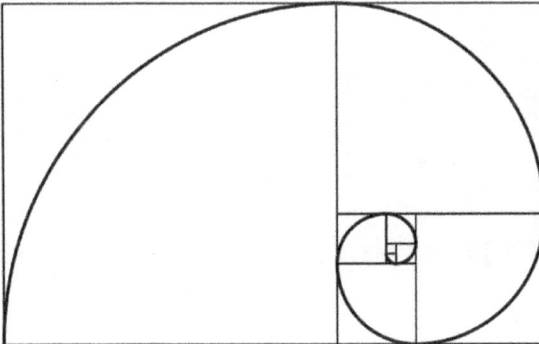

While the individual rectangles that make up the whole are in the Golden Ratio to each other, we can notice another phenomenon that is represented by the spiral beginning at the innermost rectangle and continuing through all subsequent rectangles. What does this mean?

This is called a Fibonacci spiral, and is based on another mathematical curiosity called the Fibonacci Series. The Fibonacci Series and the Golden Section are intimately related, as we shall see in a moment.

If we number each rectangle in accordance with its length—the first, smallest rectangle being equal to 1—the following sequence of numbers appears:

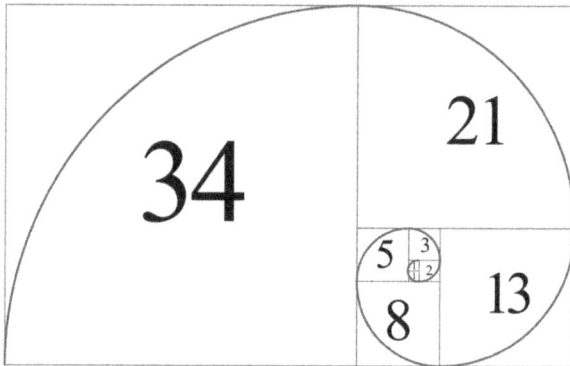

You will see that we have a number series as follows:

1, 1, 2, 3, 5, 8, 13, 21, 34.

$1 + 1 = 2$

$1 + 2 = 3$

$3 + 2 = 5$

$5 + 3 = 8$

$8 + 5 = 13$

And so forth.

THE GOLDEN SECTION AND THE FIBONACCI SERIES

In other words, this series is created when we add the next number to the previous number. This can go on forever, in ever-widening spirals or ever-increasing numbers. That number series is called the Fibonacci Series, and the resulting spiral in this diagram is called the Fibonacci Spiral. The Spiral occurs frequently in nature (the most common illustration is that of a snail shell). It is often used as a symbol for evolution but it can also represent other phenomena. For instance, Thelemites might see an echo of the spiral dance performed by the Priestess during the Gnostic Mass.

There are mathematical formulas that offer us a method for calculating these phenomena.

As mentioned above, the symbol for the Golden Section is the Greek letter Phi, or Φ. In math terms, $\varphi = \frac{1+\sqrt{5}}{2}$ The square root of 5 = 2.2360679. Thus 1+ 2.2360679 = 3.2360679. Divided by 2 = 1.6180339. Thus, the Golden Section—Φ—equals 1.6180339. That number does not seem to say much on its own; it's only by observing it "in the wild" that we can appreciate its power.

The square root of 5 is a key to understanding its importance among the ancients. There have been many studies and extrapolations of this number in analyses of the pentagram, for instance: a symbol not without attraction for ceremonial magicians, but which is also found in many other cultures as a sacred sign.

In a pentagram there are ten isosceles triangles (five acute and five obtuse) in which the ratio of the longer side to the shorter side is the Golden Section. In fact, the acute triangles themselves are considered "golden triangles" because of this ratio, since in an isosceles triangle there are two sides of equal length and a base side, and the ratio of the side to the base is in the Golden Ratio.

And then, of course:

AL I: 60. My number is 11, as all their numbers who are of us. The Five Pointed Star, with a Circle in the Middle, & the circle is Red.

My colour is black to the blind, but the blue & gold are seen of the seeing. Also I have a secret glory for them that love me.

A five-pointed star with a circle in the middle is an extremely specific construction. It seems deliberately to challenge the form we normally see: a pentagram in the center of a circle. In this case, the image is reversed. There is a pentagram, and within the pentagram is the circle. In Euclidean geometry, this is known as an "incircle."

The space in the center of the traditional pentagram is a pentagon. It is possible to draw a circle within the pentagon so that it touches each of its five sides.

But what does it mean to say, "My number is 11" and then go on to describe a pentagram with a red circle in the middle ... and then speak of colors black, blue and gold? And a secret glory?

Are we to understand from this that the number 11 is some kind of measurement that could be applied to either the pentagram or the circle? Or is the number 11 a pointer, alerting us to the fact that this quite different combination of Pentagram and Circle is the new Magic?

The most famous diagram of Star and Circle is the one everyone has seen at some time in their lives, the Leonardo Da Vinci drawing of a man stretched out in pentagram form in the center of a circle, referred to as "Vitruvian Man."

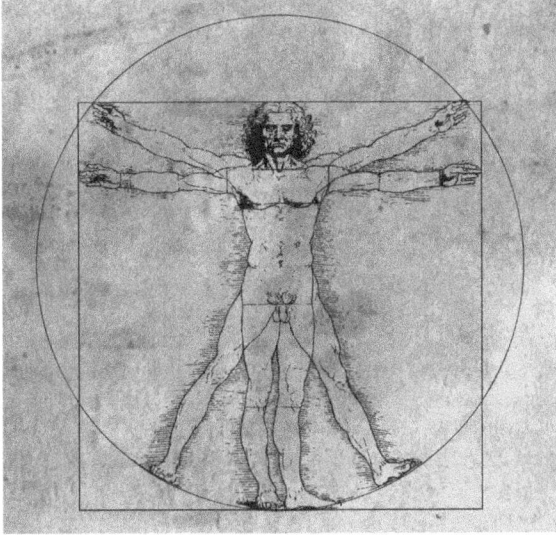

It has been claimed that this drawing is in the Golden Ratio itself, but another drawing—not as well known, except to occultists per-haps—demonstrates this quality more specifically:

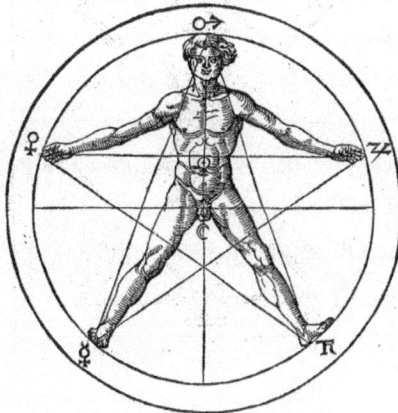

However, by contracting the Circle to the Middle of the Star— situating it above the torso, in the region of the sex organs and the lower abdomen—we may be emphasizing something essential to the Thelemic worldview and to its system of magic. It is, we contend, the magic of Da'ath and of the Tunnels of Set. This is because the Circle is no longer surrounding (and therefore protecting) the entire body, but has been concentrated on the lower chakras themselves, withdrawing from the limbs and even from the head and heart. It may be reference to the method in *Liber Yod*: the magic "of drawing all to a point," which consists of banishing all signs, all planets, and especially its "Second Method," which involves dissociating from one's limbs and eventually from one's entire physical body. The Death Posture employed by the K'rla Cell may have had a similar effect by way of binding the entire body except for the glans penis: which would be located in the center of the Circle that is Red.

This is referenced in the phrase "a secret glory for them that love me." In Greek, the phrase "a secret glory" translates as μια μυστική δόξα. This phrase adds to 1164 in isopsephy. This is the number of the Egyptian goddess known in Greek as Nephthys, the sister of Isis, who is depicted with a crown in the shape of the throne hieroglyphic (the same throne as shown in the Stele of Revealing) and the basket hieroglyphic meaning "mistress" or "lady." Thus, her name means "Lady of the Temple." Further, her role in the embalming rituals of the mummification process was critical, as she was the figure most associated with giving life to the deceased pharaoh. The power of Nephthys was the life-giving power, and this is yet another amplification of the Death Posture ritual used by the K'rla Cell.

As the following diagram illustrates, the angles we find in a pentagram are suggestive of a world of hidden meanings.

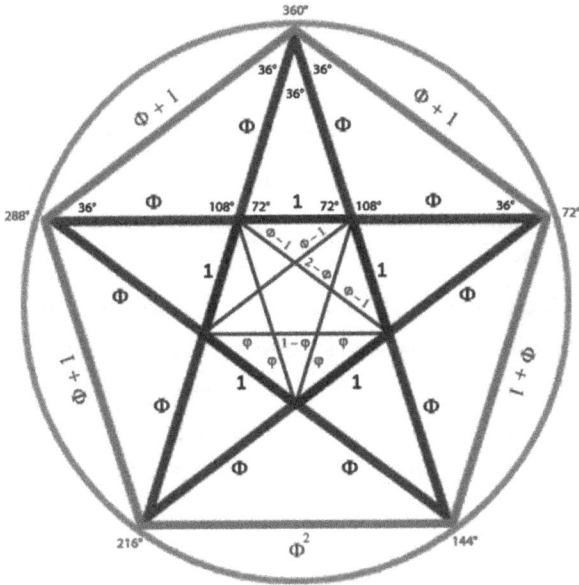

$$\Phi^{-1} = \frac{\sqrt{5}-1}{2} \qquad \Phi - 1 = \varphi \qquad \Phi = \frac{\sqrt{5}+1}{2} \qquad \Phi^2 = \Phi + 1 \qquad \Phi^2 = \frac{\sqrt{5}+3}{2}$$

$$\Phi^{-1} = \Phi - 1 \qquad 0.618... \qquad 1.618... \qquad 2.618...$$

$$\qquad\qquad\qquad\qquad \varphi$$

Dimensions of the pentagram and pentagon with relation to Phi-Φ
"The Golden Ratio." Diagram © Birol Koç eyephi.com

In this diagram we can see a number of important correspondences to Gnostic, Hermetic, and Thelemic concepts. The Golden
Triangle—which is an isosceles triangle consisting of two 72-degree
angles and one 36-degree angle—reveals a geometric condition for the
Schemhamphoras (the 72 lettered name of God) and the 36 decanates
of the Zodiac (36 divisions of 360 degrees of 10 degrees each). This
is reprised in a triangle of two 36-degree angles and one 108-degree
angle. Anyone versed in Buddhist and Hindu religion recognizes the
importance of 108 degrees. There are 108 beads in a *mala*—an Indian
rosary—and it is believed there are 108 *marmas* in the human body,

which are reflected in 108 *pithas*: sacred sites in India. (These may be connected to the *points-chauds* in the conception of the body-as-cosmos in the cosmology of Michael Bertiaux).

But what is even more striking is the preponderance of Φ in the above diagram. The Golden Mean or Golden Section is to be found everywhere in the Pentagram, which indicates a close relation between the Golden Mean and Nuit—whose symbol is a Pentagram with an inscribed Circle. This multiplication of Φ throughout the Pentagram and its various angles indicates a hidden Qabalah not only of Φ but also of 5: the Lovecraftian number *par excellence*. The first ritual anyone learns in the Golden Dawn as well as in the A∴A∴ is a version of the Lesser Banishing Ritual of the Pentagram, but it is anyone's guess whether or not the aspiring initiate actually understands the profundity of the geometric allusion.

Those who affect the tradition of the ceremonial magician—with its circles and triangles—are probably equally unaware of the significance of those shapes with reference to sacred geometry, and we shall attempt to remedy that shortcoming in the following chapter.

CHAPTER TWELVE

The Triangles of Art

One of the most comprehensive and complete repositories of the Typhonian Tradition survives today in the form of the Hindu Sri Chakra. Its complex system of yantras and mandalas constitutes a map of magico-mystical forces, and of power-zones in alien dimensions to which most other ancient signposts have been obliterated by time or distorted by misrepresentation. ... the Sri Chakra contains formulae of immense potency waiting to be restored and used again by those competent to do so.[83]

W e will study the Sri Chakra of which Kenneth Grant writes later in this book, but at this time we wish to point out the most obvious fact about the Sri Chakra—and about yantras and mandalas generally: they are geometric designs, and it is in their design that their power is to be found. The arrangements of squares, circles, and triangles in various numbers and combinations are all very deliberate and structured according to specific purposes. The closest we have in the West are the seals and sigils of the ceremonial art, including its magic circles and triangles.

The measurement of the sides of triangles and the areas of triangles, as well as the ratios inherent in various types of triangles—isosceles, right, equilateral, etc.—is the focus of trigonometry, a branch of

---

83   Kenneth Grant, *Beyond the Mauve Zone*, Starfire Publishing, London, (1999) 2016, p. 39.

mathematics that has its formal origins in the 3rd century BCE when the ancient Greeks were looking for ways to calculate astronomical phenomena. The famous Pythagorean Theorem, for instance, is a method of calculating the length of the side of a right triangle when the lengths of two sides are known. Terms like *sine, cosine,* and *tangent* come to us from this branch of mathematics as they pertain to ratios of sides to each other in a triangle. While modern Western magicians may ignore these relationships as having nothing to do with magic, this perception is in error. The progenitors of much of Western hermeticism—such as Plato, Pythagoras, and Plotinus—were well aware of these ratios and while they focused on their practical applications in architecture and science, as well as their philosophical implications, they did not spare discussions on their mystical characteristics.

For instance, Plato—in his *Republic*—states quite clearly:

> The knowledge of which geometry aims is the knowledge of the eternal.[84]

And in his *Timaeus* he goes more deeply into the idea that triangles and their proportions are at the root of creation:

> In the first place, then, as is evident to all, fire and earth and water and air are bodies. And every sort of body possesses solidity, and every solid must necessarily be contained in planes; and every plane rectilinear figure is composed of triangles; and all triangles are originally of two kinds, both of which are made up of one right and two acute angles; one of them has at either end of the base the half of a divided right angle, having equal sides, while in the other the right angle is divided into unequal parts, having unequal sides. These, then, proceeding by a combination of probability with demonstration, we assume to be the original elements of fire and the other bodies ...[85]

---

84 Plato, Republic, VII, 52.
85 Plato, Timaeus, B. Jowett, trans. *The Dialogues of Plato*, Vol. Two, Random House, NY, 1892 (1920), p.35.

In this, we see the beginning of the demonstration of the Platonic solids, for Plato goes on to describe other combinations of triangles of different proportions and continues into descriptions of the solids for fire (triangle), earth (cube), etc. While the idea of the Platonic solids has been mentioned, almost in passing, by other occult authors, what is not so well-known is Plato's description of the triangle as being the first form of a solid, and specific rectilinear figures being representative of the elements. This idea was so respected by scholars for centuries that they tried to apply it towards the solar system. The following illustration by Kepler—the astronomer who was also an astrologer—in his aptly-named *Mysterium Cosmographicum* (1597) depicts this attempt well:

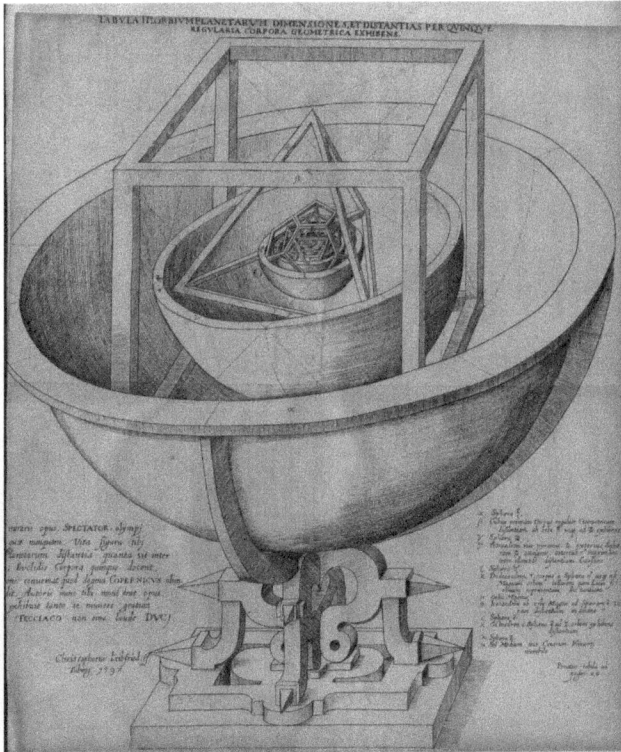

Here we have nested Platonic solids, from the sphere representing the orbit of the planet Saturn enclosing the cube representing the element of Earth, the tetrahedron representing Fire, the octahedron representing Air, and the icosohedron representing Water, all contained within the orbits of planets. These wire-frame type solids can be deconstructed into their various triangular component parts. In the Kepler diagram above, one can see the dotted lines representing connections between angles and vertices, for instance, and in the following diagrams (taken from Kepler's 1619 study *Harmonices Mundi*) we can see the structure of these solids a little more clearly:

Fire, the Tetrahedron.

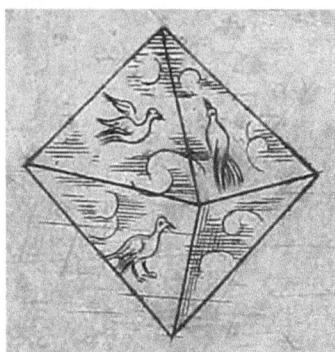

Air, the Octahedron.

Water, the Icosohedron.

Earth, the Cube.

The Dodecahedron, representing the Universe itself. One will notice that the pentagons that comprise the faces of the Dodecahedron can be inscribed with pentagrams, which reprises the Platonic and Pythagorean ideal of the Pentagram as the symbol *par excellence* of perfection, and of the interface between microcosm and macrocosm: an essential concept to occultism, hermeticism, and alchemy in general and specifically to Kenneth Grant's understanding of the Sri Chakra and its relation to the Tantric practices of the Typhonian Order.

• • •

This idea that geometry was a means of apprehending the non-material was well-known to the ancients, particularly to the Greeks and the Egyptians. Plato is said to have received this inspiration from Pythagoras and his school through Socrates, and then communicated the same to his student, Aristotle. Pythagoras is believed to have borrowed his ideas on the transmigration of souls and other mystical ideas from the Egyptians. Later, Plotinus expands on this idea of Number and its relation to creation and the cosmos in his *Enneads*, specifically the Sixth Ennead, the Sixth and the Seventh Tractates.[86] The two tractates read as if they were a Neoplatonist attempt to explain

---

86   Plotinus, *The Enneads*, Stephen MacKenna, trans. Faber & Faber Ltd., London, 1917-1930, pp. 541-595.

the idea of creation represented by the Sri Chakra, particularly the idea of the One expanding into multiple forms to establish the created world. Plotinus (204–270 CE) was an influential philosopher of the Neoplatonist school who combined elements of Christianity with Greek philosophy (especially Plato) and composed what became a response to all of these and to Gnosticism as well. There is thus a line of succession going back to ancient Egypt through the Greek philosophers concerning the mystical dimensions of sacred geometry. In the grimoires of ceremonial magic going back to at least the fifteenth century CE one discovers interesting facts about geometry and geometric relationships. One of these involves the function of the triangle.

In the *Lesser Key of Solomon* (also known as the *Goetia*), the triangle is used to materialize the summoned demon. We are told that the triangle must be drawn on the ground two feet from the magic circle (the nine-foot diameter circle where the magician stands during the conjuration) and that it must be three feet to a side. While the instructions do not explicitly state that the triangle must be an equilateral triangle (with each side measuring three feet) the actual drawing of the triangle in the grimoire is of an equilateral triangle (see illustration on page 141). Further, the base of the triangle faces the circle, and the apex of the triangle points in the direction from whence the demon is supposed to arrive.

In the edition of the *Lesser Key* with which most are familiar—the translation that bears a foreword by Aleister Crowley[87]—the triangle contains a circle inscribed within it as well as the name of Archangel Michael; in another edition, this one by Ebenezer Sibley and Frederick Hockley,[88] the triangle is quite plain and inscribed within a circle.

---

87   Aleister Crowley, ed., *The Book of the Goetia of Solomon the King*, Magickal Childe, New York, 1989, frontispiece.
88   Joseph Peterson, ed., *The Clavis or Key to the Magic of Solomon*, Ibis Press, Lake Worth, 2009, p.232.

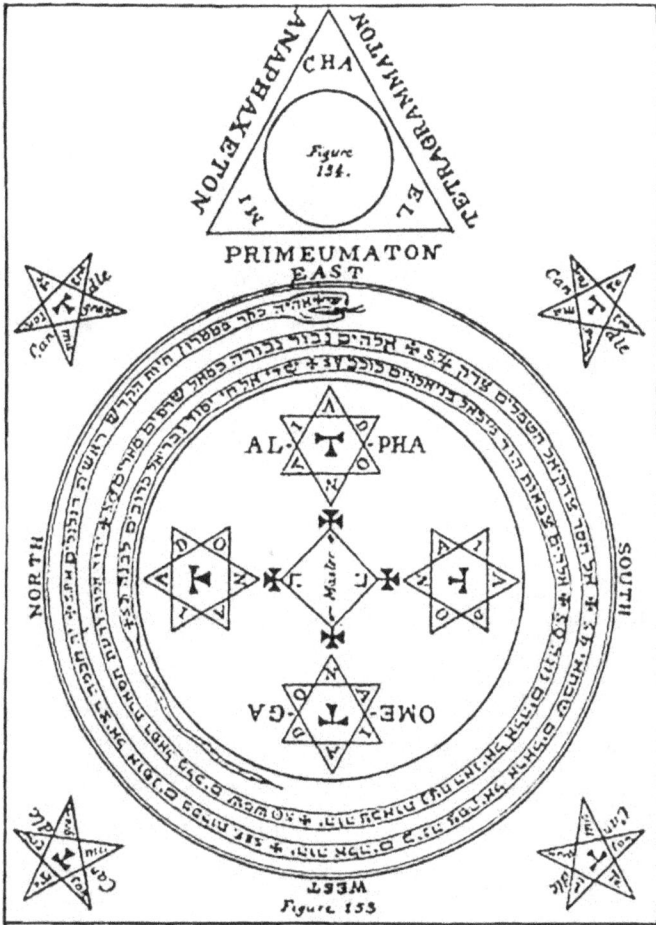

Figure 155

This exploration of—and mysticism pertaining to—triangles began with archaic astronomy. This involved the orientation of sacred spaces in alignment with astronomical phenomena—such as we see at Stonehenge, but which is not limited to megalithic sites. There was astronomical orientation among the indigenous peoples of North America, as well, at sites such as the Serpent Mound or Kahokia. In India and China, astronomical orientation of buildings and sacred spaces is a key component of Vaastu (India) and Feng Shui (China): both systems employ mathematics, astronomy, and terrestrial site selection on the

RITES OF THE MUMMY

basis of topographical features resulting in a harmonious balance of terrestrial and celestial forces.

Recent publications by authors who are experts in Vaastu reinforce the idea that the Golden Section is just as important to their science as the yantras and mandalas of East Asian religion and mysticism.[89]

Thus, we must ask ourselves if we have been neglecting to analyze the grimoires and other texts of ceremonial magic on mathematical grounds due to our ignorance of mathematical concepts—our collective innumeracy. Since we have all learned how to add, subtract, multiply, and divide, we have no problem applying that basic arithmetic to sacred texts in the form of gematria and isopsephy. But if we had more scrupulous training in higher mathematics, wouldn't we be able to apply that knowledge to the grimoires as well? Perhaps it was that mathematical ignorance that caused us to miss important clues in *Liber AL*, and quite possibly in other texts—both received, and deliberately crafted—to the detriment of our understanding, a defect that only could be remedied by the intense ritual practices of the K'rla Cell.

What we miss also is the experience of the beauty of the substructure of texts like *AL*. If we begin to realize that there is a mathematical harmony and symmetry underlying texts like these—and not only texts, but images and other forms of representation—we would be blown away by the view. The magic triangle of evocation takes on multiple dimensions of *meaning* as well as of application. The fact of the triangle as medium for manifestation reveals a wealth of useful information. It connects that simple diagram to the calculations of ancient astronomers and high priests, who invoked the gods from the planets and the stars to return to the Earth in visible appearance. It suggests that the triangle is more than just three lines on the ground, but a symbol of multi-dimensional manifestation incorporated in the ratios of its sides and the size and placement of its angles. The triangle is not

---

89   For instance, N.H. Sahasrabudhe & R.D. Mahatme, *Secrets of Vastushastra*, Sterling Paperbacks, New Delhi, 1999, pp. 73-76.

meant as a flat, two-dimensional tracing but as the basis for a multi-dimensional gateway between worlds. It helps to see the triangle first as a three-dimensional structure, like a pyramid, and the three-dimensional structure as a representation of a multi-dimensional portal. This is much the same way we draw perspective on a flat canvas to suggest foreground and background in a landscape; only now we are moving from the two-dimensional canvas to a three-dimensional "canvas" in which we represent a four-dime, five-dime, or greater structure.

While *Goetia* tells us to trace the triangle three feet across, and the diagram itself suggests an equilateral triangle of three feet on each side, with angles of 60 degrees each, what if we altered the design of the triangle, and thereby modified not only the type of triangle from equilateral to, perhaps, a right triangle but also the size of the base and the size of the angles? Would that produce a different type of gateway for manifestation?

To enable us to see the possibility, we may refer to the famous Asian diagram of manifestation, known as the *Sri Chakra* or the *Sri Yantra*. Here we see a comparable figure of concentric circles and stars composed of interlaced triangles:

In this diagram we are offered an embarrassment of riches. There are four upward-pointing equilateral triangles (associated with the male generative force, Shiva) and five downward-pointing equilateral triangles (associated with the female generative force, Shakti) making up the star in the center circle. In the very center, downward-pointing triangle there is a single dot—called a *bindu*—and it is of upmost importance. It represents the Goddess of Creation, the *Tripurasundari* ("Goddess of the Three Worlds"), and the downward-pointing triangle wherein she resides is the Womb of Creation itself.

The Shri Yantra or Shri Chakra is a diagram showing the moment of creation. The translation of the word *yantra* is "device" or "machine." While we see it as a two-dimensional figure, it is often constructed as a three-dimensional mandala. Even then, it represents a moment that is beyond the three dimensions that we know. It is still a diagram of a deeper structure, and to gaze into the center of the Yantra—from outside, in—is to approach the moment of what scientists call the Big Bang. That dot in the center, the bindu, is a singularity: that brief moment before Time when everything came into being. The triangles that radiate out from that center dot represent matter in all its forms coming into existence: stars, gases, elements, cosmic rays, even the concepts of space and of time themselves.

Those nine basic triangles explode in an array of an additional forty-three triangles formed by their intersections, and each of these triangles is occupied by its own deity and qualification of force and energy.

It is worth pointing out that Kenneth Grant devoted *three* chapters in *Beyond the Mauve Zone* to explaining and amplifying the meaning of the Sri Chakra and its mantras, and that the chapter in the same book concerning the K'rla Cell follows directly upon those three chapters. *Beyond the Mauve Zone* is basically a meditation on the diagram from a Thelemic perspective. In fact, he links the Cell with the Sri Chakra explicitly when he writes:

As in the case of the *Sri Chakra* the K'rla Cell is, fundamentally, a battery of limitless potential.[90]

He refers several times to the Sri Chakra in this chapter, connecting it quite deliberately with the K'rla Cell, even going so far as to show relationships between the mantras, deities, and seed syllables of the Sri Chakra and the gematria and other characteristics of the Cell. It is obvious that Grant was quite enthused over the discoveries made by the Cell and, indeed, this was expressed directly to Evans in conversation and correspondence as well. What the K'rla Cell had discovered were links not only to the Typhonian Tradition as expressed in Grant's *Typhonian Trilogies*, but also to earlier ritual experimentation of Grant and his circle that predated even the formal creation of the Nu Isis Lodge that was the core of what would become the Typhonian O.T.O.

While the Sri Chakra is well-known in the west to those who study Indian religion and mysticism, and especially Tantra, what is not so well-known is the depth of meaning and power inherent in that particular arrangement of triangles, circles, lotus petals, and squares. This is what inspired Grant and is the reason why he associated the practices surrounding the worship and utilization of the Sri Chakra with the rituals of the K'rla Cell.

There is much more than can be explained regarding the circles, the lotus petals, and the surrounding structure of four doors, but we believe that interested readers will have no difficulty in discovering all of that for themselves. We may even suggest a close reading of *AL* I:51 and *AL* III:64-67 for more inspiration along those lines.

For the Western ceremonial magician, the triangle still represents that moment of creation, of materialization, consciously constructed and employed to bring invisible beings to visible appearance. And the circle the magician stands in represents what Jung called the mandala:

90   Kenneth Grant, *Beyond the Mauve Zone*, Starfire Publishing, London, (1999) 2016, p. 91.

the proof of individuation, of the magician who has made contact with the Holy Guardian Angel (to use an *Abramelin* and Crowley reference). Both the Sri Yantra and the Mandala are geometric forms representing the balance of forces in harmonious interplay. It represents the perspective that this cosmos—seemingly full of contradictions, tensions, and negativity—is actually in balance; it is also a means towards achieving that same perspective.

In India, that means meditation on the diagrams themselves, accompanied by the appropriate mantras (words of power) as well as incenses, mudras (gestures) and the like in a mechanism for approaching the center of the diagram and walking backwards through time to the moment when everything came into existence through the action of Desire.

In the modern Western tradition represented by the Golden Dawn and, later, the A∴A∴, it means walking upward along the paths on the Tree of Life in an attempt to approach that same singularity on the other side of the Abyss. That includes mantras and mudras as well, albeit the Western forms of the same in the incantations, the ritual gestures, and the application of the aspirant's will to overcome all obstacles along the way.

In the Indian context, that means worshipping the *Tripurasundari*, the Goddess of the Three Worlds; in Thelema, it means giving the last drop of one's blood to the Goddess of the City of the Pyramids: Babalon.

CHAPTER THIRTEEN

Aleister Crowley and the Mathematics of *Liber AL*

The Apologia for this System is that our purest conceptions are symbolized in Mathematics. "God is the great Arithmetician." "God is the Grand Geometer." It is best therefore to apprehend Him by formulating our minds according to these measures. [...] We know infinitesimally little of the material Universe. Our detailed knowledge is so contemptibly minute, that it is hardly worth reference [...] Such knowledge as we have got is of a very general and abstruse, of a philosophical and almost magical character. This consists principally of the conceptions of pure mathematics. It is, therefore, almost legitimate to say that pure mathematics is our link with the rest of the Universe and with "God."—Aleister Crowley, *Magick in Theory and Practice*, Chapter 0: "The Magickal theory of the universe."

Aleister Crowley believed that there were mathematical secrets buried within the text of *Liber AL* and he enlisted the aid of mathematicians to discover what they were. Norman Mudd (Frater O.P.V.) was a mathematician; Edmund Saayman (Frater ADNI IHVH) was a mathematician. Even J.W.N. Sullivan—a well-known science writer whose specialty was making topics such as Einstein's theory of relativity accessible to general audiences—had been asked to take a look and to write a thesis on the subject. Crowley dropped hints to the mathematics encoded in *Liber AL* throughout his published work, including what is arguably his most famous book: *Magick in Theory and Practice*, quoted above. His *Confessions* include mentions of his desire to have *Liber AL* analyzed for mathematical and scientific clues and his absolute certainty of their existence is every-where in his *oeuvre*. Yet, neither Mudd nor Saayman nor Sullivan were able to identify these clues, much less to decode them:

> We were joined shortly afterwards by Eddie Saayman, an old pupil of Frater O.P.V.'s in Bloemfontein, and now a mathematical scholar at New College, Oxford, one of the most brilliant students in the university. He became interested in the mathematical theorems of *The Book of the Law*, which he thought, no less than myself and O.P.V., capable of revolutionizing mathematical ideas and mark-ing a new epoch in that science. [Aleister Crowley, *Confessions*, p. 921]

> [*Liber AL*] claims to be the statement of transcendental truth, and to have overcome the difficulty of expressing such truth in human lan-guage by what really amounts to the invention of a new method of communicating thought, not merely a new language, but a new type of language; a literal and numerical cipher involving the Greek and Hebrew Cabbalas, the highest mathematics etc. It also claims to be the utterance of an illuminated mind co-extensive with the ultimate ideas of which the universe is composed. [*Confessions*, p. 397]

> I had it in my mind to put spiritual research on a scientific basis. ... We already possess a universal language which does not depend on grammar. The fundamentals of mathematics are the basis of the Holy Cabbala. It is natural and proper to represent the cosmos, or any part of it, or any operation of it, or the operation of any part of it, by the symbols of pure mathematics. [*Confessions*, p. 465]

Sullivan came of the people. His brilliant brain had pulled him up to the position of "mathematical and scientific reviewer" for *The Times* and the *Athenaeum*, besides casual contributions to various papers. ...

The dialogue reverted after this short digression to the subject that enthralled us—*The Book of the Law*. I astounded his science by setting forth the facts of its origin, and the evidence of its contents that the author possessed the key to several problems insoluble by any intellect hitherto incarnate. We talked day and night for a fortnight. On his part, he showed me a great many mysteries in *The Book of the Law* that I had not suspected till then. I may indeed say that more than once he asked me some questions on a subject of which I was quite ignorant, and that on searching *The Book of the Law* I discovered a satisfactory reply in a text whose meaning had escaped me through my ignorance of the subject in question.
[*Confessions*, p. 870]

Alas, with all of this brainpower assembled over the years, the code resisted all attempts to discover it. Indeed, the only way the code could be discovered was by using the same methods by which it was encoded in the first place: the application of magical ritual to the problem. This was not the original intent of the K'rla Cell, however, since they had no idea that there was a code, much less try to discover what it was. The intention was to make contact with the non-terrestrial forces of the Dark Side of the Tree of Life and to use every tool at their disposal to do so. They came from a school of thought that assumed that there was more to Thelema than even Crowley himself knew: that the romance of Egyptology concealed more than it revealed and that Lovecraft might have had an angle on what had happened to Crowley in Cairo in 1904 that had escaped conscious understanding, both by Crowley's followers and by Crowley himself. "Let's use the tools of the O.T.O. combined with the terminology of the Cthulhu Mythos and the environment of mummification rituals to create a scenario that will blow open the doors of perception," they seemed to say. The K'rla Cell was a cabal of tomb raiders, and the tomb in question was Cthulhu's own, at the bottom of a deep, dark well at R'lyeh.

And when they surfaced, these Thelemic tomb raiders, they brought with them the Golden Key mentioned in the Amalantrah Workings (February 3, 1918).

And it unlocked the mathematical mysteries of *AL*.

CHAPTER FOURTEEN

Divide, Add, Multiply, and ... ?

Divide, add, multiply, and understand. (*AL* I:25)

The verse is quite clear in its cataloging of the operations of arithmetic, but it misses one. Why is "subtract" not included with the rest of the commands? Actually, there is a reason and it has to do with the code itself.

To understand this, we need to think about number like Pythagoreans or Hermeticists. In the early days of European mathematics, zero did not exist. Zero was an invention (or discovery) of mathematicians both in India and in Mexico at about the same time and made its way into Europe through the Middle East and the Arabian philosophers. These four operations—addition, multiplication, division, subtraction—have esoteric analogues that are quite close to their more mundane usages. In this system, multiplication and addition are cognate:

Multiplication is a kind of addition: 2 *times* 3 is basically 3 *plus* 3. 10 times 6 is basically 10 plus 10 plus 10 plus 10 plus 10 plus 10. Each method gives the same answer. Even God told Adam to "Be fruitful, and multiply" (Genesis 1:28). (A scary thing to say to a slow child in first grade arithmetic class!) And as Adam "multiplies" he is *adding* members to his family.

But what about division? To Hermeticists, division is another form of multiplication. When a cell divides, it multiplies itself into two exact copies. And then again. And then again. The result—in the case of human cell mitosis—is an embryo. And the embryo becomes a fetus, and the fetus a human being. Thus, the process of division results in multiplication. 60 divided by 10 gives us 6. The end result of the division points towards the first material. "For I am divided for love's sake, for the chance of union" (*AL* I:29)

Subtraction, however, is a different process altogether. Subtraction reduces a number, reverses the processes of addition, multiplication, and division. Subtraction tends towards Zero, towards the erasure of growth, of production. (Think of Cain "subtracting" Abel.) This may not seem obvious at first glance, but the verse itself contains the revelation.

As we have seen, the verse conceals the proportion known as the Golden Mean, or Φ. Phi is present in functions of growth and reproduction. Its cognate is the Fibonacci Series, which is identifiable in organic systems of growth: in plant life, in animal life, and in organic processes in general. Thus, this verse contains the seed of growth within it, a pointer towards growth in proportion, i.e., alchemical growth.

> The Golden Number does not act solely as a function of an ideal proportion, but serves as the basis for a philosophy that makes the connection between the metaphysical state and the physical state. It is in this connection that the Golden Number's "sacred" character consists. Furthermore, the human body develops in terms of this number.[91]

All subtraction tends towards zero and results eventually in a sum of Zero. Ten *divided* by ten equals 1. Ten *subtracted* from ten equals 0. There is a form of Christian mysticism that utilizes a meditation on subtraction. It is called "negative apophatism." It is a means of

---

91   R.A. Schwaller de Lubicz, *The Temple in Man: Sacred Architecture and the Perfect Man*, Inner Traditions International, Rochester (VT), 1977, p. 66

knowing God by refusing to accept any definition or characteristic of God, by saying—in effect—God is *not* this, God is *not* that, endlessly through every possible idea, every possible characteristic, until one reaches a form of satori. This can be understood as a kind of Advaita: a non-duality meditation in which one refuses to accept any substitution for the direct experience of God as a Unity. In that case, the pilgrimage towards Zero becomes a hajj towards One.

But what about the last word of that verse? "Understand." This word has an unusual etymology and seems to arrive in English after a complicated journey of concepts with the idea of "standing under" something, as if supporting it, or as if perceiving its base or foundation. It could also be a sly reference to a mathematical function or process, perhaps something as simple as the way we write a fraction, as one number standing under another. In which case it is also a symbol for division.

Squaring the Thelemic Circle

Further, if we study *AL* III:47 we find the following intriguing reference:

> 47. This book shall be translated into all tongues: but always with the original in the writing of the Beast; for in the chance shape of the letters and their position to one another: in these are mysteries that no Beast shall divine. Let him not seek to try: but one cometh after him, whence I say not, who shall discover the Key of it all. Then this line drawn is a key: then this circle squared in its failure is a key also. And Abrahadabra. It shall be his child & that strangely. Let him not seek after this; for thereby alone can he fall from it.

We will begin with the phrase "this circle squared in its failure is a key also," because it refers specifically to a problem in geometry which is insoluble due to the transcendent nature of Pi (π).

For centuries, mathematicians have tried—and failed—to discover a way by which a circle could be squared. Both the circle and the square contain 360 degrees, so the temptation to find a mathematical formula for converting one to the other was overpowering. However, there is no solution due to the nature of π. There is no fraction that can equal the full immensity of this number for there is no end to π's decimal places. Thus "the circle squared in its failure." However, there were many attempts to come up with a fraction that could stand in for π, and some came close to within 8 decimal points or so.

One was the intriguing fraction 256/81 which is equivalent to 3.1605: close, but no cigar. It is interesting to see these very suggestive values, however, as $256 = 4^4$ and $81 = 9^2$. 256 is the number of servient squares in the four Enochian Watchtowers, and 81 is the number of squares in the kame'a of the Moon.

But in the 1990s, mathematician Robert Dixon came up with an interesting attempt, and it involves the application of the Golden Section, or Φ. His result is:

$$6/5 \times (1 + \Phi) = 3.141640$$

Which is π correct to three decimal places. This is the only proof of concept for squaring the circle we have seen that uses Φ, and it made us wonder if that was what *AL* III:47 intended. Intriguingly, the fraction 6/5 is equivalent to the decimal 1.20. If we refer to *AL* I:20, we read "The key of the rituals is in the secret word which I have given unto him." Thus, another reference to a "key." Coincidental, perhaps. But since we are entertaining coincidences:

If we apply the same mathematical process to *AL* III:47 that we did to *AL* I:25 of "Divide, add, multiply, and understand," then $3/47 = 0.064; + 3 = 3.064; \times 47 = 144$.

144 equals 12 squared, or 12 times 12. It is the twelfth number in the Fibonacci series, and the largest Fibonacci number to be a square. In other words, it is another (similarly coded) reference to the Golden Section.

BOOK FIVE

The Grimoire of the K'rla Cell

*Being a selection of the collected writings and discoveries of
Frater Khepra-ma-Ast 481∴ and the K'rla Cell
(known as Jeffrey D. Evans in the Outer)*

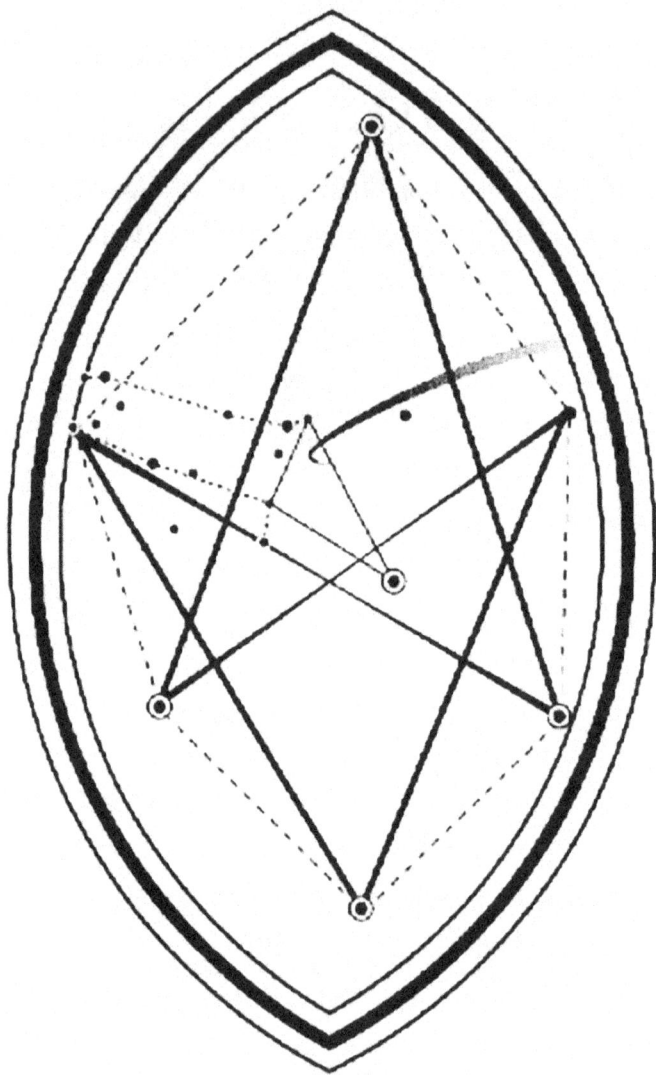

The Seal or Lamen of the K'rla Cell

A Brief Biography

J effrey Evans was born on July 4th, 1950, in Washington, D.C. at 10:05 a.m. and moved to Miami, Florida, in December of 1957. His childhood interests were science (and of course, science fiction, as was typical of his generation) but after becoming a member of the Order of St. John in the Lutheran church on July 4th, 1964, ritual worship enhanced his flair for the dramatic and he became an actor in both community and professional theaters in Miami. He had already studied the symbolism of ancient Egyptian mythology and their culture—even memorizing nearly 200 hieroglyphs at the age of ten—when he found Aleister Crowley's *Book 4, part 3* (Weiser ed.) in 1966. Following that, he began to systematically purchase books on Thelema in order to help himself get a grasp on the system. They seemed so much better than most of the trite paperbacks about "psychism," etc., of the time.

His mother provided his early education, teaching him to read before the age of five; and he could read and spell thirteen- and fifteen-lettered dinosaur names by the age of six. As a result, he was usually the top reader and speller in his classes, and frequently in his schools. Arithmetic, however, was a different matter. Taken out of school after three months of second grade, and not put back in until after the first three months of third grade, he missed nine months of schooling at a crucial time and did not take well to numbers. The basics of addition and subtraction were simple. Multiplication, division, decimals, fractions, and so forth, were of a different nature altogether.

Jeffery's mother was a registered nurse with a degree from the University of Pennsylvania, but his father dropped out of school in the tenth grade to join the service when his oldest brother died on D-day. However, his father was too young to enlist, so he simply never went back. He spent his teens at home on a chicken farm in the town of Woodstock, Virginia, tending the family still. As a result, Jeffrey's dad was an alcoholic for most of his life. He also didn't believe that an education was necessary for males: they needed to "get their hands dirty" in order to be men. Jeffrey's mother had to argue his father into allowing him to go to college, and subsequently Jeffrey entered Miami Dade Junior College. Jeffrey's sister, on the other hand, went to Florida State and she never let Jeffrey forget it—it was "superior" to Jeffrey's college. To her, a Junior College implied that Jeffrey was *"stupid,"* a characterization that haunted him most of his life. To make matters worse, Jeffrey's chosen major was Drama. Winning awards in high-school plays made no difference. To his father, acting wasn't "work." "That's why they *call* them 'plays'," he used to say!

During his community theater work, Jeffrey met Mal Jones and worked with noted Florida actor Karl Redcoff: Mal was the Florida State President of S.A.G. at the time. Mal had given Jeffrey the best advice he ever got as an aspiring actor: "Drop out of school. If you want to be an actor, get *work*. People who major in Drama at colleges become drama teachers," Mal told him.

On one of his 1971 visits to a bookstore in Coconut Grove, Florida (where the clerk had been helping him organize his knowledge of Crowley's books) Jeffrey saw a note on a bulletin-board that said simply, "Those persons wishing to contact the O.T.O. should write to....," giving an address in Fort Myers. He knew little about the O.T.O., being primarily interested in the Golden Dawn, but wrote and received a reply. It told him to begin a self-chosen magical or mystical practice, to keep a daily record of it for nine months, and then when finished, turn it in to that address. Easy enough, it seemed. He chose *dharana*, the yoga practice of focusing the mind on an object (in this case, a blue circle) without allowing thoughts to interfere with the focus. This was not as easy as it sounded.

Prior to this, he'd worked as an assistant manager at the Dadeland Twin movie-theater in South Florida, the first Twin theater in the South of the State. There, he met Harry Troeger, a man in his sixties, who (he was warned by the manager) was "an odd man," but who'd been with the company for years since it had opened its first theater on Miami Beach in the early 1930's. He was a doorman then. With the opening of the Twin theater, was *still* a doorman! Friends with all the company big-wigs, Mr. Troeger could have been wealthy, and a big man in the company. Instead, he dedicated his life to simplicity, and at his age was still making only $17 a week. The signs were clear. He walked to and from work, only wearing outdoor clothes; went into a back room where he shined shoes calmly for 30 minutes; and then came out dressed in a tuxedo and tore tickets calmly. Rarely speaking unless spoken to, he was difficult to know. One night, however, a candy-girl whispered "Mr. Evans...*look!!*," pointing to older Mr, Troeger. His eyes were pure white. After a few seconds they rolled down from his *ajnacakkra* and he gazed blissfully into the distance with just the barest trace of a smile on his lips, and he continued to tear tickets.

One night Jeffrey offered Mr. Troeger a ride home, and was told "I never ride in cars, or buses, or trains; they seem to disturb certain.... er....*vibrations* I try to set up in my body." A few days later, Jeffrey asked the man about these "vibrations," and got the answer "Well, Mr. Evans—in the 1950's I was building a cabin for myself in the woods, and while lifting heavy rocks felt a kind of 'pain' in my back. I did some research and found out that I'd awakened my *kundalini*." It was startling to hear an elderly man use such a word in the 1960's. It also seemed unique that a man claiming kundalini experience was working at the first Twin Theater in South Florida. The two vast towers that advertised it seemed suggestive of the *nadis*.

Shortly after the Twin opened, there was a great hustle-and-bustle there: Jack Mitchell, the head of the company's theater division, was coming for a visit. Mr. Mitchell pulled up in a limousine. He walked into the theater, and one of the first things he did was walk up to Mr. Troeger, looking him squarely in the face. "How about a *raise*, Harry?" Mr. Mitchell asked. Mr. Troeger closed his eyes and slowly shook his head "no"; Jack Mitchell walked away laughing.

While working there, Jeffrey also met Vivian Jones, a British-American woman working as a candy-girl. Her parents were "genuine Wiccans," she claimed, and she'd heard of Crowley (being British). One day, though, Jeffrey got a call from Karl Redcoff, offering him a job with a dinner-theater company ("Gold Coast Players") that operated out of Hollywood in Broward County, and he took it, working for two years without pay. The company traveled up and down the east coast of Florida doing plays at hotels and restaurants (for free meals); taking down sets, driving to another town, and putting the sets back up for another two or three performances. It was grueling work, but taught him the basics of carpentry, and lighting techniques, and helped him get his membership in the actors' union, Screen Actor's Guild (SAG).

He probationed for Kenneth Grant's Typhonian O.T.O. in 1972, becoming a member in 1973 (and adopting the Magical Motto *Kpra-ma-Ast*, 481∴ which means "To Come into Being out of Isis") before turning to devotional work to the Hindu deity Krishna in 1974. While Probationing, he called Vivian Jones (whom he'd met at the Twin Theater), who was just getting a divorce. They got together and she became his first magical partner, beginning a Probation practice herself.

When his Fifth Degree sponsor came to Miami to visit them, he recommended reading *The Magical Revival*. He was two years younger than Jeffrey Evans. However, he also made suspicious advances toward

Vivian, which proved to be true when he failed Jeffrey's Record, and subsequently passed hers. Almost immediately, Vivian gave the news that he was going to England with her and her parents. Adopting a Thelemic attitude, Jeffrey wished her good luck and let it go. At that time he was still an actor, and—having become a member of SAG—returned to the city of his birth in December of 1974 to perform in the first government-sponsored production of a play by Shakespeare in U.S. history (sponsored by ex-actor Ronald Reagan). There, Jeffrey underwent a Dark Night of the Soul for two years, and, while in a greatly depressed state one night at midnight, he had what has been called K&C of HGA (Knowledge and Conversation of the Holy Guardian Angel) over the Potomac River on July 23rd, 1977. The bridge connects Virginia (with his boyhood hometown of Alexandria) and Washington, D.C. (where he met Ruth Keenan).

Potomac comes from an Algonquin word that means "the river of swans." The swan is a symbol of Aphrodite and is therefore cognate with the dove on the O.T.O. Seal (see *Liber 777*, col. Xxxviii, line 14) and is רוברב in Hebrew, with a gematria of 410; the number of שודק, "sacred" or "Saint" (see *Liber D*).

This so-called "Dark Night of the Soul" came about as a result of three things: the huge delay and under-funding of the Shakespearean production; being thrown out by the first family that had offered to take him in; and having the second couple that took him in accuse him of *"molesting"* their 4-year-old child. The police were called; Jeffrey was hand-cuffed, stood in line-ups, given a lie-detector test, and spent a night in jail. When he returned, all his things were thrown out on the street. All of this, apparently, was because he'd become known as a Thelemite, and when the local occult bookstore (ironically called "Yes! Inc.") got wind of it, all he heard was "NO!" They refused to let him in the store, and would not sell him books. After this, his sister turned the whole paternal side of his family against him; they denounced him as a "bum" for being an actor, and told him he "didn't have a right to be an Evans." One week later, his mother came to Washington on a visit, but with a new husband, since Jeffrey's father had passed away. The step-father was despicable, and wouldn't allow his mother to see him.

The Name of his Angel was *Karla*, but she communicated no Book; only a Number: 251. He has designated her as his "Angel" only due to the other-worldly nature of the experience. It occurred at midnight, and over a bridge. She came out of a fog, approached, and after a brief exchange, *invited herself* to his apartment. At first he thought *"she must be a prostitute, or something, "* but when they got there she asked him about the books he had lining the borders of the single room. Pointing to a line of books, she asked: "Is that the *Encyclopedia Britannica?*" He replied, "No, that's something called *The Equinox,*" of course expecting her to not know what he meant. Instead, she asked with amazement, "That's *The Equinox*?!!"

It turned out she knew all about Crowley and his writings; she said she'd been practicing magical rituals for years *"with a boyfriend"* but wouldn't give his name or allow a meeting. Also, she professed to have no affiliation with any group or circle—not even Wiccan. She knew more about Thelema "off the top of her head," so to speak, than he would ever expect of a total stranger. However, she'd never heard of Kenneth Grant. He showed her the first three books of the *Trilogies*, and when she saw the quote from Charles Beatty's book *Gate of Dreams* about a re-incarnation memory experienced by Joan Grant (in K.G.'s *Cults of the Shadow)*, she told him she and her "boyfriend" had experimented with that rite.

They talked until nearly dawn about the Typhonian nature of Kenneth's books, and before the sun rose, she said "I have to go, now." He asked to walk her back, but she said no. He replied, "At least let me walk you back to where we met, since it's so late," and she agreed, asking for a promise not to follow her. They walked back to the middle of Key Bridge, where it was still foggy. She said goodbye, and walked toward the fog, at the last minute turning to say "Now, don't follow me!" He said he wouldn't, and she walked into the mist. He never saw her again.

When he returned to his one-room apartment, he realized that he'd never touched her and that the predominant colors he recalled were blue, gold, and white (her jeans and the penetrating color of her eyes; her blonde hair; and a white top). Also, she'd never told him her *last* name. When he got back, he reflected that there must be something in the fact that where they met was *Key* Bridge. Named, of course, for Francis Scott Key—while his mundane birth was the fourth of July— he nevertheless looked it up in an English-Greek dictionary out of curiosity, and found that the spelling of the Greek word for "key" was κλειτoρις—"clitoris," with the final Sigma counted as 31. The total value was 576, or (481+95), and (576+95) = 671, אערת, the Gate; and ארעת the Law (see *Liber D*). It was all-too overwhelming. This happened on July 23rd of 1977; at first reluctant to call it K&C of HGA, he adopted that terminology after describing the experience in a letter to Kenneth Grant, who replied on September 23rd with no objections, and even some excitement.

With this event, he gave up his career as an actor and devoted his life and his work entirely to the direction of his Angel, and to the Order.

By then he held the Grade of V° in the Typhonian O.T.O. and began monthly communication with Kenneth Grant, meeting Ruth Keenan three months later. She Probationed for the Order and was admitted in 1979, taking the Motto of Maiat, 352∵ Jeffrey met Kenneth Grant in the U.K. for the first time in December of 1977, staying for three days with Mike Magee and Jan Bailey. They were both extremely friendly, and the first day he was there, took him on a "surprise visit" to someplace they wouldn't name. Assuming it to be his meeting with Kenneth, he was disappointed to find himself taken to Stonehenge. Mike and Jan were amazed, saying they'd never met an American who didn't want to see Stonehenge the first time they were in England! Jeffrey had seen it too

Jeffrey D. Evans in the library of Kenneth Grant, at the latter's house in Golder's Green, London, October 31, 1989 e.v.

Ruth Keenan Evans with Kenneth Grant at the latter's residence in London, October 31, 1989 e.v.

many times on television; it didn't seem that impressive. He asked about Vivian Jones and her paramour while he was in the U.K. on this first visit, and didn't hear very good things. Vivian was well-liked by members of the U.K. Power Zone, but the boyfriend wasn't. They didn't like "the way he treated her," according to some accounts, such as getting her pregnant and forcing her to have an abortion when she didn't want one. It had apparently left her in a slightly unstable emotional state. The boyfriend gained his MA at Antioch University and a PhD at the University of London (Kings College); then divorced her and moved back to the U.S. where he's now a Professor of Philosophy whose books are regularly reviewed by the *New York Times*. He's cut all ties with his occult past but was briefly back in touch with Jeffrey to brag about his success; until a mention of their previous acquaintance in Miami made him cut off their contact as well.

As pointed out above, when his HGA had first begun instruction, she mentioned the ritual vividly described by Joan Grant, author of several novels drawing on her experiences of past lives. It is also mentioned by Kenneth Grant in *Cults of the Shadow* (p. 135) in a quote from a book by Charles Beatty titled *Gate of Dreams* (London, 1972), and depicted in the drawing *The Rite* by Margaret Ingalls ("Nema") in Kenneth Grant's *Beyond the Mauve Zone* (Starfire 2016 edition, Plate 8). The drawing depicts a Priestess of Isis being bound as if for death, to be *buried alive* in a highly sexually-charged state. She was to serve the Pharaoh as his slave, his seer, and his concubine in Amenta (the underworld).

Karla (in Hebrew אלרכ, with the numerical value of 251) suggested that it be turned into a Rite of *Alien Abduction*. The second half of the formula became 152, the reflex of 251 and the number of the Greek word for Cell, as in a Lodge or monastery of monks and nuns. Kenneth Grant suggested turning it into a ritual for contacting the Old Ones of H. P. Lovecraft's Cthulhu Cultus that so terrified Jeffrey in nightmares over which he had no control. He instructed the Cell to focus on the star Ibt al Ghauzi, or Betelgeuse, so focus was directed on the Winter Hexagon and the constellation Orion, eventually discovering that the four Hexagrams in *Liber 0 vel Manus et Sagittae (sub figura V)* were actually constellations.

Ruth Keenan had moved to Miami with Jeffrey on his return, and they were initiated into an *Ile di Yemanja* ("House" of *Yemanja*) in the Afro-Cuban cult of Santeria under Padrino (or "Godfather") *Omi Ademi* (literally "Sea Water" in the sacred language of Santeria, called *Lucumi*). The orisha *Yemanja* is the orisha of water.

They received their *ileke* ("collars," or prayer-beads), yet for only *five* orishas: Elegba (also called Eshu); Shango; Obatala; Yemanja; and Oshun. (These can be recognized as the Sephiroth Yesod, Geburah, Kether, Binah, and Netzach to those familiar with the symbolism of the Qabalah—and the sum of these numbers, $9+5+1+3+7 = 5^2$, the significance of which will become apparent later). Initiates into the cult traditionally receive *ileke* for Orunmila as well, yet Jeffrey and Ruth did not. The significant fact about this is that they had been instructed to achieve communication with the Old Ones, whose *number* is 5. Also, curiously, the number of beads on Evans' *ileke* for Yemanja was 251—this was entirely arbitrary, as he did not choose the number of beads. They had entered a House of Yemanja, yet one that did not practice animal sacrifice. Kenneth Grant felt that the Order should "not work with arterial blood," and they chose to respect and follow those wishes.

Jeffrey began to notice the predominance of water symbolism in his Magickal career at this time. St. John (the Baptist) was the Christian disciple of water; his tropical birth-sign (Cancer) was a water sign. In the Shakesperean play he was in (*Romeo and Juliet*) for the bicentennial, he opened the play as a water seller on the streets of Verona, crying "Water!" He met his HGA over water. He met Ruth Keenan where he worked, at the M-Street Newsstand (M is the letter of Water). They had been admitted to a House of the orisha of water. Their Santero had the magical name of "Sea Water." They each had five sets of prayer-beads,

Omi Ademi's Botanica in Miami, Florida in 1979.

and 5 is the numerical value of the Hebrew letter He, which stands for water as the mother in the formula of tetragrammaton.

The receipt of the *jagunjagun* (called *guerreros* or "warriors" in Spanish) is the second step in the cult of Santeria. These are magical weapons comprised of icons that represent the three orishas Eshu, Ogun, Ochosi, as well as the guardian Osun. They are fashioned by the *Padrino*, or the Santero. Eshu is a small clay head with twin faces, equivalent to the dual nature of Heru-Ra-Ha as Ra-Hoor-Khuit and Hoor-Paar-Kraat; or, Horus and Set. In the center of the icon a special occult stone is placed. Inside of our Eshu is a piece of amber; and it can be spelled in Greek as αμβηρ, which = 151, the number of κρλα, or אלרכ as it is transliterated into Greek. Ogun is an iron cauldron filled with iron tools, representative of the Strength of Geburah. Ochosi is an iron crossbow-and-arrow, placed inside Ogun (and therefore suggestive of Sagittarius, Ruth's natal sign). They all sit on a reed mat behind the front door of the practitioner's home, as Eshu is the Guardian of the Door or the Gate. He corresponds to the *dikpalas* of Tibetan Buddhism that serve as Guardians of the Quarters. Osun sits apart from the others, high up on a shelf, facing the door, and is often called "The Watcher." The Warriors are saluted every day with a morning purification of water, white rum, and tobacco smoke; and sandalwood incense can be lit for Eshu. His special day is Monday, at which time he receives coffee (traditionally his sacred drink, along with rum); fruits that are sacred to him; and candies with toys (he is depicted as a trickster-child; the messenger of the Supreme deity Olodumare: yet always ready to surprisingly deceive). Every Monday, a red 7-day candle is lit for Eshu.

Jeffrey Evans was divined by a *Babalawo* or Priest if Ifa as having Obatala for his *ori inu* ("ruler of the head"). Ruth Keenan was divined as having Chango. They correspond to the Sephiroth Kether and Geburah respectively, and the beads for Obatala are white, with four equally-spaced red beads. The beads for Chango are alternating red-and-white. The *ori inu or* "inner ruler" is distinct from the Western concept of the Holy Guardian Angel or *Augoeides*. For each Initiate on the Western Path, the Angel is a personal, distinct being. There is an Angel of Dark, and an Angel of Light. The orishas, however, correspond to the Grades of the Western Path. One cannot say that his or her angel is an orisha such as Ochun. That is like affirming that one's Angel "is" Netzach. The HGA can, of course, have the *qualities* of Netzach.

The ori inu is a communal experience, not a personal one.

Kenneth Grant arranged for Jeffrey and Ruth Keenan to stay with another member in Ithaca, New York, to begin to create the K'rla Cell Rite. This was Frater Otz PTN, 690, who had originally printed the

Typhonian O.T.O.'s American newsletter, *Mezla*, along with Janice Ayers of Buffalo, New York. Frater Otz PTN wrote offering to let them stay for free (as he put it) for the Working, but problems ensued. At their first rite he insisted that they partake of "magic mushrooms" or "there will be no ritual." They obliged.

He told them to begin, and Ruth did the Invoking Ritual of the Pentagram. Jeffrey followed with the Lesser Ritual of the Hexagram from *Liber O*, which probably took about 20 minutes. Afterward, he did *Liber V vel Manus et Sagittae*, with the full tripetal spiral dance, both widdershins and deosil, while Ruth beat a rhythm on a small drum. It was followed by a recitation of the "paeon" following the rite; and Ruth closed with the Banishing Ritual of the Pentagram. Altogether, this was certainly over an hour.

When it came time for Fr. OTz PTN to do his ritual, he turned off the lights. He'd had four Enochian Tablets put up on the walls. A small spotlight went on, and he shined it on one of the Tablets. Then, he shined it on a second one. Then it went off. It came on again, and went off suddenly. Then it came on and trailed across one of them. They realized he was going to present a simple "light show," without any music! The light went off again.

Suddenly, the Frater broke the circle, and ran upstairs, screaming. His girlfriend (ex-Soror Omaku, 137) had to go upstairs and calm him down with a bubble bath. The relationship was strained after that, to say the least.

The Priestess presiding at the first K'rla Cell Rite was a member of the Typhonian Order named Deborah Davis, who had recently become a Priestess of Isis (on October 7th, 1980) in the Fellowship of Isis headed by Olivia Robertson.

Fourteen days later, the Priestess of Isis willingly presided at the first performance of the K'rla Cell Rite in the same Temple. No other Typhonian Order members were present for this, and nine months later Frater OTz PTN threw them out for "refusing to pay rent," as he put it

Frater Kphr-Ma-Ast in his Deborah Davis persona. He was permitted to change his legal name to Deborah Davis and get a driver's license in the new identity, and all in record time. He functioned socially as Deborah Davis full-time for years until Kenneth Grant advised him to reserve the female persona for ritual magic work.

online. He also made the claim that they "threw a hissy-fit and trashed their Temple, leaving us to clean up the mess."

He'd apparently never heard of banishing.

After they returned to Miami, the Priestess of the K'rla Cell of the Typhonian O.T.O. became entranced and began to gaze at verse I:25 of *The Book of the Law*. Applying the command of the goddess to "Divide, add, multiply, and understand," she discovered the Golden Ratio in the text. (See "Iunci CXXV: The Golden Line." *Iunci* is Latin for "Papyrus.") They immediately saw the significance of the permutations of 251; 152; 125 (= 5 times 5^2); ... not to mention the fact that $512 = (481+31)$.

Unable to grasp the significance of this fact at first, it took years of research for a non-mathematician to unravel it. Kenneth Grant remarked, "Your numbers overwhelm me!" and provided Jeffrey with the names and addresses of several Order members to send the material to. He got everything from no response at all, to angry comments such as "Pure mathematics! Non-occult!!" Mathematicians were similarly unwilling to work on it, viewing it as simply "mysticism." Jeffrey Evans and the K'rla Cell (or Lodge) of the Typhonian O.T.O. became despised and feared by most members of the Typhonian order, and by most mathematicians we contacted for help.

Kenneth's concept of the Typhonian O.T.O. had great potential, to Jeffrey's mind. It separated the wheat from the chaff. Yet in his experience, he felt he only met two genuine Initiates in the group: Kenneth Grant, and Mike Magee. The latter has become an acknowledged Tantric scholar, and is translating written works from Sanskrit into English. He was the publisher of the Typhonian Order's first British organ, "Sothis," and his magical partner (now ex-wife) Jan Magee (nee Bailey) is a superb artist.

The number given by Nuit in *The Book of the Law* is truly unique. It is $5^{0.5} \times 0.5 + 0.5$, and also $2\cos(36^{\circ})$; while two times 36 is $(360^{\circ} \div 5)$ or one-fifth of the Circle. It is the square root of 1.25 plus 0.5; and $\cos(60^{\circ}) = 0.5$ while $\cos(36^{\circ}) = (\frac{1}{2}\Phi)$. Note that $36 = 6^2$, thus it truly unites the 5 and the 6, one of the definitions of the Great Work. Also,

$$\Phi^{-1} = 0.61803398875$$

$$\Phi = 1.61803398875$$

$$\text{and } \Phi^2 = 2.61803398875$$

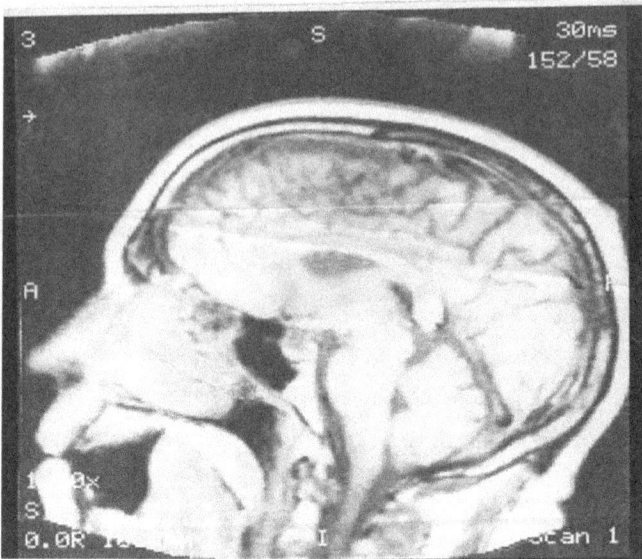

A CT-scan of Jeffrey Evans's brain. There is no identifiable source for his seizures, even after decades of attempts by medical specialists to discover the cause. That the seizures began as a consequence of occult workings cannot, therefore, be discounted entirely.

Due to material such as the above (and more, as will be revealed in future writings) received by the priestess of the K'rla Cell[92]—and it's interpretations by Jeffrey Evans due to years of research virtually unaided—he passed through the Sovereign Sanctuary of the Typhonian O.T.O. swiftly, and was appointed to the position of X° (Administrative Head of the Order) in America in 1987. He and his magickal partner Ruth Keenan married on April 9th of 1985, and she took the legal name of Ruth Keenan-Evans. She was admitted to the Sovereign Sanctuary of the Typhonian order on Halloween, 1989.

---

92   Miami, Florida is "a land of palms," thus Deborah Davis, the Priestess of the K'rla Cell of the Typhonian order, is the new "Deborah of the Palms." See Judges, chapter 4; also Judges, chapter 5, *The Song of Deborah*. Also, notice that the bottom left corner of the last page of Kenneth Grant's "The Dikpala of the Way of Silence—the Lam Statement" at *https://documents.pub* reads "London and Miami; Spring Equinox, 1987 e.v."

During his tenure in this Office in America, Jeffrey D. Evans straightened up the Typhonian Order in America, setting it on its proper course. He got rid of a drug-dealer attempting to use order channels for personal gain. He got rid of members-in-name-only, simply by asking for Magical Records (a requirement of the Oath of Membership under Kenneth Grant's structure) and was even called a "slave-driver" for making that request. He attempted to get members to see their need to follow the instructions of the O.H.O. ("or his authorized representative," as the Oath of Admission read), and was accused of "stabbing members in the back," and of "magically attacking" others. While attempting to oversee Kenneth Grant's "Nightside Tarot Project," he saw participants in the project pull away from it, publish *"their own"* completed decks, and claim to have initiated the concept. Finally, Kenneth Grant saw that this was all too heavy a burden for Jeffrey, and asked him to turn the Office of X° (Administrative Head of the Order) in America over to Michael Staley. He did so willingly, and even with a letter of congratulations to Mr. Staley.

For this, he was passed into the Grade of XI°, a Degree which gave him "the Right to Form an Order along Typhonian Lines," formulating the new motto of Shemsw-nn-Ast, 576∴ meaning "To Pass (Back) into Isis."

He was not "expelled," as Michael Staley has intimated online. Nor was he "the cause of the downfall of the Order in America," as has been claimed by others. In fact, he and his wife are attempting to formulate an order based upon material and a grade-structure received by the K'rla Cell Rites, and any and all willing to participate in this venture are urged to contact them at email *yhvvh32@yahoo.com.*

Typhonian O.T.O. Structure

♆ ---- DA'aTh: XI° (Outside the Order): Member is given the right to found their own Order along Typhonian lines, based on their own Work.

♀ ---- KthR: X° Outer Head of the Order (or Administrative Head of the Order in any Country).

♅ ---- ChVKMH: IX° Heterosexual Magical Work with a partner.

♄ ---- BINH: VIII° Masturbatory Magical Work (Degree conferred when the X° Administrative Head of one's Country or O.H.O. deems applicable).

♃ ---- ChSD: VII° (Intermediate Degree/Period of study in a self-chosen area. Begin correspondence with the X° Administrative Head of one's Country).

♂ ---- GBVRH VI° (Requires an Essay to the X° Administrative Head on what your progress in the Order has taught you).

☉---- TphARTh: V° The practice of *Liber HHH* and the beginning of the creation of a V° Circle of Probationers under your charge (a Power Zone).

♀ ---- NeTzCh: IV° Conferred after the successful completion of a Work of *bhakti* to a deity of the member's own choosing. The Record of the practice is judged by one's V° Superior.

☿ ---- HVD: III° Conferred after turning in an essay to one's V° Superior on the importance of the Order to your own Path, and to the 93 Current.

☽ ---- YSVD: II° Conferred after completion of a self-chosen mag./ myst. Practice.

⊗ ---- MLKVTh: I° *(Outside the Order):* On the physical plane. Comprised of those persons seeking admission to the Order.

It is specifically stated on the member's Oath of Admission that "The O.T.O. is *not* a Teaching Order." However, adherence to "The Instructions of the O.H.O., or his Authorized Representative," are required. The "Grade" of 0° is considered to be Qliphotic, while XI° confers entrance to the Nightside of the Tree of Life. "Secrecy" is required, although not strictly enforced, as there are no Group Workings, no Lodges, or Passwords, etc., as such. The "Power-Zones" are the V° Circles. Work is essentially "Self-Initiation." Each PZ is left up to the Direction of its V° Superior.

Timeline of the K'rla Cell

Vernal Equinox, 1973: Admission to II° of Frater KPhRA-Ma-AST, 481∴

Vernal Equinox, 1973:Admission to III° of Frater KPhRA-Ma-AST, 481∴

Vernal Equinox, 1974:Admission to IV° of Frater KPhRA-Ma-AST, 481∴ (After bhakti-yoga to Krishna as Radha)

July 23, 1977: K&C of HGA, Midnight on Key Bridge (Nearly exactly 3 months later I met Ruth)

Autumnal Equinox, 1977: Admission to V° of Frater KPhRA-Ma-AST, 481∴ (Fantasized that "the fiendious children" would become my V° Circle. No way.)

First two weeks of Dec. 1977: Met Mike Magee, Jan Bailey (her maiden-name), and Kenneth Grant for the first time.

First week of Jan. 1979: Had my first true seizure at a big party for Ruth. Fell down a stairwell; no memory of this at all. Simply woke up in a hospital feeling like I'd been run through a kitchen-blender. I could barely move for about three days after that and was surprised I hadn't broken any bones. Ruth and I moved to Miami.

Kenneth Grant admitted me to the VI° immediately, and I headed a Miami PZ of 5 Florida members (as I recall). But by now one of our members was heavily into Santeria, and had decided to receive Osha. Mid-Summer, 1979: We discovered the ile of Silo Crespo (Omi Ademi), and found such an easy-going, happy, and Thelemic Santero that we allowed him to take us in immediately. He was totally accepting of *Liber AL*, and of the attributions in *777*. When I demonstrated its value to him, he pointed to me and shouted to Ruth, "Wow!! He's a *real magician!*" He was a black man with an African dialect, and only charged us what we could afford. We got Ileke for Yemanja (the Mother of our Ile, i.e. his ori inu), Ochun, Elegba, Shango, and Obatala. We got five, and other aborishas started asking us where our Ileke for Orunmila were. We could only say, "Well, these are the ones we got." I thought it was significant that we got five, as it was the number of Horus, Mars, etc. I hadn't even considered the Old Ones yet. I was divined by a Babalawo as having Obatala. Ruth was divined Shango. I also got our guerreros, and we were told they should belong to both of us, as we were priest & priestess. She got the exceptionally large Ogun, "...for the strength she'll need," he told us. He used to call us his "crazy American Godchildren" and our guerreros underwent full charging-ceremonies with arterial blood, but we weren't present for these ceremonies, only his fully initiated God-Children. I wrote immediately to Grant and asked him about animal sacrifice, and when he said "no," we went straight to Omi Ademi and asked him what he thought. "Use Water!" he said, reminding us that the Mother-of-our Ile was Yemanja.

Beginning of the year, 1980: Ruth met Kenneth Grant for the first time. He interviewed her, but (as she claimed) didn't take her anywhere else but his den. Mike Magee had left the Order by then, and even Jan wasn't at a party the British PZ was holding (possibly a Vernal observation).

That's the evening I had my first meeting with Mick Staley, so Ruth met him, but never Mike Magee or Jan. I'm sorry for that.

We did both meet Caroline Wise then, though, and then Mick found out that I was given a LAM picture also. He told me that Mikhailovic-Slavinsky had also been given one. Mick told me that the three of us were not supposed to be in contact with each other over this business, and Kenneth had apparently done it all secretly, except that I know that Ruth was present when he gave one to us. Still, it was in darkness, and in secret.

October 7th, 1980: Admission to the Fellowship of Isis with a Certificate dated October 7th, 1980, signifying Deborah Davis as "…a Priestess of Isis," sealed by Olivia Durdin-Robertson, with accompanying letter from her, addressed to Deborah, with a side-note stating, "I shall light a Candle & use Brighid's Well-Water for you at 7.30 this evening. FOI Centre: SANDRA HELTON (Morgana) Centre of Sothis-Sirius, 7th OCTOBER 1980." Vivian Jones (ex-Soror NTRT PShT, 658·.·) gained her Admittance.

Dec. 31st, 1980–Jan.1st, 1981: Opening of experimental series of Cell Rites, following with the first Egyptian-styled Working we'd done. I'd heard in 1960: MAKARE. I had never heard the "name" before then, and only recognized it as a Formula in the Typhonian Trilogies, later.

End of March, 1984: Recognition of the Celestial Winter Hexagon, began researching it, and was able to correlate 17 Alpha-class stars that comprised these hexagons, and how they corresponded with those in the Lesser Ritual of the Hexagram. Discovery of al-hanah (Gamma Geminorum) in Richard Hinckley Allen's *Star Names: Their Lore and Meaning*, identifying it as "The Mark," i.e., a beast's mark.

April 2nd, 1984: The discovery of the Golden Mean equation in *AL* I:25.

LIBER 561
vel
Το βιβλίο της μούμιας

THE BOOK
OF THE MUMMY

I

Psions from Space

The Cthulhu Gnosis that is expressed in fictional form by writers such as H. P. Lovecraft, and others, is a viable dimension of consciousness that is amenable to contact by one having the proper keys, or who has "made the sacred alignments," as Zos vel Thanatos has said. Lovecraft readily admitted that much of his inspiration came from his dreams; that, in fact, many of his stories were transcribed directly from dream experiences[93] with little changed but the names of characters. On at least one occasion, he began to write before fully awake: The incident is reported in one of the published Volumes of his letters.[94] Control of the dream-state is one of the keys to making "the sacred alignments," and by "dream state"[95] is meant the entire gamut of dreaming, daydreaming, and imagination—especially, the creative imagination of the magician and the artist. The dream-state comprises also the phenomena of psychism [96]; and the theories of some recent researchers into the relationship between dreams and psychic phenomena such as telepathy and precognition, posit

---

93 Lovecraft's own position was, actually, that "occasionally—but not often—a dream of mine forms a usable fictional plot." See *Selected Letters*, Vol. V, p. 355 (Arkham House,1976 e.v.). However, see also Vol. I, pps. 97, 119, 160-162, 266; Vol. 11, p. 202; Vol. IV, pps. 242-243, 289-290, 317,326, 402, 413; Vol. V, pps. 70, 159, 181-162, 201, and 335.

94 Vol. I, p. 160 (letter to Reinhardt Kleiner).

95 *Svapna.*

96 See *Dream Telepathy: Experiments in Nocturnal ESP,* by Montague Ullman, MD, and Stanley Krippner, PhD, with Alan Vaughan. Macmillan, New York, 1973 e.v.). Also, *The Medium, The Mystic, and the Physicist* by Lawrence LeShan, Viking *Press,* 1974 e.v.

the existence of a particle, dubbed the psion to which the neurophysiological organism is more receptive when asleep and/or dreaming. Thus during sleep, scores of psi-particles bombarding the brain, which in the waking state go unnoticed, are picked up and occasionally even fine-focused by the more receptive type of neurological antenna.[97] Investigations into telepathy have even suggested that, when a sleeper passes into the REM state—the state of the most active dreaming, accompanied by Rapid Eye Movements—a telepathic field is created around the dreamer. Whether new information is obtained, or memory traces are stimulated in some unknown way by distant phenomena (i.e., distant in time or in space), is here irrelevant.[98] The important thing is that modern dream-research has begun to link svapna with the telepathic state.

The *psion* is named for the phenomena which are generally classed by psychic researchers under the heading of "psi," after the Greek letter: Ψ. The form of Psi is that of the Trident, the symbol which signifies Da'ath,[99] the Sphere of Knowledge in the Qabalistic scheme: the *"hole"* or Door to the Nightside of the Tree of Life; or in the Tantric terminology of the centres of subtle anatomy, Viśuddha Chakra. The letter traditionally occupies the 28th Path of the Tree,[100] and as both 7x4, and the Mystic Number of Netzach or Σ (1---7), 28 is a number of Venus in the Qabalistic scheme. It is the double or reflection of the 12th kala, represented by β the letter-name of which is—βήτα—equal to the number 311. This is the number of the Greek words δϝναμις (DFNAMIS), power, and οικιας (OIKIAS), house, thus signifying the Power-House or Source of the energy (shakti) here symbolized by Mercury, the Astro-mythic glyph of this kala.

---

97 That is, according to the Radiation Theory of Telepathy. However, *see The Medium, the Mystic, and the Physicist*, cptr. 1, and also *Extra Sensory Perception*, J.D. Rhine, PhD, (Bruce Humphries, Boston, 19(4 e.v.), cptr. 10, for arguments suggesting the unique nature of the supposed-X01 particle.
98 Current writers on psi-phenomena are divided on this point, and others. See *The Medium, the Mystic, and the Physicist*, appendix E: "Telepathic Perception in the Dream State.'
99 See *Nightside of Eden* by Kenneth Grant, Muller, London, 1977 e.v., page 9 (Pt. 1); also p. 259 (Glossary, under "Shin").
100 See any standard text on the Qabalah.

The Chaldean letter-glyph of the 12th kala, and the Semitic Linguistic equivalent of the Greek letter, is ב : BITh. The letter-name BITh or Beth signifies the House of the Womb; the Source of the Power of the "restless" Mercury—who was the messenger of the Gods.

In the Western attributions of the letters of various *"sacred"* alphabets to the Tree of Life, the 28th Path is also glyphed by the Semitic letter, Tzaddi (צ).[101] Psi therefore Qabalistically *"equates"* with Tzaddi. Both are given in New-Aeon symbolism to Atu IV, *The Emperor,* according to an instruction in *Liber AL vel Legis* the prime Tantra of the New-Aeon or 93 Current, in which it is exclaimed that "צ is not the star." Accordingly, Aleister Crowley switched the Tarotic attribution of Tzaddi from Atu XVII, The Star, to Atu IV, The Emperor.[102] This aligns The Star with the letter Hé (ה), which means a window—an important point to which I will return later. However, if Hé is The Star, and not Tzaddi, what happens if we switch not only the Atu attributions of these letters, but their actual positions on the Tree of Life? Hé then connects Yesod with Netzach and Tzaddi (or Psi) is seen to be raying down through the Abyss from Chokmah (the Logos) to Tiphareth (the Sun!) Thus it is a fitting symbol of the proposed psion, whether as the double of the 12th kala, with the "messenger" Mercury, its Ruler—or as raying down through the Abyss (of space) from the Sphere of the Logos ... the Word!

The letter-name Psi has the numerical value of 710. There are several interesting correspondences to 710: it is the number of LAM (71) times 10 (the number of Earth as Malkuth); of ARGUREOS[103], silver, of silver; of the combined letter-names of the three Paths which ray down from Kether, Chokmah and Binah, i.e. GAMMA+HTA+ZHTA[104] of

---

101 Chapter 1, verse 57.
102 See *The Book of Thoth*, Weiser, NY, 1969 e.v., pps 9-10.
103 $1 + 100 + 3 + 400 + 100 + 5 + 70 + 31 = 710$.
104 $(3 + 1 + 40 + 40 + 1) + (8 + 300 + 1) + (7 + 8 + 300 + 1) = 710$.

KUDISTOS[105], most glorious. When added to the numbers of the Spheres it links $2 + 710 + 6 = 718$—"the Abomination of Desolation!"—the magical name of the Stele of Revealing, the Supreme Yantra in the Cult of Thelema.

Commenting on an observation made by Dr. George Devereux (in *Psychoanalysis and the Occult*) [106] that the high incidence of telepathic coincidences between patients and their analysts implies that the patients are "spying" on their analysts in what seems like an aggressive act, the Dream-Researcher Ann Faraday wrote:

> [T]he observation that telepathy seems like prying or spying is interesting, for it makes the *"receiver"* of the information *the* active agent reading the other person's mind, in contrast to the model of *"mental radio"* on which most telepathy experiments are based. The mental radio model implies someone actively trying to send out messages to a relatively passive recipient, whereas the alternative model, which immediately sprang to my mind after reading about telepathy in the consulting room, was that of radar scanning the environment for something either threatening or desired. This is congruous with the mind's *"normal"* ability to pick up subtle impressions and vibes without our being aware of than until they turn up in dreams. The radar model also puts telepathy *in* the same category as clairvoyance and pre-cognition which do not involve a sender.[107]

In magical terms, the subconscious throws up a *"radar screen'*— the *"telepathic field"* associated with the REM state—in an effort to accomplish its Desire. As Dr. Faraday points out, the radar model puts telepathy in the same category as clairvoyance and precognition; and is also cognate with the nature of our other senses or skandhas, from which comes the modern English word scanners.

---

105 $20 + 400 + 4 + 10 + 6 + 70 + 200 = 710$.

106 New York: International Universities Press, 1953 e.v.

107 The other two of the main types of ESP. *The Dream Game*, Harper & Row, New York, 1976 e.v., pps 318-319.

II

Geographical Gateways

T he discovery, in the 1970's e.v., of triangular areas on the surface of the earth that are connected with high incidences of psychism and other unexplainable phenomena[108] may shed some
light on the tremendous impetus behind H. P. Lovecraft's dream-world of
the Old Ones. A highly significant fact is that *Lovecraft lived very near to
one of these triangles*, or "windows" as they have also been called. They
are, according to Fortean researcher Loren Coleman, locations of "focused
unexplained activity."[109] The Bridgewater Bay Triangle, in Massachusetts,
has long been associated with inexplicable phenomena of the type reported
by Charles Fort in his celebrated *Book of the Damned*: gigantic birds large
enough to carry off a human being; spirit-presences; phantom creatures with
tracks that are unidentifiable by normal classifications, and which are never
caught, only *halfway seen*; and similar manifestations of other-worldly or
extra-dimensional interpenetrations or visitations.[110] The sensitive artist will
often perceive what the purely rational mind cannot (or will not). Lovecraft
was such an artist, a true natural sensitive, the value of whose work is only
just beginning to be perceived by the occult community-at-large.

---

108 See *The Bermuda Triangle* by Charles Berlitz, and similar studies.
109 *Mysterious America*, by Loren Coleman, Faber & Faber, London and Boston, 1983 e.v., page 28.
110 See chapter four of *Mysterious America*.

Lovecraft made his home near the Bridgewater Bay Triangle, the boundaries of which include the Hockamock Swamp. The swamp itself seems to be the focus of much of the mysterious activity that occurs within the boundaries of the Triangle. The mysterious creatures that haunt the area, creatures such as the New England Man-Ape, or North American *yeti*, and giant birds which stand six feet tall, seem to disappear into the swamp, as well as come from it. Scores of reports by locals have noted the mysterious and chilling *sounds* that come from the swamp. The Hockomock Swamp has a long history in legend,[111] not only Indian legend but in the continuing reports that describe "unexplained activity," which are persistent up to this day. The swamp covers an area of nearly 200 square miles. In the Cthulhu Mythos as elaborated by Lovecraft, the areas he knew and loved in New England, are a prime focus of activity for the Cult of the Old Ones. What is suggested by the considerations here put forth is that this may not have been merely because he knew these areas but because Lovecraft the Dreamer became psychically sensitive to the proximity of the Bridgewater Bay Triangle in its possible function as a Gateway between dimensions.

The Triangle is the Yoni, or *place of manifestation*, but it is also the Pyramid of Fire, the Fire associated with the letter Shin, which is also representative of Spirit. In the formal system of ceremonial magic, the spirit is evoked into the Triangle of Art whereas the Goddess or God is invoked into the Circle. Such Triangles as the Bridgewater Bay Triangle are found all over the world, one of the most well-known being the infamous Bermuda Triangle, off the coast of South Florida. The former is associated with the Hockomock Swamp as the focus of its activity, and the latter with an area between Florida and Bimini which is associated with the Sargasso Sea—a seaweed "swamp'—and is known as Poseidonis, or Atlantis to the popular mind. A curious fact to be noted

---

111 Evidence of weird phenomena in this area prior to Lovecraft includes Indian legends, the descriptions in Cotton Mathers' *Wonders of the Invisible World*, and the Salem (or "Arkham') witch cult.

here is that Chozzar, the god of Atlantean Magick, has for his symbol the Trident (see Chapter 1). The modern-day twin-islands of Bimini are supposed to be the remnants of the twin islands called *Ruta* and *Daitya*, which existed before the final catastrophe that obliterated the remnants of the great Atlantean civilization.[112] Whatever the phenomena—whether the *disappearance* of people and objects (planes, boats, etc.) or the *appearance* of strange creatures and inexplicable phenomena—the area in which they occur (and especially where local legend is supported by an overwhelming abundance of modern-day reports) can usually be mapped out as *roughly triangular in shape.*[113]

According to the Field-theory of telepathic transmission,[114] the dreaming mind of Lovecraft may have served as a sensitive neuro-physiological antenna, transmitting via dreams the knowledge of the activities of the Old Ones; such activities being somehow connected with the Gateway of the Bridgewater Bay Triangle. That the Triangle is such a Gateway has been well-attested to. In *Mysterious America*, Loren Coleman reports a typical incident:

> Several years ago, an expedition of Massachusetts Archaeologists discovered an eight thousand year old Indian burial site on Grassy Island in the Hockomock Swamp. When the graves were opened, the red ochre within the tombs bubbled and dissolved mysteriously and every photograph taken of the site failed to develop.[115]

---

112 Cf. *The Story of Atlantis & The Lost Lemuria*, by W. Scott-Elliot; the Theosophical Publishing House, 1968 e.v. However, according to Mr. Scott-Elliot's maps, it would seem that the modern-day Bahamas and Bimini could only be remnants of Ruta, the larger and most northward of the two islands. But see *Atlantis: the Autobiography of a Search*, by Robert Perro and Michael Grumley; Bell Publishing Company, NY, 1970 e.v. The authors suggest that the name of the twin-islands of Bimini is a corruption of "Gemini."

113 *Mysterious America*, pps. 28-29.

114 See *Dream Telepathy*, p. 222, where it is called the "psi vigilance" theory, a term originated by Dr. Rex Stanford. See Chapter 1.

115 *Mysterious America*, p. 26.

Coleman also notes that, "for the Indians, it has been a site that is especially sacred and sometimes *especially evil*."[116] I have emphasized the last two words because via Greek gematria the word *evil*—κακος— has a numerical value of 311.[117] What is here suggested is that Lovecraft's dreaming mind focused on an influx from the Windows (Hé) of the Stars (ChABS = 311), manifesting via the "Gateway" of the Hockomock Swamp Triangle; that, in effect, his dreams were *mnemonic recordings of inter-dimensional activity*, due partially to his natural psychism; and partially to his proximity to the Triangle. From accounts of the Hockomock legends it can readily be seen that the New England area has long been a focus of activity for the Cult of the Old Ones, their agents, and those ever-ready to open the Gate and call Them through.

---

116 Ibid.
117 20 + 1 + 20 + 70 + 200.

III

Celestial Gateways

Researchers of strange phenomena have dubbed such Triangles as the Bridgewater Bay and Bermuda Triangles "gateways," or *window areas*,[118] two images which are especially interesting when viewed from the standpoint of occult symbology. The Chaldean letter ה (Hé) means "a window" and its numerical value is 5, which is a number especially associated with the Old Ones. Furthermore, it is *The Star* in the Tarot. That the Stars are the Windows or Gateways *to the spaces beyond* is the occult doctrine indicated by these correspondences. According to Yakut shamans, the stars are the *windows of the world*. As it is put by Mircea Eliade, they are "openings provided for ventilating the various celestial spheres (usually 9 in number, but sometimes also 12, 5, or 7) ..."[119]

> In the middle of the sky shines the Pole Star, holding the celestial tent like a stake. The Samoyed call it the *"Sky Nail'*; the Chukchee and the Koryak the *"Nail Star."* The same image and terminology are found among the Lapps, Finns, and Estonians. The Turko-Altaians conceive the Pole Star as a pillar; it is the *"Golden Pillar"* of the Mongols, the Kalmyk, the Buryat, the *"Iron Pillar"* of the Kirgiz, the Bashkir, the Siberian Tartars, the *"Solar Pillar"*

---

118 *Mysterious America*, p. 26
119 *Shamanism*, by Mircea Eliade; Princeton University Press , 1974 e.v., p. 260.

of the Teleut, and so on. A complimentary mythical image is that of the stars as invisibly linked to the Pole Star. The Buryat picture the stars as a herd of horses, and the Pole Star (the "Pillar of the World") is the stake to which they are tethered.[120]

This last analogy is especially important, due to research[121] performed by Dr. Jonathan Shear on one of the yoga sutras attributed to the sage Patañjali: "By performing *samyama* on the Pole Star, one gains knowledge of the motion of the stars." Since *samyama* is a meditational technique which can be learned, and there is a predicted result ("knowledge of the motion of the stars"), this is a scientifically verifiable statement. Dr. Shear therefore collated the results of this experiment from hundreds of subjects around the world who were skilled in the meditational technique and had recorded their experiences. In the paper presented on the experiment, he reported, in part, that ...

> [O]ne would expect to perceive the motion of the stars in the context of the heavens as we are accustomed to perceive and think about them. And in fact such perceptions do represent early phases of the experience produced by the technique in question. But in many cases the experience quickly develops into something quite different. The Pole-star is seen at the end of a long, rotating shaft of light. Rays of light come out the shaft like the ribs of an umbrella. The umbrella-like structure on which the stars are embedded is seen rotating. Along the axis of light are other umbrella-like structures, one nested within the other, each rotating at its own rate, each with its own color, and each making a pure, lovely sound. The whole experience is described as quite spectacular, blissful, colorful and melodious.[122]

Shear goes on to say...

---

120 Ibid., pps 260-261.
121 Reported in *The Tao of Symbols* by James N. Powell; Quill, NY, 1982 e.v., in the chapter titled "Druids."
122 Ibid., pps 71-73.

[T]he experience is the innocent by-product of the proper practice of the technique. The logical conclusion is that the specific content of the experience represents the mind's own contribution arising in response to the practice of the technique. This is, the technique enlivens ... specific, non-learned or innate responses, and allows us to experience what can, I think, properly be called an innate archetype or structure of the human mind.[123]

Such an experience, verified and recorded by hundreds of subjects, is more than a little suggestive of that Vision of supreme importance in the Magickal career of TO MHGA ThRION, 666 , the Vision which he called "the Star-Sponge,"[124] and which finally flowered on the shores of Lake Pasquaney, in New Hampshire. This is an area not far at all from Lovecraft's own territory, and the influence of the mysterious Hockomock Swamp and its Triangular region the Bridgewater Bay Triangle, Window, or Gateway.

Among the Old Ones, the quasi-entity Yog-Sothoth is "the Key, the Gate, and the Guardian of the Gate,"[125] its position on the Qabalistic Tree of Life (תעד)[126] indicates a connection with the Abyss of Space, through which flows the Path of *The Star* and its Nightside counterpart, the *Tunnel* of Hemethterith. This Tunnel informs the Black Sun of Tiphareth with the glittering darkness of that Titanic Globe of Living Black Flame, Chokmah, the *Sphere* of the Stars. The sponge, octopus, squid, and coral as oceanic types of the informing energies of the Old Ones, are the astral counterparts of Beings that tread the Deeps (or Waters) of Space *between the stars*. The concept of *inbetweenness*

---

123 Ibid., p. 73.

124 Described in *The Confessions of Aleister Crowley*, Arkana Books, London, 1989 e.v., pps 81-811.

125 The *Necronomicon* of Abdul Alhazred, in Olaus Wormius' Latin version, printed in Spain in the 17th century; this is page 751 "of the complete edition," as it is stated in *The Dunwich Horror*, Lancer Books, New York, 1963 e.v., page 126.

126 Cf. *Nightside of Eden* by Kenneth Grant, Muller, London, 1977 e.v., page 3 et seq., where Da'ath is equated with The Gate.

figures prominently in Zos Kia Cultus,[127] and points indirectly to that state of consciousness which Dr. Shear calls "perception of an innate archetype or structure of the human mind"; but which is also, in some sense, a future development of the human mind. Zos understood this when he wrote:

> The law of evolution is retrogression of function governing progression of attainment, i.e., the more wonderful our attainments, the lower in the scale of life the function that governs them.[128]

Or, put another way, the unsealing and resurgence of primal atavisms leads directly to the original most ancient state of consciousness. This being pure, is cosmic, and of unlimited potential. See *Aleister Crowley & The Hidden God* by Kenneth Grant,[129] where this matter is discussed in relation to the mysteries of the Kundalini Shakti: the Primal Power behind all our "wonderful attainments.'[130]

---

127 The magical Cult of the Artist-Occultist Austin Spare, d. 1956 e.v.

128 *The Book of Pleasure (Self-Love): The Psychology of Ecstasy*, by Austin Osman Spare, 93 Publishing, 1975 e.v., p. 47. This is the doctrine of atavistic resurgence, for which see also *Images and Oracles of Austin Osman Spare* by Kenneth Grant, Weiser, NY, 1975 e.v., page 42 et seq.

129 Weiser, 1974 e.v., p. 98

130 Also cf. Gopi Krishna, *Kundalini: the Evolutionary Energy in Man*, Shambhala 1971 e.v.

IV

The Mummy Cult

Through the grimoire of Yog-Sothoth, the *Νεκρονομικον* or "Book of Dead Names," the Cult of the Old Ones links with the Cult of the Dead, which has existed in innumerable forms since prehistoric times. Nowhere has the Death Cult achieved greater proportions than in Egypt, in the form of the Mummy Cult. What at first glance may seem like a worship of death was in actuality *the Cult of Revival*. *The Book of Coming Forth by Day*, often erroneously called "The Egyptian Book of the Dead," contained the supreme spells for reviving the mummy *in amenta*, and all magic connected with the burial rites was geared toward this end. The 17th Chapter of that book, however, demonstrates that the Initiated interpretation of the text refers to the *physiological phenomena* upon which the text is based, and not upon metaphysical theory.[131] According to the texts of the *Coming Forth by Day*, the first power to revive in amenta is the sexual power. Amenta—the Underworld—is the Subconsciousness; or more properly in a Magickal context, the intertwining network of dream cells and Tunnels which have been approximately tabulated in part II of Kenneth Grant's *Nightside of Eden* as "The Tunnels of Set." The place of entry to the Tunnels has been located at Da'ath, the *Gateway* or Door on the Tree of Life: Viśuddha Chakra.

---

131 As pointed out by Kenneth Grant in the Introduction to *The Magical Revival*; Weiser, New York, 1973 e.v. and SKOOB Publishing LTD., London, 1991 e.v.

RITES OF THE MUMMY

The power of the mummy to revive from a magical sleep is a recurring theme in gnostic lore, and Graeco-Egyptian legend attributes the source of this power to the mystical *tana* leaf, which was distilled and heated in a chalice or vessel before being fed to the magically-entranced mummy. Via Greek gematria, the numerical value of ταυα is 352, a number associated by Frater Achad with the Aeon of Maat. That the revival hints at some inner, initiated tradition, is suggested by the fact that the Great Pyramid itself was designed, not as a burial-chamber, but as a Temple of Initiation; also, by references in ancient writings to the rite of the "little death," and the mock-burial of the Initiate. The height of the Great Pyramid is 481 feet[132], and when measured against the base and converted to the great cubit of 55 Egyptian Cubits, is in the ratio 8:5, or the Golden Mean: Φ.[133] In the Greek Qabalah, the value of Phi is 500, which is the value of the Middle Pillar on the Tree of Life (Sephiroth plus Paths: $10 + 400 + 9 + 60 + 6 + 11 + 3 + 1 = 500$); thus exhibiting the same symbolism in this Qabalistic *inner temple* as is found to be embodied in the Temple of the Pyramid. With the Pyramid's base as the unit of measurement, the Golden Mean Phi, capped by the Pyramid, equates with the Middle Pillar as Phi, capped by the "pyramid" of the Supernal Triad. Why should these symbols of Initiation embody similar—if not the same—ideas? On the Tree of Life, there are five *Spheres* placed along the Middle Pillar, from Malkuth to Kether (including Da'ath). Architecturally and geometrically, the quantity Φ embodies the formula of pentagram & pentagon. Accordingly, it holds an important ratio to the square root of five: a quantity which is equal to both *phi plus its reciprocal, and the square of phi minus its reciprocal.* According to Lovecraft, the occult-architectural-geometric-mathematical system of the Old Ones, *was based upon the quantity five.*

---

132 Given as 480.5 feet by John Michell in *The View Over Atlantis*, Ballantine Books, New York, 1973 e.v.; note xxii, between pps 89-90. Other writers vary, between 480 and 481.

133 Ibid., p. 96. Φ is the glyph of the Greek letter, Phi.

In the Chaldean alphabet, the letter ה (Hé) is the number 5 and means *a window*.[134] It is the letter of the female, the Mother-Daughter of the Divine Tetragram, and thus of the five days of flow in the female physiological cycle. As Gerald Massey has shown, the five-day flow of the female was considered *disruptive* from prehistoric times. It was the time of the "break" in the cycle or circle that allowed for the influx of Forces from Outside. Thus at this time the yoni was bandaged *or bound up* as a magical preventative against such an incursion, and in ancient times the sight of the female to be bound signified her right to be married; to this day, we speak of "tying the knot" in reference to marriage. The historical result of such customs led to the first laws of marriage, which were based on the legalized capture of females *from outside the tribe or clan*, females who "had the right" to be bound.[135] The etymology of the Chaldean word QShRITh, for bridal gown, reveals the origin of the law in the custom: for the "attire of the bride," QShRITh, comes from the root QShR, to tie or bind. In fact, the KR, or "victim bound for sacrifice" (cf. the Theosophical SKR[136]), is the origin of the Graeco-Gnostic Charis, a pre-Christian image of "the bloody savior." As Massey (and others) have shown, the original image of the *bloody savior* was *feminine*. This concept harks back to the earliest creation myths, involving the sacrifice of the goddess: in which the body of the goddess is dismembered, torn into bits, "sacrificed" *so that creation might take place*. In later patriarchal times, the early feminine symbol *became masculinized*, and the image of the goddess, dismembered, achieved its culmination in the image of the Osiris, dismembered and scattered about Khem, the symbol of the world as a whole. In the Egyptian myth, the body of Osiris is gathered together by Isis and

---

134 See Chapter 3.

135 See *The Natural Genesis* by Gerald Massey, Weiser, New York, 1974 e.v., vol. 1, section 11, titled "Natural Genesis and Typology of Primitive Customs."

136 See *The Secret Doctrine* by H. P. Blavatsky, Theosophical University Press, 1952 e.v., Vol. II, p. 467.

re-assembled sans phallus; the bandaged, feminized Osiris completing the cycle of the myth and returning to the earlier, feminine image. Thus: as the Yoni, bloody & bound; Isis, bound up and pregnant; Osiris, de-masculinized, bloody, bandaged; Charis, the bloody female "savior" who was celebrated in the eu*charis*t; or Christ, long-haired, gentle, effeminate, sweating "tears of blood" in the *garden* (an ancient image of the Yoni); we find that the KR, or sacrificial victim, renews all these ideas in one of the earliest Typhonian images of the female in her lunar phase. The gnostic goddess *Charis* is especially indicative of the female flow, for Charis was the wife of Hephaestos, the Lord of Fire; and in the saṃdhyā bhāṣā of the āgamas, the female flow is equated with *rajas*, the *guṇa* which is predominantly active in fire.

Control of the inner fire is one of the most archaic of magical techniques.[137] Traces of its practice can be found in aboriginal and shamanistic cults around the world, and many of these shamanistic techniques were later adapted and developed by Yoga along experimental lines.[138] According to the kinetic theory of heat, all mechanical energy can be turned into heat, and vice versa. In fact, there is no essential difference between heat energy and mechanical energy, for the energy of heat is only the motion or vibration of the molecules that compose a substance. The one difference lies in the fact that in heat energy the molecules move in a random, clashing manner, whereas in mechanical energy all the molecules are moving in the same direction. The ancients sought to direct the *Inner* Heat, the body's biological heat, a technique which is perfectly in accord with the primary aim of Yoga (ekāgratā: one-pointedness), and which culminated in the development of Hāthā Yoga: a science of controlling the body's "subtle" energies. As is well known, the accomplished Hāthā Yogi is often able to control these ener-

137 Eliade, *Shamanism*, p. 474 et seq., "Magical Heat."
138 See Mircea Eliade's *Yoga: Immortality & Freedom*, Princeton University Press, 1971 e.v., p. 106, "Tapas and Yoga."

gies to such a degree that control even over the so-called "involuntary" muscles (such as the heart, the muscles that govern digestion, etc.) is possible. That this can be (and has been) done, is well-documented by scientists and physicians, although as usual in such cases they cannot "explain" the phenomenon. Such an accomplishment, however, could well be described in modern physical terms as the transformation of heat energy into mechanical energy, since it transforms or translates the energy of the Fire Snake into the electro-chemical energy of a major nerve-plexus; and control of the neural energies automatically implies control of those "involuntary" muscular (i.e., *mechanical*) functions over which the particular nerve-plexus or center presides.

In the Cult of Thelema, the injunction "*Do* what thou wilt ..." implies *action*, and especially the *control* of action (it must be "under will"). Action, whether physical or mental, is mechanical action, for even mental processes are a special development and refinement of prakṛti.[139] Thus, even *thought* is mechanical action, being the result of the *motion of matter*. Control over such mechanical (physical) actions implies magical control of the Inner Fire, which tradition says can be accomplished through the control of one or more of the body's main "fires": the pneumatic fire; the digestive fire; or the sexual fire. Hence the formula "*Do what thou wilt* shall be the whole of the Law," and its corollary "Love is the law, *love under will*," demonstrates the specific direction of the Thelemic or Ophidian Current, since it indicates the *control of action* through *control of the sexual fire*, and vice-versa. This is the ancient, Typhonian technique, which achieved its apotheosis in the Indian system of Tantra-Yoga; as the control of action through control of the pneumatic fire achieved its culmination in the "classic" system of Yoga, as syncretized by Patanjali.

Cults of the Shadow, the third book in the Typhonian Trilogies of Kenneth Grant, contains a brief description of an occult experience

---

139 The subtle "matter" of which all elements are composed.

undergone by Joan Grant,[140] and which is perfectly understandable in terms of the thesis outlined above:

> She was looking down at what appeared to be an Egyptian mummy on a ritual bier. But this woman was still alive, and her body was being used as a kind of battery. There had been a tremendous build-up of libido by various means, including an unguent which worked like the witch-ointment of Europe, massage of a peculiar kind, and the cumulative effect of bandages. The face was masked as a corpse would be, and over the genitals was a gold plaque inscribed with the cartouche of Sekmet and other gods of the Shadow. The climax of the repulsive ritual released accumulated energy in such a way that it was available for projection at the will of the priests.[141]

The Fire Snake, after being aroused in the basal chakra or Seat of its Emanations, is led to whichever of the centers or higher chakras in which its manifestation is desired. This will, of course, depend on the nature of the Operation in question. The results of a successful Operation may vary, depending upon which channel or *nadi* of the occult anatomy Shakti takes as She streaks up the column of the body of the priestess chosen for the rite. She has varying characteristics in each of the centers, as well. In addition, there are various *granthis* or *"knots"* to be pierced as Shakti forces Her way up *suṣumna*.[142] The opening of these granthis, and the *"cleansing"* of the associated nadis, is of the utmost importance; for they tend to choke off the channel, and deflect the Serpent Power into areas of the subtle anatomy that may be totally unprepared for Her influx. The piercing of the granthis involves considerable danger, and sometimes even disease and death. There are three primary granthis along the nadi suṣumna, plus many smaller,

---

140 The author of several reincarnation novels.

141 *Cults of the Shadow*, by Kenneth Grant, Muller, 1975 e.v., p. 135, where it is quoted from Charles Beatty's *Gate of Dreams*.

142 The central channel or nadi of the human occult anatomy.

less *"knotty"* complexes associated with one or more of these three *"primaries."* The first is called *Rudra-granthi*, and is associated with the Mūlādhāra-Svādhiṣṭhāna complex. It is, properly speaking, *the point of divergence* of the nadis associated with these chakras. The second is called *Viṣṇu-granthi*, associated with Manipūra-Anāhata. The third is called the *Brahma-granthi*, and is associated with Visuddha-Ājnā. It is *the point of convergence* of the three primary nadis. In terms of the Qabalah of the Tree of Life, these granthis are symbolized by *the three cross-paths on the horizontal plane of the Tree*: glyphed by the letters Pe—Teth—Daleth ... which are equal to 93, the number of Will and Love.

V

The K'rla Cell

The Mummy Posture is a Tantric form of the Death Posture, and the Mummy-Priestess or Priestess in Amenta is MKR, phonetically Ma-Ka-Ra. As the Mummy She is a form of the vessel or vehicle of *K'rla*. This is the feminine sexual vibration, or in the language of the Tantras, the *spanda*[143] of Kundalini Shakti in the left sympathetic chain of the subtle anatomy—the nadi, *ida*. The conception is that of an infinitely expanding field, the k'r-field, its feminine vibration K'rla. Woman is thus seen as the biological embodiment of K'r (Desire) as K'rla: *a vortex in the Field*. The corresponding masculine vibration is exhibited in the formula *K'ral*; hence both male and female are forms of the "crystallization of Desire." As 220, the number of *Liber AL vel Legis*, K'r unites Will and Desire, and provides a Qabalistic link between Zos Kia Cultus, Thelema, and Tantra sastra:

K'rla / ida / Luna / Agape
K'ral / pingala / Sol / Thelema

In *Outside the Circles of Time*,[144] p. 234, appears the following remarkable statement:

---

143 Vibration.
144 Kenneth Grant, Muller, London, 1980 e.v.

The Elder Gods are the Maatians who, when manifesting as the Ophidian Current are known as the Great Old Ones.

Earlier in that work, one of the functions of a Priestess of Maat is described as being,

[T]o wield and direct the "titanic power of the Elder Gods to arouse the sleeping child—through the use of nightmare, if need be.[145]

The "sleeping child" equates with the Sleeping or Entranced Priestess, the Child who is the Daughter of COPH NIA. One of the glyphs of COPH NIA is the frog, an amphibious being with tongue anchored firmly *backwards* in its throat. In the Cult of the Old Ones, the frog is Cthulhu's totem, Cthulhu who is described as being in the semblance of death, and yet but "asleep and dreaming," " in that place under ye great waters ...," namely the Sunken City called R'lyeh,

[T]oward which at once all His minions swam and strove against all manner of obstacles, and arrang'd themselves to wait for His awaken'g powerless to touch ye Elder Sign and fearful of its great pow'r know'g that ye Cycle returneth, and He shall be freed to embrace ye Earth again and make of it His Kingdom and defy ye Elder Gods anew.[146]

In terms of human physiology, the Sunken City of R'lyeh suggests the Womb; Cthulhu "asleep and dreaming" suggests the unfertilized Ovum; and "His minions" suggests the semen virile.

The Mummy-Priestess Makara is an iṣṭa-devātā evolved for use in the Cell Operations. As the living Priestess in the bandages of mummification, she is a type of Life-in-Death, paralleling the "semblance of death" which the Elder Gods placed upon the great Cthulhu. She therefore equates with the Daughter, fertile and receptive to the Current.

---

145 Ibid., p. 158.
146 The *Necronomicon*, quoted in *The Lurker at the Threshold*, by H. P. Lovecraft, Beagle Books, New York, 1971 e.v., p. 93.

As the vessel or vehicle of Desire, K'rla, she becomes a "battery of Desire": K'rla-MKR = K'r-LAM-K'r; tapping into the power (Shakti) at the seat of its emanations, the "root-Lotus" in the human occult anatomy, Mūlādhāra Chakra … and the *bija-mantra* of that chakra is the root-vibration LAM, the Name of that Most Ancient One of the Elder Gods, who is yet the Avatar of an Aeon-to-come.

In the tantro-qabalistic saṃdhya bhāṣā the three lowest chakras, Mūlādhāra, Svādhiṣṭhāna, and Manipūra, are associated with the Sephiroth Yesod, Hod, and Netzach, respectively.[147] These comprise the lowest of the inverted triangles on the Tree of Life which are above the pendant, Malkuth. Yesod is connected through occult physiology with the sexual energies, and as the "inverted apex" of the triangle is *a reflection of Tiphareth*, the Solar Center of the Tree. Thus the identity of Phallic Power with Solar Power is exhibited, and the problem for the Adept who is working with these energies is the rending of the first of the Veils, the *Veil of Paroketh*, which is associated with the lowest of the three cross-Paths on the Tree, attributed to the letter Pe. The *direct Path* through this Veil, that is along the Pillar of Mildness or the Middle Pillar, is that of Samekh, the Virgin luminous and quick as a lightning-flash being a totem of this Path and its corresponding Tunnel. The energies of the Tunnel flash up from the sub-Cthonian cell which is associated with the Nightside of Yesod, and from where it connects to Tiphareth, the Current continues up to Kether via the 13th Path. The letters of these two Paths, Samekh and Gimel, when added together equal 63: a number of the Old One, Dagon. Therefore, the Sacrifice (Tav) *to* Dagon (63) is the sacrifice *of* the Virgin Priestess (Samekh-Gimel), these three Paths of the Middle Pillar (Tav, Samekh, Gimel) together being equal to the number 463. This number begins the series of "numbers & … words" (*AL* II, 75) of the 76th verse of the Second Chapter of *Liber AL*. The following six characters, 8A B K 2 4,

---

147 *Liber 777*, col. cxviii.

add up to 37, the number of IChIDH (Jechidah), the Kether-aspect of the *jivātmā*, or embodied soul. 37 is also the sum of the Sephiroth along the Middle Pillar *plus Da'ath*, and the Sephiroth (37) plus the Paths (463) yields the sum 500, the value of the Middle Pillar or Pillar of Mildness itself. This exhibits the link, by gematria, of the Middle Pillar to the glyph Phi, which is Qabalistically identified with the stau-sign, ℸ , or *double letter* ST: a glyph of Set.[148]

The Union of Set and Pillar, or *Yug Set-Tat*, displayed in the cipher of *AL* II, 76 suggests that it might be a formula for evoking the Old Ones. Investigation into the formula by gematria yields interesting results, for, transliterating character by character, the "half" of the phrase (i.e., the first 15 characters) reads: D V G Ch A B K B D A L G M O R. Interpreted as a clue which was inserted into the text by Aiwass in no one particular language, it can quite easily be seen to suggest *a particular astronomical phenomenon*, i.e., the exaltation (KBD) of the Dog Star (DVG ChAB) and Orion (ALGMOR). The word KBD is an Arabic technical term signifying "the exaltation of a star."[149] ChAB of course suggests the Chaldean ChABS, Star, thus making DVG ChAB an Anglo-Semitic *"pun"* suggesting Sothis, the Dog Star. From ancient times, Sothis has been associated with the asterism of Orion, which was called by the Arabs *Al Gbor*.[150] The B devolves through elision into the letter M, suggesting ALGMOR as an ancient Name of this constellation. Looked at in another way, the letter M replacing the letter B suggests the Daughter superseding the Magician, or the onset of the Lesser Cycle of the Ma-Ion. It seems also significant that a title of Orion is tripater,[151] for the next three characters in the cipher indicate that very thing: 3 Y X. 3 = "tri," and YX = the Male Chromosomal Pair!

---

148 Φ = 500 = σ(200) + τ = 300). Also, the old Greek letter Digamma (ϝ) replaced phonetically and alphabetically by Φ was replaced numerically by ℸ (=6).

149 *Star Names: Their Lore and Meaning*, by Richard Hinckley Allen; Dover, New York, 1963 e.v., p. 116.

150 Ibid., p. 307, where it is also given as *Al Jabbār*. On p. 309 of the same work it is stated that ..."the Jews called Orion Gibbōr, the Giant ..."

151 Ibid., p. 308.

Working with the Priestess in the Mummy Posture, who is charged with the energy of K'r, may result eventually in the piercing of the Rudra-granthi. The key is the feminine technique of karezza, gly-phed by the number 89: silence, and restriction. It is the Silence of the True Black Brother, and the Restriction which "...is the word of Sin." (*AL* I, 41). The word, *Sin*, is here interpreted as the Name of a Lunar Deity, hence the Sphere of Yesod is implied. The vibration of Yesod-Mūlādhāra is LAM, being interpreted as LA + Ma-kara, or the letter M. Besides being the "M-maker," or name of the letter M, *Makara* is the Name of the horned sea-serpent or goat-fish which is attributed to Svādhiṣṭhāna chakra. Thus, these Yesodian-Netzachian Workings fol-low the formulation: K'rla + Makara = K'r-LAM-K'r, or the Name (i.e. *vibration*) of that Elder God who is the energy (Shakti) that Rends the Veil of Paroketh: the Rudra-granthi.

In the Hindu system of the *Nakshatras*, or Mansions of the Moon, Rudra is the Deva of the 5th Nakshatra when counting by the most ancient reckoning; and this Nakshatra[152] is ruled by the star Betel-geuse—identified by Lovecraft as *the home of the Elder Gods!*

> Ubbo-Sathia is that unforgotten source whence came those daring
> to oppose the Elder Gods who ruled from Betelgeuse ...[153]

The technique of karezza, on the Priestess Silent and Restricted (formula of 89), exalts the Priestess to the Sphere of Netzach from that of Yesod. In other words, the Lunar energies (Yesod) are exalted to Venusian (Netzach). Connecting these two Spheres on the Tree is the 28th Path, traditionally identified with the letter Tzaddi as noted earlier. However, by reversing the positions of these letters on the mandala of the Tree, the letter Tzaddi or Psi not only becomes a fitting image of the psion-kala raying down from the Sphere of the Stars (Chokmah), but Hé then becomes the connecting link between Yesod and Netzach. This

---

152 Called *Ardra*, Moist.
153 *The Lurker at the Threshold*, p. 146.

is a significant result, for The Star then connects the two Spheres whose numbers (9 + 7) are equal to 16! The sixteen kalas are implied, and the exaltation of the Priestess in the Mummy Posture becomes an invocation of the kalas. Significantly, 9 x 7 = 63, the number of Dagon (see above). We can thus see why the Path of Nun is attributed to "Death" and the Ritual Slaying of the sexually-entranced Priestess; for it is but one aspect of the Formula of the Sacrifice of the Virgin as displayed in the lower two Paths of the Middle Pillar. In either case, Shakti is invoked into Anāhata chakra (Tiphareth). Tiphareth is the Sphere of the Lord or Lady of the Mummy Cult, either as Osiris *without* phallus or as ithyphallic Makara. Hence the Sphere of Tiphareth is Androgynous, the conception obtaining from the masculinized female, and the feminized male, united in one image.

The Ritual Slaying of the Priestess that occurs in the Tunnel of Niantiel during the course of the evocations is not the slaying of the physical body; the Death implied is the Death of the Ego, for Ego is that which is born, and which dies; it is the only Death. The Ego is the Double or Twin; in this Cult of K'rla, *the Shadow of an Old One*. As the Shadow of the physical body is *"slain"* at noon at the time of the Equinoxes, so is the Magical Shade slain in the Tunnel of Niantiel. This Tunnel, it will be noted, connects the Spheres of Netzach and Tiphareth on the Tree: Tiphareth being the Sun; and Netzach, Venus, that is AHATHOOR who is given to the *noon* Position in *Liber Resh* ... the Adoration of the Sun!

Ahamkara, or the "I-maker," is *the symbolizer*. Pure Consciousness can have no meaning in and of itself, for when there is *no thing*, there is *nothing to symbolize*, Pure Consciousness being Static Potential in an illogical *"present'*: a now-moment that is a random collection of ever-changing symbols, that has no relation to any *thing* except as a point-of-contact with Continuum. The Blind One is an image of the Conscious One, that is, the One *Conscious of* Whole-Mind, the Old One which casts the Shadow, or *doubles*. The Twins (or Doubles) is an image of the Lovers, for this Atu (VI) is given to the constellation of the Twins, that is, Gemini. A clue to these identities is given in a variation of the English Cabbala Simplex, in which A = 5, B = 10, C = 15, etc., for the word SLAY is equal to 285, the factors of which are 3 x 5 x 19, or 15 x 19, the number of the Goddess (15) times the Feminine Glyph (19). It is the Aspiration to Binah—the Sphere of the Goddess as Understanding, and which is invoked, from Tiphareth, via the Path of ZIN (Zain)—the Sign of the Twins. Counting in the same manner, 285 is also the number of MOON, which is of a dual nature; of ABRAH-DABRA, which is a dually-constructed formula; of GEMINI, the name of the Sign of the Twins itself; and of THESE, which is especially interesting in this connection due to *AL* II, 47, a verse in which Hadit exclaims: "Where I am *these* are not."

According to the previous verse,[154] "these" are identified as "failure," "sorrow," and "fear"; three attributes due only to ahamkara, and the belief in an Ego which IS—but which "really" IS NOT.

In Cthulhu Cultus, the Blind One is AZATOTH, the CHAOS which is at the Center of All, and of whom it is said, he "shal arise from ye middle of ye World" where He waits, "till there shall come again ye winds & ye Voices which drove Them forth before & That which Walketh on yc Winds over ye Earth & in ye spaces that are among ye Stars for'r."[155] In the Mythos of the Old Ones, the Substance which will allow Azatoth to manifest to visible appearance, is the *Powder of Ibn Ghazi*, which appears to be a corrupted form of the Arabic Ibṭ al Ghauzi, or the Star (kala) that rules the *Fifth Nakshatra* –Betelgeuse! As pointed out above, this red star is called in Sanskrit after the Storm God, Rudra, or that Power which is behind "That which Walketh on ye Winds over ye Earth," and therefore also of those beings which tread the Deeps of Space *between the stars*. The number of IBN GHAZI is

---

154 Verse 46 of Chapter II.
155 The *Necronomicon*, from The Lurker at the Threshold, p. 94.

88 in the Semitic Qabalah, or 8 + 80 (cf. *AL* I, 46). Via Greek numerical exegesis, 88 is the number of αζαοθ, a spelling of AZOTh, the Alchemical "solvent" or creator of ubiquitousness of Consciousness. The similarity of Azoth to Azatoth cannot be ignored, for the Name of this Old One by the spelling AZTATh is equal to 418.

The ignition of the Powder of Ibn Ghazi (88), is the inflammation of that Power or Shakti which finally rends the Veil of Paroketh, or the first of the Major Veils over the Typhonian forces. The exaltation of the Star from Yesodian to Netzachian realms has its parallel in the Solar kala (Resh) which precisely balances it, and rays from Yesod to Hod, or Svādhiṣṭhāna chakra in the Tantric systems. The Path of the Sun leads to the Pillar of Severity, the *"Feminine"* Pillar on the Tree; and of the three main nadis in the human occult anatomy, pingala is attributed to the Sun. A very subtle androgyny can be seen to be developing among these symbols, and the inflammation of the Powder of Ibn Ghazi (8 + 80 = Hod + Pe) thus formulates the lowest of the Triads on the Tree, the Astral Triad or World of Yetzirah (Formation).

As though on an Astral crossbow, the tension created by the successful use of the Formula of K'r-LAM-K'r, the Battery of Power, is both the dangerous and the key element. For as on a bow, when the release of the tension occurs Shakti flashes up the Middle Pillar like lightning, or the Flashing Virgin of the Tunnel of Saksaksalim, as the *balanced energies* which have been involved into ida and pingala come together in suṣumna, to pierce Rudra-granthi. The flood of Power which subsequently informs Anāhata chakra (Tiphareth, or the Sphere of the Sun), is the manifestation "to visible appearance" of Azatoth, one of Whose numbers is 418: a number described by 666 as the Formula of Solar Consciousness. The use of the Powder of Ibn Ghazi to manifest the Old One, Azatoth, is also necessarily an evocation of "the key, the Gate, and the Guardian of the Gate," "...upon whom are no strictures of time or space...," for 88 + 418 = 506: or the union of Set and Pillar which is YOG-SOTHOTH!

From the direction of this line of thought, it will be seen that the conception is of the Qabalistic Tree of Life as a neuro-physiological road-map, much like the Tantric *"map"* of chakras and nadis, perhaps less developed, or perhaps just *more subtle.* A mandala which is to be *turned inwards,* and applied to the structure of consciousness. It might be even better to say, "to what structure *can be perceived* in Consciousness"; for Consciousness *is* structured, and *needs* Structure, *in its dualistic mode.* As "evolution" proceeds, this so-called "structure" is ever-mutating, never the same in the Stream-of-Time; a seething mass of flesh reaching out, tentacled, over the planet, for its vehicle—blind, but for our senses, skandhas or *scanners,* like the sonar of bats, only more fully developed. The bat in the cave is an image of the power of the atavism in the Subconscious, especially the vampire bat, living off the blood of its victims. An image of the Aeon of Zain is called forth in the picture of bats, flying out of their caves in a swarm, at sunset: into the twilight of dualistic Consciousness that must precede the inevitable Night. As Consciousness evolves in time, change is perceived, new developments arrived at: better eyesight, a larger brain, facility for speech, and more able hands for making tools. This occurs at every moment, and through precisely the same function that allows embodied Consciousness to adapt from moment-to-moment. One *"moment"* of Time by itself, a ksāna,[156]—a point on the *"line"* of the Stream-of-Time—is only a *symbolizing* of impressions on the skandhas, from a perceiving by the brain of electro-chemical activity that runs along certain familiar channels; and which is itself stimulated by certain chemical changes in the sense-organs which take place in response to particular types of particle-wave activity in what is actually a Continuous energy-field. Through transformation of *symbols* into *things,*

---

156 A *"split second."* This is Buddhist terminology. According to Wei Wu Wei (*Posthumous Pieces,* Oxford University Press, 1968 e.v.) the ksāna "...should correspond exactly to the *"stills"* whose rapid succession in projection onto a screen—our *"mind"*—produces the illusion of movement ..." (p. 39).

Objective "Reality" is arrived at; but at root, each moment is the sum of the entire past, *all* past experience, Subconscious memories even of "lives" as one-celled Protozoa. The symbols change, grow, die, like the seasonal transformations of the tree; the primal symbols being the roots, virtually unchangeable in the firm grasp they have on the soil from which they suck up their nourishment.

To return to the state of Primal Chaos, to confront the blind and idiot Azatoth who, along with Yog-Sothoth, *instructed the Old Ones*, would be to reach for that Power of Transformation; and, once reaching it, to learn the secret of *transforming those symbols into other Realities* ... the secret of traversing the Deeps of Space "... that are among ye Stars for'r." This is the root of sentience, analogous to the torus-formation or ring-singularity of the physicist John Taylor,[157] called by John Lilly "the center of the Cyclone." It is the root of true physics also, since *"physics"* is but a reflection of what is created by the aforementioned process of symbolizing electro-chemical activity, or rather of *interpreting ourselves as symbolized.*

The aim of the Minions of the Old Ones is the Opening of the Gate *so that the Old Ones can be let in* and allowed to Rule where once They Ruled—Kings of the Earth forever!

Tiphareth the Sphere of the Osirified, is the plane of Azatoth in the Qabalistic scheme, the feminine aspect of which is the Daughter *Makala*, whose number is 93. This parallels the Son Horus, whose Word is Thelema, also 93. Makala + Thelema = 186, the number of QVPh, *back of head*, and KENOMA, *the outer void*. The Daughter Makala-Azatoth, or 93 + 418, is equal to 511, which identifies Her Qabalistically with the Formula K'r-LAM-K'r, the female battery or condenser of *ojas*. Tiphareth is informed from beyond the Abyss, by the 15th

---

157 See *Black Holes: The End of the Universe?* By John G. Taylor, Avon, New York, 1975 e.v., Chapter 7.

and 17th Paths, leading from Chokmah and Binah, and the 13th Path, which proceeds from Kether. Now, a curious fact should be recalled: in switching the positions of Tzaddi and Hé, the former letter now symbolizes *the kala that rays from the Sphere of the Stars* (Chokmah) ... to Tiphareth (the Sun). In *Liber AL vel Legis* I, 57 it is exclaimed by Nuit that " צ is not the Star." Since Tzaddi is now raying, nevertheless, from the Sphere of the Stars, it suggests that Radiance (kala = "a ray") which links Star to Star (and *the Sun is also a Star*). The phrase may be a title: "not the star," equivalent to "Nuit the Star"; that is, the Radiance of the Totality of the Body of Our Lady Nuit. As such it is that *radiation* that reaches Earth from Deep Space, *via the Sun*. And in the Greek Qabalah, the Path of Tzaddi—here interpreted as Path 15—is glyphed by the letter Psi; which is also used to symbolize the probable *psion*,[158] thus suggesting it as the quanta or *energy-packet,* which is the basis of interstellar communication. In the Sphere of Tiphareth, the Priestess-as-Battery is glyphed under the image of Makala-Azatoth, or the K'rla Cell receiving the Psi-kala from the Sphere of the Stars. An "energy-packet" herself, she is pure Atomic Consciousness, as shown by the equation:

K'r-LAM-K'r = 512 = DOULH[159] = ATOMOS[160]

---

158 See Chapter 1.
159 Slave girl.
160 Indivisible particle.

VI

The Fountain of Death

Between 1984 e.v. and 1988 e.v., a location in South Florida in proximity to the Bermuda Triangle served as the primary site for Operations that developed the K'rla Cell as a tool for communion with the Great Old Ones; although the seed of the Work sprouted as a series of experiments in dream control,[161] years of experimentation were conducted in South Florida, also in proximity to the Triangle.[162] The substance of these early Workings and the Egyptian mode of their symbolism has been condensed in Chapter 4. (The relevance of the Mummy Cult, and especially of that Tantric aspect of it which is embodied in the Joan Grant vision quoted in Chapter 4 to Cthulhu Cultus, can be seen in those references in the stories of H. P. Lovecraft to the Great Old Ones' callous use of other organisms for their own ends; such as the use of a phosphorescent, living organism to light their buildings and city streets.[163] That callousness towards other organisms is nowhere more apparent than in

---

161 See Chapter I.
162 See Chapter II. Also, see *Monstrum! A Wizard's Tale* (Fortean Tomes, London, 1990 e.v.) by Tony *"Doc"* Shiels, who makes the case that most human experience of truly "monstrous" beings takes place under, on, or very near to the larger bodies of water on the globe. Florida, being a peninsula, is surrounded by water on three sides.
163 "...they used a curious phosphorescent organism to furnish light," *Mountains of Madness*, p. 59.

Lovecraft's *The Whisperer in Darkness,*[164] a particularly horrifying short story in which it is made clear that the skill of the Old Ones enabled Them to convey human beings in "the seemingly impossible flight across the interstellar void." But by then, they were no longer truly *"human beings."* The Old Ones, in other words, had no use for their *humanity.*) Other indications that Florida is geographically and topographically ideal for the evocation of such entities as Cthulhu and Dagon are the fact that geologically the region is composed of primarily coral, which is the melded bones of dead colonies of the type of primal sea-creatures that represent the Old Ones, astrally; and the fact that its shores are lined with mangrove hammocks, swampy areas actually *created* by the presence of the mangrove: a type of tree that is especially representative of the Old Ones.[165] There is the Everglades, a vast "Sea of Grass" serving as a filter system to the inland waters of North America as they flow into the sea; as well as serving as home to the alligator, a descendant of that ancient terror of mammals, the dinosaur. Then there are the "bones of Florida," great quantities of ancient bones, some of them belonging to animals now extinct, that crowd and clog the limestone-and-coral caverns and *tunnels* that underlie the northern two-thirds of the state. The porous limestone has helped to create the phenomenon known as the sinkhole; wherein even large tracts of land have been literally swallowed into the ground. One such sinkhole north of Lake Okeechobee has been associated with suggestively evil phenomena at times in the past, and is known as "The Devil's Millhopper"! As the author Loren Coleman notes, the use of the word "devil" in place-names often denotes their peculiarly evil reputation.[166] Finally, since 1960 e.v. South Florida has become a fertile ground for the spread of the ancient African cults in their forms of Santeria; Palo;

---

164 First appeared in *Weird Tales*, August, 1931 e.v., Copyright by the Popular Fiction Publishing Company. Copyright 1939 e.v. by August Derleth and Donald Wandrei for *The Outsider and Others* (Arkham House).

165 *Outside the Circles of Time*, by Kenneth Grant, Muller, London, 1980 e.v., page 232.

166 *Mysterious America*, p. 20.

Obeah; and Voodoo: represented by the Cuban, South American, and Haitian communities that have been settling in that American State as a result of the instabilities of their native governments. These magical currents are quite popular and their constant and extended use charges the astral atmosphere with primal African imagery and totems. And there is the sand, everywhere in South Florida ...

We first began to develop the Tantric rite of the K'rla Cell in 1976 e.v. in Washington, D.C. Within four years the Cell was Operating in Florida, and it became necessary to establish our occult links with the Afro-Cuban magical community. In 1980 e.v. through our initiator Omi Ademi of Miami, Florida, we received the *eleke* or specially-prepared beads appropriate to *five* of the orishas: Eleggua; Obatala; Chango; Ochun; and Yemaya; the last being the Great Mother of All Waters under Whose auspices was our own *Ile* or Spiritual House. Omi Ademi[167] and his Madrina and other Santeras[168] brought us through the formal rites: Omi himself provided the oral instruction. It was from his Eleggua that our own Eleggua was "born" when, less than a year later, we received the Guerreros or "Warriors," a trinity of protective orishas comprised of Eleggua, Ogun, and Ochosi as Guardians of the Door (and especially as their nature is three-in-one, 5 orishas + 3 Guerreros = 8 and the ratio 5:8 indicates Φ as we will see in the next chapter).

By 1980 we had also visited a Babalawo or Priest of Ifa[169] for consultation. He revealed the perfect blend of my *ori inu*[170] with that of my magical partner, Ruth Keenan. In the symbolism of the system of the lucumi religion of the people of Western Nigeria, the magical religion commonly known as Santeria in its Cuban recension, Ms. Keenan is said to "have" Chango, the African equivalent of Ra-Hoor-Khuit. The

---

167 Literally, "Water is the Crown of my Head." For many years he operated a botanica called "The House of Miracles" on 5th Street in the old Overtown section of downtown Miami.
168 Priestesses in the Santeria tradition. The Priest is a Santero. "Madrina" means "Godmother."
169 The orisha of the oracle.
170 Ruler of the Head.

reading diagnosed my ori inu as Obatala, in this sense an aspect of Hoor-paar-Kraat. The sacred color of Obatala is white, but in many myths and representations he is depicted as enveloped in, and one with, his wife Odudua, who is black.[171] In this view, Obatala represents the potential of Kether in the stress of the Ain, or Odudua. The two orishas are often depicted as one in the symbol of the coconut, which is dark on the outside but white on the inside.

The color sacred to Chango is red ... Thus in the two orishas, the four primary colors of the Sacred Mysteries are represented: red and white, with the black (and gold) implied.[172] (The consultation of Ifa revealed something else, as well: the presence of three Oyeku, one of the four major Odu[173], and the one that means *Death*.)

Florida means "the Land of Flowers,"[174] an intriguingly tantric designation for the land in which Ponce de Leon,[175] among others, searched for the mystical *Fuente de la Juventud*, the so-called Fountain of Youth. The Fountain, transcendent to geography but immanent occultly, is synonymous with Hecate's Fountain[176], and as such might be more aptly described by the phrase *Fuente de la Muerte*, the Fountain of Death, or the infinite extension of old age and fleshly decay. The Fountain of Death equates with the Tree of Death, i.e. the *Nightside* of the Tree of Life, to which the Gateway or Door is Da'ath, the Knowledge which obtains upon the Death of egoidal awareness.[177] In

---

171 There is another *Odudua* of later mythology. This *Odudua* was an historical Warrior-King whose myths tended to become confused with those of the earlier *Odudua*, the Great Mother.

172 "Red, black, gold, are equivalent terms. The menstruum or vehicle of Light (Gold), on the physical plane, is blood, the liquid source of manifestation. The Mystical Water, the Sea of Infinite Space represented by Nuit (Nu) equates with red, gold, or black, all of which are One Principle, One *Tattva*, One Truth." Kenneth Grant, *The Magical Revival*, SKOOB Books, London, 1991 e.v., p.142.

173 Geometric figures produced by lots, or sometimes by a type of geomancy.

174 *Kalas*, in Sanskrit.

175 Discoverer of Florida in 1513 e.v.

176 The title of a book by Kenneth Grant.

177 It is the "Knowledge" that is neither "knowledge" nor "ignorance," neither "knowledge" nor "no-knowledge," for therein is No One(=Nu) to know. See the works of Wei Wu Wei, especially *Posthumous Pieces*.

the magical and mythological traditions of the world there are many references to Doors both dangerous and sacred, and in the system of the lucumi, Eleggua (which is the Hispanic form of the African Elegba) is the Guardian of the Door; and as a primal African form of Set is a component of the union (*yug*) of Set and Toth that is reflected in the imagery of Cthulhu Cultus as *Yog-Sothoth*—"The Key, the Gate, and the Guardian of the Gate."[178] This Gate is the Gate of Da'ath, or Death.

"We are composed of flesh and death; Turn and return, father of trans-formations," is part of one Babalawo's[179] comment on Oyeku Meji. The phrase describes well the *necrophilic nature* of certain visionary experiences undergone by the Cell in the early 1980s, and continu-ing well into the middle of the decade. That such experiences should occur *subsequent* to launching the Cell through the Gate of Da'ath and into the Tunnels of the Nightside in preparation for *"launching"* Her into "… the seemingly impossible flight across the interstellar void," is not surprising. The contents of the Visions could easily provide sub-ject matter for a modern novel of weird fiction or horror: images of mysteriously-robed skeletal figures, as if in secret conference, bathed in a strangely evil purple glow; the continuous destruction and decay of the world, as if it were the single purpose of all life to die; the contorted crumbling of bones and grinning skulls, melding into the corruption and decomposition of flesh—agglutinous flesh expanding amoeba-like as it decayed.

---

178 See Chapter III, note 8.

179 Awotunde Aworinde, quoted by Judith Gleason in *A Rec. of Ifa: Oracle of the Yoruba*, Grossman, NY, 1973 e.v.

VII

Algebra from Al G'bor

O n April 2nd, 1984 e.v., the nature of the information being received by the Cell underwent a dramatic change, that is, from Visionary *to mathematical*. We have described this (in magical records and accounts of the Cell Operations) as the date of the Cell's "magickal impregnation," and only months later was it recalled to me[180] that this is a *reversal* of Frater Achad's date for the Inauguration of the Aeon of Maat (April 2, 1948 e.v.)! Particular mathematical symbols, such as Φ (Phi), soon became central to the mathemagical system slowly being reified. The Qabalistic import of Φ has been discussed in Chapter 4. The mathematical importance of Φ lies hidden in the fact that it is the basis of the root of five,[181] which connects it magically with the Cult of the Old Ones, whose complete mathematical-geometric-architectural-artistic system is *based* on the quantity five![182] The metaphysical significance of Φ can be suggested by the equation $1/\Phi = (\Phi-1)$: *phi inverted is equal to phi minus one* (that is, minus ego). This statement is true of no other quantity. Finally, the significance of Φ *in nature* lies in the fact that it is the guiding ratio of the growth of the

---

180 By Mr. Kenneth Grant. Private communication, dated New Moon, October 1985 e.v.
181 And therefore also, of the Pentagram, the Star of Nuit or Infinite Space.
182 See the collective tales of H.P. Lovecraft, especially those that deal directly with the Cthulhu Mythos, such as *At the Mountains of Madness*. (Available under the title *At the Mountains of Madness & Other Novels*, Arkham House, Sauk City, Wisconsin, 1964 e.v.)

spiral, especially physiologically: in everything from the curling tendrils of floral vines and the spiralene chambers in the shells of primitive mollusks, to the double helix of DNA.

"Divide, add, multiply, and understand," says Nuit in *AL* I, 25. The mathematical function appropriate to Nuit is that of infinite exponential progression. The reverse would be true for Hadit (i.e., infinite exponential *regression*, or $1/n\infty$ in contradistinction to $n\infty$). Infinite contraction as opposed to infinite expansion. The function of the exponent, or powers of n, is one that is easily describable in terms of both division and multiplication (which is just the inverse of division). Nuit, however, tells us to "Divide, *add*, multiply, and understand," in phrasing that implies the evolution of a single mathematical function. Or perhaps, the application of all three functions to a single formula? One formula describable in terms of all three functions is that of the *exponential progression of ϕ*, an application that is similarly true of no other quantity. In other words, greater powers of Φ are the products of the lesser powers *and also the sums*, whereas (for example) two plus its square does not equal its cube. Two *times* its square equals its cube, just as Φ times *its* square equals its cube. But Φ *plus* its square is equal to its cube also. Hence, the formula "Divide, add, multiply ..." (a command of Nuit), in relation to the formula of exponential progression-regression (*formulae of Nuit & Hadit*), is applicable to Φ alone. Since infinity can never be greater or less than infinity, the expression $\Phi\infty$ and its reciprocal as numerical symbols for Nuit (infinite expansion) and Hadit (infinite contraction) are just as valid as any $n\infty$. Perhaps more so, since Φ (the Circle "... divided for love's sake ..."[183] i.e., Nuit) is Qabalistically identified with ܩ (*stau*, a letter of SET or Hadit), and their sum by gematria is 506, which can be read Qabalistically as the combined numbers 50 and 6. In *AL* I, 24, the verse prior to that just under discussion, Nuit exclaims that Her "...word is *six and fifty*."

---

183 *AL* I, 29.

"*The ceaseless five-pointedness* [184]of the surrounding architecture and of the few distinguishable mural arabesques had a dimly sinister suggestiveness we could not escape, and gave us a touch of terrible subconscious certainty concerning the primal entities which had reared and dwelt in this unhallowed place," wrote Lovecraft in *At the Mountains of Madness*,[185] and also, "The arabesques displayed a profound use of mathematical principles, and were made up of obscurely symmetrical curves and angles *based on the quantity of five.*"[186] Why are the Old Ones depicted as so obsessed with quantities and ratios based on the number five? The important mathematical fact here is that, as previously stated, the *root* of five is the sum of Φ and its invert (or $1/\Phi$) ... and $(1/\Phi)$ is equal to $(\Phi-1)$. The metaphysical implications of this relationship of Φ to its invert suggest Śakti and Śiva, respectively. More importantly, the geometric ratio of Φ is that of the spiral, which is also the nature of the power of Śakti. Śiva and Śakti are thus depicted as one in the equation $(\Phi + 1/\Phi) = \sqrt{5}$, but this is *the root of five*, not the integer itself. In order to obtain the integer, it is necessary to multiply the root times itself, as every schoolchild knows, and this too suggests the union of Śiva and Śakti. The function of Śakti being *negation*,[187] She ought more properly to be represented by a negative number, i.e., in this case $(-\sqrt{5})$ as opposed to $\sqrt{5}$ for Śiva, and this is an interesting formulation, for *the negative root times the positive root is negative five*, not 5. This negative represents the Advaitist metaphysical *Pūrna*, the One Irreducible Reality that is the Whole. But this Whole[188] is not Dual, not is it Singular either. *It is Negative.* Not the "ordinary negative" that is the polarized opposite of "the positive," but the absence of both kinds of positivity (of concept), i.e., both positive and negative

---

184 Italics by present author.

185 *At the Mountains of Madness and Other Novels*, Arkham 1964 e.v., page 40.

186 Ibid., p. 52. Italics by present author.

187 Ibid., p. 33.

188 i.e., Whole-Mind. See the writings of Wei Wu Wei.

positivity. Therefore a negative number, while still a positive concept in the sense that it is the opposite of a positive number, is a more fitting numerical symbol to suggest that Absolute Absence that is represented in Advaita-Vedanta as *Sat-Çit-Ānanda*: Being-Consciousness-Bliss.

In the Qabalah, the number 5 is the letter Hé;[189] the letter attributed to Atu XVII of *The Book of Thoth*. Atu XVII (The Star) is especially relevant to Aquarius and the Waters of Space, the "Infinite Space and the Infinite Stars thereof"[190] that are the Body of Nuit. Her nature being Void,[191] it is again to the negative that we must look for the more fitting symbol, i.e., to (-5). Negative five is divisible into $\sqrt{5}$ and $(-\sqrt{5})$, and these must represent Śiva-Śakti in Their forms as Çit and Çidrūpiṇī if (-5) is to be a glyph for that which is transcendental and changeless, That which is called *Para-saṁvit* in the Tantric scheme of the 36 Tattvas or Principles of Existence. In that Cosmology, the next Tattva produced following *Para-saṁvit* is the *Śiva-Śakti-Tattva*, and it is produced by the *negatizing* action of Śakti, Who "negates Herself as the object of experience, leaving the Śiva consciousness as a mere 'I', 'not looking towards another'."[192] Mathematically, this could be represented by the equation: $(-5) / (-\sqrt{5}) = \sqrt{5}$: the act of division by $(-\sqrt{5})$ *negates* $(-\sqrt{5})$, i.e., leaves the positive of $(\sqrt{5})$ alone. But in that positive root is another Union of Śakti and Her Divine Counterpart Śiva in the form of Phi, and its invert. This Śakti (Φ) *is therefore Vimarśa-Śakti*, Whose action on the *Śiva-Śakti-Tattva* results in the appearance of incipient Dualism.

From the "I" (Aham) and "This" (Idam) of $\sqrt{5}$ and $(-\sqrt{5})$ that are united in (-5), the negatizing action of Śakti as symbolized by the equation $(-5) / (-\sqrt{5}) = \sqrt{5}$ leaves the "I" (Aham)[193] alone. It is important to

189 See Chapter III.
190 *AL* I, 22.
191 "None, breathed the light, faint & faery, of the stars, and two." *AL* I, 28. Also, "Nothing is the secret key of this law." *AL* I, 46.
192 *The Serpent Power*, p. 33.
193 Here represented by the root of five.

realize, though, that ultimately They are not-two.[194] At such an early stage in the Descent of Consciousness into Matter, Duality is as yet unknown. When it first appears, it is symbolized by $\sqrt{5} = (\Phi + 1/\Phi)$, in other words it is the *spiralene power* Φ of Śakti that brings about the first transformation of Consciousness known as *Sadākhya-Tattva*: the state called Nāda in the Mantra-Śastra, or the primary movement in the genesis of cosmic consciousness culminating in the *Śabda-brahman*. This is the Brahman as Sound "...whence all ideas, the language in which they are expressed (*Śabda*), and the *objects* (*Artha*) which they denote, are derived."[195] In *Sadākhya-Tattva*, Consciousness is divided into "I" and "This," with the emphasis on "This" or mathematically, $(\sqrt{5} / 2) = \frac{1}{2}\sqrt{5}$.

The mathematical analysis of negative five thus brings it symbolically into alignment with the scheme of the Tattvas down to, and including, Sadākhya-Tattva! This can be done with no other number, and is only possible with (-5) due to the equation:

$$(-5) = \sqrt{5} \times (-\sqrt{5}); \text{ where } \sqrt{5} = (\Phi + 1/\Phi) = [\Phi + (\Phi{-}1)]$$

In other words, *Paraśiva* as (-5) contains within itself both $\sqrt{5}$ (Śiva) and $(-\sqrt{5})$, or Śakti, *Whose function is negative*, the act of division by which leaves $\sqrt{5}$ to represent *Sadākhya-Tattva, which Tattva is of the nature of Śiva.* But this *Tattva* (as $\sqrt{5}$) is still the Union of Śiva and Śakti; mathematically, $[1/\Phi = (\Phi\text{-}1)] + \Phi$. Utilizing such irrational numbers as Φ to represent cosmic and extra-cosmic processes indicates the non-conceptual nature of these matters and implies the "inbetweenness concepts" of Zos Kia Cultus[196]; such numbers themselves being in

---

194 That is, Aham and Idam. Also, Śiva and Śakti, Çit and Çidrūpiṇī, $\sqrt{5}$ and $(-\sqrt{5})$, $1/\Phi$ and Φ, and all such symbols.

195 Ibid., p. 34.

196 See Bibliography under Spare, Austin Osman. Also, see part 2 of *Images & Oracles of Austin Osman Spare* by Kenneth Grant (Weiser, NY, 1975 e.v.) and chapters 11 and 12 of Grant's *The Magical Revival*, Skoob Books, London, 1991 e.v.

between the integers which are used in classical Qabalistic exegesis.[197] It may be, that in such an "inbetween number" as Φ lies a clue to the "strange geometries" of the Old Ones so often hinted at by Lovecraft in his stories. That this is entirely possible, is indicated by Their passionate devotion to the numerical and geometric properties inherent in the quantity, five.[198]

Returning to the scheme of the Tattvas, in *Sadākhya-Tattva* the emphasis is placed on the Idam, or "This." Due to the action of Śakti and the initial stages of Dualism, this can be shown mathe*magically*:

$$(\sqrt{5} \, / \, 2) = \tfrac{1}{2}\sqrt{5} = Sadākhya\text{-}Tattva$$

The next Tattva in the scheme, *Īsvara-Tattva*, represents the universe-experiencer as Lord (*Īsvara*), hence the emphasis shifts to the "I," or Aham aspect of Consciousness. As Lord of the Cross of 4 Quarters, ($\tfrac{1}{2}\sqrt{5}$ x 4) yields ($2\sqrt{5}$), *the implied Dualism of Worshipped and Worshipper*. The significance of ($2\sqrt{5}$) representing *Īsvara-Tattva* becomes apparent when it is realized that in the scheme of the Tattvas the force of Māyā-Śakti begins to stir at this point; and if we multiply the two numbers representing the Tattvas below *Śiva-Śakti-Tattva* (*Sadākhya-Tattva and Īsvara-Tattva*) i.e., ($\tfrac{1}{2}\sqrt{5}$ x $2\sqrt{5}$), the product is 5 … which, as the number of the Female Power or Sakti in the symbolism of the Qabalah, is the number of *Māyā-Śakti* Herself!

The next stage appearing in the Tattvic scheme that represents the Descent of Consciousness into Matter, is *Śuddha-Vidyā-Tattva*. After the appearance of *Śuddha-Vidyā-Tattva*, the action of Māyā severs the United Consciousness, and the world of Objects begins to evolve. This can be mathemagically demonstrated in a peculiarly unique way by here applying the command of Nuit to "Divide, add, multiply," *since a trifold*

---

197 i.e., Φ, being equal to 1.618033989… is *in between* the integers one and two.

198 A passion shared by the ancients of humanity, many cultures of which patterned their Shrines, Temples and other Initiatory sites on the geometry of Φ.

function can only be applied to four elements, even if one or more of those elements is equivalent to another. That is, out of four elements, a, b, c, and d, we can begin with a; divide by b; add c; and multiply by d. Any order, of course, is possible. In the foregoing mathemagical analysis of negative five, we have now arrived at four elements with which it is possible to symbolize the four highest "Pure'[199] *Tattvas: Para-saṁvit; Śiva-Śakti-Tattva; Sadākhya-Tattva*; and *Īsvara-Tattva*. The mathemagical elements, or symbols, are (-5); $(-\sqrt{5})$; $(\frac{1}{2}\sqrt{5})$; and $(2\sqrt{5})$; or, negative five; the negative of the root of five; one-half the root of five; and twice the root of five. Applying the function of *AL* I, 25, results in:

$$[(-5)/(-\sqrt{5}) + (\tfrac{1}{2}\sqrt{5})]\,(2\sqrt{5}) = 15$$

Thus suggesting *fifteen kalas* representing the function of Māyā "and the multitudinous objects of the universe," although technically at this stage the kalas have not yet appeared in the Tattvic scheme of the Tantras.

The trifold function of "divide, add, multiply" suggests the *trib-indu*; and indeed since a mathemagical analysis of (-5) can be applied to the symbolism of *Tattvic* evolution inherent in the *Tantra-Śastra*, it can be applied to the Mantra aspect of the *Śastra* as well. In this application, both (-5) and $(-\sqrt{5})$, or the *negative* of the root, being aspects of the Metaphysical Whole (*Pūrna*), are Motionless (*Nih-spanda*) and Soundless (*Nih-śabda*). Or it might be better put, they represent the Motionlessness and Soundlessness of *Paraśiva*. The stage of *Nāda*, literally "sound"—actually the initial *vibration* in the ideating cosmic Consciousness that culminates in Brāhman-as-Sound [200]– equates with *Sadākhya-Tattva*. Therefore in the mathemagical scheme, it equates with $\frac{1}{2}\sqrt{5}$. The next stage in the Descent of Consciousness according to the *Mantra-Śastra* is the stage of *Para Bindu*, which is called *Para*[201] to distinguish it from the *bindu,* which appears later in the scheme; the

---

199 *Śuddha-Tattva*

200 *Śabda-Brahman.*

201 Supreme.

bindu, which is one element of the *Tribindu* composed of *bindu, nāda,* and *bija,* that are *Śiva, Śiva-Śakti,* and *Śakti,* respectively.

In the *Mantra-Śastra, bindu* is the dot (*Anusvāra*) which indicates the nasal breathing, and is placed in the *Candra-bindu* above *Nāda.* In the *Pranāva*[202], the *Anusvāra* "colors" the *Ma-kara,* the "M-maker" or sound of the letter M which is sacred to the Priestess of the Mummy Cult and of the K'rla Cell alike.[203]

The mathemagical results obtained via the K'rla Cell over nearly a four-month period in 1984 e.v.—from April 2nd until almost the end of August—kept turning us back again and again to the "strange geometries" of the Cult of the Old Ones. But there was another side to the matter (as just demonstrated), which pointed in the direction of the *Mantra-Śastra* as a key to the Work. This was the continuing emphasis on *bindu,* and the importance of *japa*[204] as a focal tool for the K'rla Cell. During the initial months of mathemagical material that came through via the Cell, this emphasis on more "traditional" methods such as *mantram* persisted, and by August we had formulated a plan to use "the numbers & the words" of *AL* II, 76 ourselves, in this manner.[205]

On the night of August 25th, 1984 e.v., those of us involved in the K'rla Cell experiments gathered in the Temple for another kind of experiment. The Altar, decorated with figurines of the Great Old Ones and surmounted by a goat-skull, sat in the half-shadow created by the several candles around the small room. The screened-in area which served as our Temple allowed the chirping and screeching of sub-Tropical insects to pierce the room, creating an especially eerie effect with its reminder of the legendary source of the name *Al Azif.*[206] We began loudly, and slowly:

---

202 The sacred mantric syllable, OM.
203 See chapters IV and V.
204 Concentrated repetition of a sound or syllable.
205 See chapter V in. re. this phrase as a possible formula of the Old Ones.
206 Said to be imitative of such nighttime insect sounds.

"Four; Six; Three;
Eight; A; B; ..."

The mantra continued to revolve, gradually picking up speed, and at the same time becoming softer. As the *japa* went from *sthula* to *suksma*,[207] it began to seem as though the buzzing of the insects was increasing, adding to the chilling suggestion that they were as a single voice, screeching "*Azif! Azif! Azif!*" in contrasting rhythm to our increasingly faster mantra.

Then, a curious thing occurred. After almost an hour of *suksma-japa*, in the flickering half-light that filled the Temple, a group of strangely alien sigils appeared on the wall in a manifestation that was seen by all who were present! Without hesitation, we copied them carefully, *after which they disappeared.* After months of mathemagical results obtained via the Cell, we were wont to read the characters as some kind of "alien equation,"[208] and all present agreed that it did, certainly, suggest that:

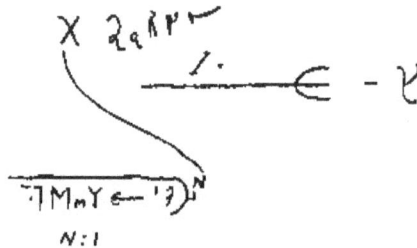

It is, in fact, the equation of the K'rla Cell Herself, as transmitted by the Old Ones ... a sort of algebra from Al G'bor!

---

207 "Gross" to "subtle."
208 Also referred to as "alien physics" in Records detailing the Working.

LIBER DE FIBONACCI
SUB FIGURA DLV

Geometria de radix quadrata de quinque, in mathematica de Vetus Ones, sicut scriptum est in Libro Legis.

I

The Numbers of the K'rla Cell

In the simplest theories of K'rla Cell experimentation, the eigenstates of the Hamiltonian describing single-state excitation are identified with the terran gender-state "female," denoted (φ) in the Dirac bra-ket notation which uses (μ) for "male" and (φ) for "female." Because of the Uncertainty Principle, statements about the position and mobility of the φ-body used in the creation of the K'rla cell can only assign a probability that its position or mobility will have some numerical value. When the φ-body can be definitely restricted, it is said to possess an eigenstate; and the more extreme the restriction, the higher will be the level of excitability.

Self-interactions involving a solitary φ-body are more difficult to observe, although examples have been documented that involve highly excited states. Unfortunately, the resulting fluxes or flows are not often well-measured.

The tendency of one object to impose another adjoining or inter-connected object into such a resulting flux is referred to as a forced vibration; more definite evidence for the theory seems to be emerging from situations involving extreme restriction. Although the theory is qualitatively successful, we need more experimental data to pin down the parameters for a more highly restricted cell. It is not certain, for example, whether some form of binding force can be identified.

The רכ force has been labeled the Spirit or שׁ, the libido, orgone, animal magnetism, vital force, and many other names. We have chosen *k'r* since רכ = 220. When I met my Augoeides on Key Bridge over the Potomac River on 23 July 1977 she gave me the formula k'rla but not the spelling. Working with it by the literal Qabalistic method of gematria, I discovered that the name of the river, "Potomac," was very likely a corruption of the Greek word for "river," ποταμακ. It equals 512, a temurah of 251 and 152. The number 152 is the gematria of the Greek word ναος, "cell," and this is the reversal or reflective of 251, the sum of 220 (רכ) and 31 (אל). 521 is the sum of 31 and 481, my Magickal Number in the O∴T∴O∴ at the time of the meeting. Also, 481 is the value of a hidden formula behind the K'rla Cell.

A Greek formula for "key" exists in the word κλειτόρις = 576, indicating the Negative Terminal of the Cell. The רכ energy is measured as the energy-flow between the eight psychic centres or cakkras in the form of the inverted Fibonacci powers of the aurea media (= τ) from the first, or One, to the eighth, or Forty-Seven. Thus:

$$\Sigma \left[\tau^{-1} + \tau^{-2} + \tau^{-3} + \tau^{-4} \dots \tau^{-47} \right] = \Phi = 1.61803399\dots$$

… and, by the Law of the Inverted Squares,

576 x $1/\Phi^2$ = 220 or,

Κλειτόρις x $1/\Phi^2$ = רכ

The mathematical progression runs:

τ^{-1} = 0.6180339887504…*sahasraracakkra*

$\Sigma \left[\tau^{-1} + \dots \tau^{-3} \right]$ = 1.2360679774910…*ajñacakkra*

$\Sigma \left[\tau^{-1} + \dots \tau^{-4} \right]$ = 1.3819660112508…*viṣuddhacakkra*

$\Sigma \left[\tau^{-1} + \dots \tau^{-7} \right]$ = 1.5623058987480…*anahatacakkra*

$\Sigma \left[\tau^{-1} + \dots \tau^{-11} \right]$ = 1.6099033699940…*manipūracakkra*

$\Sigma \left[\tau^{-1} + \dots \tau^{-18} \right]$ = 1.6177539551670…*svadisthanacakkra*

$$\Sigma\,[\tau^{-1} + \ldots \tau^{-29}] = 1.6180325815810\ldots muladharacakkra$$
$$\Sigma\,[\tau^{-1} + \ldots \tau^{-47}] = 1.6180339887504\ldots brahmacakkra$$

The first of my five Magickal Orders was the Christian O.S.J., for which I chose the number 336. I hadn't discovered the 93-current yet, so I had no idea how significant the number would prove to be (336 = 6 x 56). I'd always been verbally oriented and had no ability for mathematics. By the age of ten I thought I wanted to become an archaeologist and had become fascinated with ancient Egypt. In 1960 I discovered a copy of *Egyptian Hieroglyphics* by E.A. Wallis Budge in an old bookstore in downtown Coral Gables in Miami, Florida and within several months I'd taught myself nearly 200 hieroglyphics.

I had a dream that year which influenced my interest in ancient Egypt. I was a Priestess being wrapped as if for death, while still alive, for placement in the tomb of a Pharaoh. My name was M'kar, which has the value by Hebrew gematria of 261 (ראכמ). When I was living in Washington, D.C., seventeen years later, I discovered that 261 was the numeration by Greek Gematria of the Motto that gave me 336 in the O.S.J. By the English gematria of *Liber Trigrammaton* it has the numeration 107, and the sum of those three numbers (336 + 261 + 107) = 704 = (2 x 352), and therefore the duplicative form of the Number chosen by my Magickal Partner when we met in Washington in 1977.

I'd already taken two years of Latin in school, and when I discovered *Magick in Theory and Practice* in 1966 I began teaching myself the rudiments of Hebrew. Ten years later I was starting to explore Greek, and discovered that the numerical values for my O∴T∴O∴ motto in Hebrew, Greek, and English—481; 381; and 100—add up to 962, the duplicative of 481. We moved to Miami in 1978 and joined the *Ilé de Yemanja* (the primal orisha of Water: *Yemanja* can be translated "Mermaid"). We received *iléké* or prayer-beads for Elegba, Chango, Obatala, Yemanja and Ochun (orishas for Moon, Mars, Mercury, Jupiter,

Venus) and later received the *jagunjagun*, called Guerreros or "Warriors" in Spanish. These are Magickal Weapons for Elegba, Ogun, and Ochosi. Ochosi is represented by an iron crossbow hidden inside Ogun, who is himself represented by an iron pot filled with iron tools such as railroad spikes. He corresponds to the strength of Chango (Mars).

352's Ori Inu, or "Ruler of the Head" Shango perfectly symbolizes her birth-sign, Sagittarius. My Ori Inu was divined as Obatala, corresponding to Kether on the Tree of Life. Osun is represented by the figure of a silver rooster on a stand from which depends four bells. He is kept on a shelf higher than the Warriors, and never allowed to fall over; ever the Guardian. For placement in Elegba I was told to bring a sacred stone to represent my birth-sign. Using the tables in *Liber 777* as a guide, I chose amber: partly because it had an ant trapped inside it; but later I discovered that רהבמא = 251, and shortly after our Padrino Omi Ademi created the tool, the Government released its now well-known "Amber Alert." I also discovered that 251 was the number of blue beads on my *iléké* for Yemanja, the ruler of our *Ilé* , and therefore chose Amber 251 as my Motto and Number for the Santeria stage of my Magickal Path.

The first true K'rla-Cell working occurred in 1981 in Ithaca, New York, soon after the Winter Solstice. I'd been admitted to the Fellowship of Isis (based in Clonegal Castle, Scotland) under Olivia Robertson and under the sponsorship of Vivienne O'Regan-Jones, a noted occult author who comes from a family-line of Wiccans, and was at one time a member of the Typhonian O∴T∴O∴. I entered the F.O.I. under the member-name שיואד הארבאד אמא, 576, and lived legally under the name Deborah Davis for nearly a year in Ithaca. It was quite an experience, as I'd already performed a work of bhakti yoga to Krishna, dressing as Radha and chanting for 9 months in 1974 in Coconut Grove, FL in Peacock Park.

I never understood the opposition I received for this line of experimentation; from everyone except Kenneth Grant, that is. I never knew another Thelemite to complain about 666's attempts to live as "Alyce Cusack" at Cefalu.

Our first cell Working was 3 hours long and followed the Winter Solstice Invocation of the Ritual of the Mark of the Beast, after which we returned to Miami and began to plan our concept for a Cult of the K'rla Cell; and for this, I adopted the Magickal Motto of טסא-ון-ןסמש, 576.

Thus, the sum of my five motto numbers, (336 + 481 + 251+ 576 + 576) totaled 2220; 10 times 222 (the number of Θεοβαλδος) and also the values of the Double Letters counted in the following manner:

	INITIAL VALUES	FINAL VALUES	
ך		500	
מ	40		
ן		700	
פ	80		
ץ		900	
Σ	120	2100	= 2220

After our return to Miami from Ithaca, we made two very remarkable discoveries that hinted we were on the right Path. First, we did a 3½ hour *japamantra* using "the numbers & the words" from *AL* II:76 that resulted in the appearance of an "equation of the Old Ones" (as we came to call it; see page 224, the "alien equation") on our Temple wall, and the discovery of the star Gamma Geminorum in the Hexagram

of the South—also known as the Winter Hexagon—called לא האנאה ,
which means "the Mark" and has value by gematria of 93. The Mark
refers to the "mark" or "brand" on the neck of the Camel (למג) , which
carries the Traveler across the Desert.

I'd also been experimenting with the Instructions of *AL* I:25 for a
number of years, "Divide, add, multiply, and understand," but hadn't
actually gotten anywhere with it. One day it dawned on me that I.25 is
a number—five-fourths—and by applying those instructions to it, the
discovery of the *aurea media* ensued, and that opened up the world
of Thelematics, the type of mathematics which seems based in Liber
AL, and ...

$$1.25/\sqrt{1.25} + 0.5 = 1.61803398875 \ldots = \Phi$$

... leading to the power-progression:

$$
\begin{aligned}
\Phi^{-1} &= 0.61803398875\ldots \\
\Phi^{0} &= 1 \\
\Phi^{1} &= 1.61803398875\ldots \\
\Phi^{2} &= 2.61803398875\ldots \\
\Phi^{3} &= 4.23606797750\ldots
\end{aligned}
$$

... and to the square-root results:

$$
\begin{aligned}
\sqrt{5} &= (\Phi^{0} + 2\Phi^{-1}) \\
&\quad (\Phi^{1} + \Phi^{-1}) \\
&\quad (\Phi^{2} - \Phi^{-2}) \\
&\quad (\Phi^{3} - \sqrt{4}) \\
&\quad [(\Phi^{4} - \Phi^{-4}) \div (\Phi^{2} + \Phi^{-2})] \\
&\quad [(\Phi^{5} + \Phi^{-5}) \div 5] \ldots \text{etc.}
\end{aligned}
$$

It turns out that $\sqrt{5}$ can be derived from every power of Φ, from which develops an entire geometry of the square root of 5, which is the basis of the mathematics of the Old Ones.

This discovery proved that we were on the right track, since $(1.25 \times 10^2) = 125$ or 5^3, and 125 is a temurah of 512, of 251, and of 152. Also, the equation

$$\Sigma\,[125 + 152 + 251 + 512] = 1040$$

gives the numeration for υοφο, the Greek word for UFO; but this can also be abbreviated in a pre-Hellenic spelling using the ancient letter Ϝ (digamma), equivalent to the Hebrew vav, which gives

$$ϜΦΟ = 576$$

There has been some question over why Kenneth Grant adopted the form of a Triple Trilogy, or set of nine books, to present his occult theorems. We shall attempt to answer these concerns here.

Consider *The Book of Thoth* or Atu of Tahuti, which begins with Zero followed by Unity. This One, or Unity, is the beginning of the Natural Numbers or Whole Numbers. What is the second number? The Magickal Theory says, "Zero equals Two." So if we add the previous Zero to the *successive One*, what is the result? A second One. Adding the *previous One* gives us the number Two: and adding the second previous One results in the number Three. We now have the beginning of the series 0, 1, 1, 2, 3 ...

Continue in the same manner, always adding the *previous* number, and you obtain the running series; 0, 1, 1, 2, 3, 5, 8 ,13, 21 ...etc. The resulting ratios eventually produce τ, the *aurea media*. In chapter 33 of *Magick Without Tears*, Crowley writes:

There is great danger in the Golden Mean, one of whose main objets is to steer clear of shipwreck, Scylla being as fatal as Charybdis. No, this lofty and equable attitude is worse than wrong unless it derives from striking the balance between two very distant opposites.

This can be seen in the development of the ratio:

$$1 \div 1 = 1$$
$$2 \div 1 = 2$$
$$3 \div 2 = 1.5$$
$$5 \div 3 = 1.666...$$
$$8 \div 5 = 1.6$$
$$13 \div 8 = 1.625$$
$$21 \div 13 = 1.615384...$$
$$34 \div 21 = 1.619047...$$
$$55 \div 34 = 1.617637...$$

The *numbers* are known as the Fibonacci Numbers after the twelfth century mathematician who discovered them, Leonardo of Pisa, better known by his nickname of Fibonacci. He traveled extensively as a young man, studying the mathematical systems of people everywhere he went; and, recognizing that arithmetical computation would be simpler and much easier with Hindu-Arabic numerals than with Roman numerals, introduced them to the Western world in his *Liber Abaci* or *Book of Calculation* (first published 1202). Section Three of that treatise discusses a number of mathematical problems including a description of the growth of a population of rabbits, which is the origin of the Fibonacci Number Sequence for which he is most famous today. The "Golden Mean" (*aurea media* = τ) develops like the swing of a pendulum, approaching the true medium ever more closely.

The numerical sequence itself is also hinted at in *AL* 2.15 (another temurah of 125, 152, 251, and 512), and note that

$$\bar{A}\Sigma\ [125 + 152 + 215 + 251 + 512] = 251 = \text{אלרכ}$$

The verse reads, "For I am perfect, being Not; and my number is nine by the Fools; but with the just I am eight, and one in eight." 8 times $\sqrt{9}$ is 24, and the 24 recurring Fibonacci Numbers produce, by Numeric Reduction (a process by which numbers are reduced to their lowest digit), as for example 89 becomes 8 via the process

$8 + 9 = 17$ and $1 + 7 = 8$

1st 12:	1	1	2	3	5	8	13	21	34	55	89	144
Reduc.	1	1	2	3	5	8	4	3	7	10	17	9
Result:	1	1	2	3	5	8	4	3	7	1	8	9

2nd 12:	233	377	610	987	1597	2584	4181	6765	10346	17711	28657	46368
Reduc.	8	17	7	24	22	19	14	24	20	17	28	27
2nd Red.	8	8	7	6	4	10	5	6	2	8	10	9
Result:	8	8	7	6	4	1	5	6	2	8	1	9

1st 12:	1	1	2	3	5	8	4	3	7	1	8	9
+2nd 12:	8	8	7	6	4	1	5	6	2	8	1	9
= Sum	9	9	9	9	9	9	9	9	9	9	9	(1+8)=9

1.61803398875 … = The Golden Mean, symbolized by the Greek letter Phi or Φ (drawn like a curl: φ) due to its properties of creating the Fibonacci Spiral which appears throughout nature, from beehives, seashells and flower-petals, to storms and the shape of spiral galaxies. The third function in the equation displays a peculiar property shared by no other number: Φ multiplied times itself gives its powers, which are equal to the sums of those powers, i.e.:

$$\Phi^0 \cdot \Phi^1 = \Phi^1 = (\Phi^{-1} + \Phi^0)$$
$$\Phi^1 \cdot \Phi^1 = \Phi^2 = (\Phi^0 + \Phi^1)$$
$$\Phi^2 \cdot \Phi^1 = \Phi^3 = (\Phi^1 + \Phi^2)$$
$$\Phi^3 \cdot \Phi^1 = \Phi^4 = (\Phi^2 + \Phi^3)$$
$$\Phi^4 \cdot \Phi^1 = \Phi^5 = (\Phi^3 + \Phi^4)$$
$$\Phi^5 \cdot \Phi^1 = \Phi^6 = (\Phi^4 + \Phi^5)$$
$$\Phi^6 \cdot \Phi^1 = \Phi^7 = (\Phi^5 + \Phi^6)$$
$$\Phi^7 \cdot \Phi^1 = \Phi^8 = (\Phi^6 + \Phi^7)$$
$$\Phi^8 \cdot \Phi^1 = \Phi^9 = (\Phi^7 + \Phi^8)$$
$$\Phi^9 \cdot \Phi^1 = \Phi^{10} = (\Phi^8 + \Phi^9)$$
$$\Phi^{10} \cdot \Phi^1 = \Phi^{11} = (\Phi^9 + \Phi^{10})$$
$$\Phi^{11} \cdot \Phi^1 = \Phi^{12} = (\Phi^{10} + \Phi^{11})$$
$$\Phi^{12} \cdot \Phi^1 = \Phi^{13} = (\Phi^{11} + \Phi^{12})$$
$$\Phi^{13} \cdot \Phi^1 = \Phi^{14} = (\Phi^{12} + \Phi^{11}) \ \dots \ \text{etc.}$$

Phi symbolizes the Union of NUIT and HADIT. Nuit is the Circumference of the Circle, while Hadit is the Center, equidistant from all points on the circumference. Therefore, the mathematical formula appropriate to Nuit is the product of Phi and twice the radius;[209] and Phi times the square of the radius symbolizes Hadit.[210]

The mathematical symbolism of RA-HOOR-KHUIT unwinds through the ancient teachings concerning the Golden Mean, which both Qabalists and mathematicians have chosen to represent by the 16th letter of the Greek alphabet, Phi. Actually, Phi (or Φ) is either the 16th or the 17th letter, depending upon whether or not the ancient letter of Digamma[211] (which was later discarded) is counted. But then again when it was a letter, Φ (which replaced it) was not, therefore the whole question of the Hindu Tantric doctrine of the 16-17 kalas may be implied.

---

209 "For I am divided for Love's sake, for the chance of Union."
210 $2\pi r$, the Circumference is the Infinity of Nuit. The Area given by πr^2 is the ability of Hadit to traverse along all points from the Center.
211 F

II

Diary Entries

♂ 11 *Nov. An XCIX (2003 e.v.)*
10:42 *pm*

Intense interest in the number 4811 and its reversal 1184, brought an insight to look into 718∴'s remarks on Frater Achad's Formula of Reversal. Investigation into them just now showed me that:

$$4811 = 17 \cdot 283$$
$$17 + 283 = ש$$
$$1184 = 2^5 \cdot 37$$
$$2^5 + 37 = 69$$
$$4811—1184 = 3^2 \cdot 13 \cdot 31$$
$$3^2 + 13 + 31 = 53$$

4:41 *pm*

What this seems to imply is that the *"old"* form of the formula IAO has been superseded by the VIAOV or ϝ IAO ϝ adumbrated by 666; but that the true type of the formula involves Φ/ στ mysteries that we have been investigating.

No, let me correct myself: not *"the true type of the formula,"* for with the digamma or vav, ϝ IAO ϝ = 93; rather a secret meaning of the formula applying to the Cult of the K'rla Cell and the Coming Androgyne.

5:28 pm

Does ꟻ IAO ꟻ imply ΦO ꟻ (I + O = Φ; A = Ayin = O; ꟻ = the Sun, Horus, whose secret name is Set), shadowed forth in the identities

$$\Phi = \text{ꟻ} = \sigma\tau$$

as has been demonstrated in so many ways, both literally and numerically? For,

ΦO ꟻ = 576.

Die Jovis, 5 June, anno CX (2014 e.v.)
5:52 pm

Today is the day of Jupiter, which rules the sign Sagittarius, the birth-sign of the Agent of the Cell; and that Agent hath chosen as her Magickal Number 352; the number of the Cell (Ναος = 152) before she even knew of that Cell, plus the number 200, the value of the letter Sigma in the Greek Qabalah, which is the ancient form of the modern-day letter "s." In its final form[212] as ς it depicts the risen Kundalini.

Thursday is also the Day of Yemanja, the Mother of our *Ilé* in the Afro-Cuban style we work with our *guerreros* or "Warriors."[213]

There is much significance in the formula received in the Working of two days ago—the day of Mars—when read in the Trumps attributed to the letters of that formula. I have just finished studying it in connection with the corresponding Atus and was overwhelmed! For example, I saw for the first time the importance of reading the symbols of the Cards *in reverse order*, and what Light that shed upon my understanding of that Formula!

---

212 "The manifestation of Nuit is *at an end*," *AL* I:66.
213 See remarks by 666∴ on Atu XVI in *The Equinox* III, 5.

I must show all this to 352∴ tonight and can only hope she picks up on it as I did.

The formula was received as the number 393 and taken as significant due to its accordance with the numbers attributed to the Aeon of Horus. Upon hearing that the conclusion of the Working was 9:33—a permutation of 393—this was confirmed, and I immediately turned it into a tetrad formula of the letters:

שׁ	=	300
פ	=	80
ח	=	8
ה	=	5
		——
	=	393

Could this correspond in some way with the Tetragrammaton of the Aeon of Osiris? There was a hidden Shin in the center of that formula that implied the forthcoming of the Messiah turning יהוה into יהושה or Yahweh into Yehashueh; Jehova into Jesus, etc. But this was no historic figure, it surely implied that the next Aeon would be one of "Force and Fire," since שׁ equals Fire in all its symbolism and as "a Tooth" would be the Messiah that "bites the hand (yod) that feeds it," or as one of our most prominent contemporary initiates[214] says, "I have sharp teeth." M.M.M. = 120 = 2·60 which equals S∴S∴ as two Samekhs. Has anyone ever noticed that the initials of *Typhonian Ordo Templi Orientis* spell Toto: the dog in *The Wizard of Oz*? That Wizard may be the one who wrote Liber OZ, hence all the symbolism of the Dog Star!

Today is also the 5th day of the 6th month, a Union of the 5 and the 6 which symbolizes the completion of the Great Work. As anno CX, the Year of the New Aeon equals $\Sigma n[1-10]$ times two, or 55 + 55, and 2014 of the vulgar era is two times 1007, which is 19 · 53. Note that (19

214 Mad Mike Magee, who was a member of the Sovereign Sanctuary of the Typhonian O∴T∴O∴

+ 53) = 72, אמאל! It is significant that yesterday was the 25th anniversary of the Tiananmen Square Massacre, and that the Dalai Lama came out after renouncing all ideas on politics two years ago, urging China to embrace democracy. 25 is, notably:

$$(2\Phi \cdot 2\Phi^{-1})$$
$$(\Phi + \Phi^{-1})$$

and ... $(2\Phi^2 \cdot 2\Phi^{-2})$
$$(\Phi^2 - \Phi^{-2})$$

The symbolism of the importance of the spiral in the Thelemic Mathematico-Philosophical view really overtook me this afternoon, especially after I learned to see the Formula both forward and *in reverse*; since 393 has no entries in *Liber D*; but I discovered that החפש in reverse is the word שפח (=388) which means "to search out diligently" preceded by the letter ה, which is a Window!

388 is (4·97), 97 being the number of זמן, "the appointed time," (i.e., the Aeon) and the 4 implies the Four Quarters, symbolized by the Stellar Hexagrams in the symbolism of the K'ρλα Ναος, but also note that 388 equals (352 + 36)!

The Formula החפש read in reverse is especially significant in light of remarks by 666∴ in Equinox III,v upon Atu XVI, "the Tower [or War]" where he says "It may be taken as the preface to Atu XX, the Last Judgement, i.e., the Coming of a New Aeon;" for in that order *that is exactly where it appears*! It is also notable that the figure of Nuit is the predominant image in the two cards that display the first and last letters of the Formula, since Nuit is the first figure to appear in Liber AL, and yet "the Manifestation of Nuit is at an end." In his remarks on ATU XVII, 666∴ says "The figure of the goddess is shown in manifestation," and reading the Formula as it was received this is where she appears ... at the end. The Beast also points out that "... every form of energy in this picture is spiral," and that is exactly what has been revealed to the Cell via *AL* I.25 and the subsequent study of spiral geometry.

7:52 pm

I could go on, and on … but want to save some of this insight to share with 352∴.

Die mercurii, 18 June, anno CX (2014 e.v.)
1:10 pm

Spent the morning attempting to construct the titlepage and sub-title to our proposed book on the Mathematics of Thelema. It is difficult, but I believe I can do it. …

III

The Alien Equation

Investigations into the *"alien equation"* caused me to notice implications of important mathematical functions in *AL* I.25, "Divide, add, multiply, and understand." The inverts of two of these operations do not affect the result, but that isn't true of the third. Nuit does not tell us whether to divide *by*, or divide *into*, and the difference can be striking.

Take Unity, for example. One divided by One, plus One, times One, equals Two. Two divided by One, plus One, times One, equals Three. Three divided by One, plus One, times One, equals Four. And so on. The function results in the succession of natural numbers. But what if we divide into One, add One, and then multiply times One successively? Dividing into One is the same as inverting the previous result, and multiplying times One doesn't affect the equation at all, and so the process becomes: One (inverted) plus One (times One); invert, add One, (times One); invert, add One, (times One); etc. where multiplication times Unity is simply implied. The result is the Sacred Proportion known throughout history as the Golden Mean.

The Golden Mean, glyphed by the 27th letter of the Greek alphabet, Phi (Φ), is not simply a number; it is "THE Number."[215] An irrational constant like Π, that cannot be worked out algebraically but can easily be determined by geometric analysis, it appears throughout nature. The first notable thing we discovered about it, is that it is the basis of

---

215 ΟΑΡΙΘΜΟΣ = 500 = Φ, by gematria.

quintile geometry and the square root of five; as we had been using the K'rla Cell to contact the Old Ones, this might have been evidence of such contact, or at least of its initial stages. According to the dream reports of Θεοβαλδος, the svapna plane of the Old Ones is based on a five-fold geometry.

The relationship of the Golden Mean to the root of five is intimate, for:

$$\Phi^1 - \Phi^{-1} = 1$$
$$\Phi^1 + \Phi^{-1} = \sqrt{5} = \Phi^2 - \Phi^{-2}$$
$$\Phi^2 + \Phi^{-2} = 3$$

Also, $\Phi = \frac{1}{2}\sqrt{5} + \frac{1}{2}$ and $2\cos36°$, thus following an old definition for the accomplishment of the Great Work: the Uniting of the Five and the Six (really, the square root of five and the square of six). And it is the formula of the Star of Nuit or Pentagram, out of which I designed a K'rla Cell talisman on 23 July 1977 e.v.

Φ is the only possible creative Duality within Unity; and is thus the formula par excellence that demonstrates the identity of magick ("creative duality") and mysticism ("Unity"). This needs to be demonstrated geometrically, but its metaphysical implications can be shown in other ways:

Magick: Φ^2 (Formula of Self-Love) $= \Phi + 1$

Mysticism: Φ^{-1} (Formula of Inversion) $= \Phi - 1$

Regarding the division of Unity by the Golden Mean, refer to *AL* I.27–30, and *AL* I.45-48.

There is direct reference to the Divine Proportion in *AL* III.47, "...then this circle squared in its failure is a key also," for there seem to be several solutions to this ancient problem, and they all involve Phi.

Besides its Qabalistic value of 500, Φ is given to Geburah in Lib. 777, the sphere of Mars, making it an appropriate mathematical-qabalistic glyph for the energies of the Aeon of Horus ... But is it?

The history of the letter reveals some interesting facts. Φ was a late addition to the Greek alphabet, replacing the obsolete letter Digamma (ϝ), which had a numerical value of 6. The first thing to notice is that Φ + ϝ = 506, or "…six and fifty" (*AL* I.24). To replace the Digamma Qabalistically and take on the numerical value of 6, the combination letter Stau (στ = σ + τ) was adopted, since σ = 200 and τ = 300. So, Φ is a letter of Horus … hiding, as it were, the letter of Set (στ)…

Further investigations into its qabalah confirms this identity, for the Qabalistic value of Φ divided by its mathematical value gives the formula:

500/Φ = 309 = שט

… while the Qabalistic value of Φ times its mathematical value gives the formula:

500 x Φ = 809 = 500 +309 = Φ + שט

As the basis of the logarithmic spiral, Φ represents the movement of the Kundalini Shakti, and its influence appears throughout nature from the structural form of the DNA and the gnomonic evolution of the human brain, to the spiral whirlpool of our galaxy, and similar *"island universes."* But the thing that really convinced us that Φ was "a key also" (*AL* III.47) was the discovery that Φ - 0.5 equals the square root of 1.25 … the number of the Chapter and Verse of *AL* that tells us to "Divide, add, multiply, and understand" !

The evidence was mounting that this was an important key to the implied *"Nu-mathematics"* of *AL* … or, at least, to a formula of the K'rla Cell. So I continued to investigate both the function of *AL* I.25, and the Golden Mean. The former resulted in an important solution to *AL* I.46 involving the declination of the star γ Geminorum. The latter resulted in an extension of the division-of-unity into fewer and fewer distinctions approaching the ultimate division into two equal parts. ("The Math of the Crystal Humm"). In other words, where $\Phi^{-1} + \Phi^{-2}$

$= 1$, we now have a value Phi-sub-one (Φ_1) which fulfills the formula $\Phi_1^{-1} + \Phi_1^{-3} = 1$. Similarly, Φ_2 yields $\Phi_2^{-1} + \Phi_2^{-4} = 1$, and Φ_3 yields $\Phi_3^{-1} + \Phi_3^{-5} = 1$. The series also relates in the following way:

$$\Phi^2 - \Phi^1 \quad = \quad 1$$
$$\Phi_1^{\ 3} + \Phi_1^{\ 2} \quad = \quad 1$$
$$\Phi_2^{\ 4} - \Phi_2^{\ 3} \quad = \quad 1$$
$$\Phi_3^{\ 5} - \Phi_3^{\ 4} \quad = \quad 1 \quad \text{etc.}$$

Only two terms in this series, Φ and Φ_3, have whole number powers which are equal to the base-power plus one:

$$\Phi^2 - \Phi^1 \quad = \quad 1$$
$$\Phi_3^{\ 3} - \Phi_3^{\ 1} \quad = \quad 1$$

The *successive inverted powers* of these two terms, which equal Unity when added together, are:

$$\Phi^{-1} + \Phi^{-2} \quad = \quad 1$$
$$\Phi_3^{\ -2} - \Phi_3^{\ -3} \quad = \quad 1$$

... the difference between the opposite terms being equal, in the number we have called Zeta (ζ), which can only be the vibrational formula of the K'rla Cell, for

$$\zeta = 0.048193697756$$

The result was too striking, and probably the main spur behind that period of ALALIA I made the S∴S∴ suffer through. I balanced the Hunchback against the Soldier on this one, for years. I don't know what the odds are against getting that particular string of numbers, not only once, but *twice*, in the curious interplay—especially when searching for a formula of the K'rla Cell! Their magickal significance cannot be overstated:

$$\zeta = 0.0\ 481\ 93\ 69\ 77\ 56$$

0.0:   Could suggest 0 = 2, and also OTO, where the bindu =
       spermatozoon = Lion-Serpent = T.

481:   The magickal number of Fra. Kephra-ma-Ast, adopted in 1971.

93:    The number of Θελεμα.

69:    Suggests the magickal formula written about in Liber 333, cptr.
       LXIX.

77:    The number of עז, and of the "Political Programme in the
       Outer" of Thelema.

56:    The "word" of Nuit (*AL* I.24). Here it appears "at an end" (*AL*
       I.66). Refers to Ma Ion since "the end is constant only when it
       is "not'" (56=NU).[216]

We adopted Zeta as a designation not only because it was phonetically apt (the Current is a vibration), but because of the correspondence
ζ ≡ Gemini and the position of that sign in the region of the Hexagram
of the South. Also, there are the implied links with the Aeon of Horus,
Achad's Aeon of Zain or of Silence[217] and the constellation of which Al
Hanah[218] forms a part and which has been the focus of the K'rla Cell
within the region of the Hexagram.

The two proportions, Φ and Φ_3, divide Unity in two different ways.
In decimal form they are:

$$\Phi = 1.61803398875\ldots$$
$$\Phi_3 = 1.32471795725\ldots$$

Phi is the only proportion that divides Unity into mean and
extreme ratios, i.e., a square and its root. Phi-sub-three, on the other

---

216 Cf. *Mauve Zone*, p. 112.

217 Note my own period of ALALIA upon making this contact.

218 γ Geminorum. *Al Hanah*, "The Mark (of the Beast)," has a numerical value of 93. The function
of *AL* I.25, when applied to its declination, offers a solution to the puzzle of *AL* I.46.

hand, makes a proportional division of Unity with its inverted *cube* and inverted square. This can be demonstrated with a Moebius-like arrangement, or a figure rather like the glyph for Infinity, or an image suggestive of a continuous flow between their functions as Primary and Secondary divisions of Unity:

$$\Phi^{-1} + \Phi^{-2} = 1 = \Phi_3^{-3} + \Phi_3^{-2}$$
$$\Phi^{-1} - \Phi_3^{-2} = \zeta = \Phi_3^{-3} - \Phi^{-2}$$

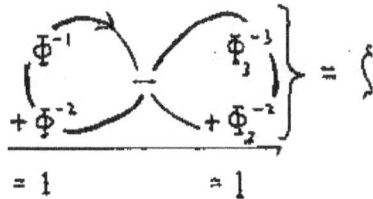

There are further implications concerning the role of Φ in this K'rla Cell complex. When on their honeymoon in Cairo in 1904, 666∴ and Ouarda[219] did an invocation in the King's Chamber of the Great Pyramid. The Beast claims that all he succeeded in doing was intensifying the Astral Light; but it may have been there, and not later at the Boulak Museum, that Rose became inspired.[220]

The base of the Pyramid is 440 cubits, and 440 = KR + KR. If the 356 cubits of the Pyramid's apothem are divided by half the base (220, or the number of AL), the result is the Golden Mean, 1.618.[221] In fact, a study of the Pyramid Complex reveals that it was designed with the Common Basic Principle named the *Pyramids Principle*, using the Common Basic Measure called the *Pyramids Common Measure*. The Pyramids Principle (PP) can be expressed as the ratio of both volume and surface area between the cube and the sphere:

---

219 Arabic for "rose." Note that in Greek Ουαρδα has a numerical value of 576, the number of "the key" (κλειτορις), and of the pos. term. of the Cell.

220 See *Confessions*, Arkana, 1989, p.372.

221 The incorporation of the Divine Proportion makes the Great Pyramid an effective system for transforming spherical areas into flat ones.

$6 : \Pi :: 5 : \Phi^2$

Or,

$\Phi^2 : \Pi :: 5 : 6$

Union of the Five and Six.

The Pyramids Common Measure (PCM) can be determined with the following formula:

PCM = Height of 2nd Pyramid/0.4 = 140.8m/0.4 = 352m[222]

… the magickal number of Soror Maiat, 352∴ - !

At the same time, we found confirmation of an earlier assertion of mine that the height of the Great Pyramid is 481 feet, or 153 meters[223] … and 153 = 481/π.

The Pyramids Common Measure (352m), the Pyramids Principle ($\Phi^2 : \pi :: 5:6$), and the Golden Mean (Φ) figure throughout the geometry of the Pyramid Complex (an image of the "City of the Pyramids"?), not to mention the magickal numbers of the bringers-through of this Cult (352∴ & 481∵) -!

The basis of the geometry of the Old Ones; keys to verses in AL; the metaphysical significance of the Golden Mean as it relates to the identity of Magick and Mysticism, to the Aeon of Horus-Set and to the formula of the Kundalini Shakti; the basis of the Math of the Crystal Humm which led to the discovery of the K'rla Cell vibration (ζ); and a Sacred Proportion on the Giza Plateau … all of this resulting from investigations into the equation of the K'rla Cell!

---

222 Source: Comet Research Inst.—Geometrical Analysis of the Great Pyramid http://www.comet-ri.com/index-e.html
223 Ibid.

IV

Analysis of *AL* II.76

"4 6 3 8 A B K 2 4 A L G M O R 3 Y X 24 89 R P S T O V A L"

AL II.76 is the 142nd verse of the Book as a whole,
and 142 = (2 x 71)

71 = LAM

(4 x 6)	=	24
(3 x 8)	=	24
A B K (or 2 x 2 x 20)	=	80
2 4	=	24
A L G M O R (by notariqon = 1+3+3+4+7+2)	=	20
3 Y X [algebraically 3(YX) = 3(2x4)]	=	24
24	=	24
89	=	89
R P S T O V A L (by notariqon = 1+8+6+7+6+1+3)	=	32
	+	
	=	341
	=	(11² + 220)
	=	א מ ש

The total number of characters in this cryptic phrase is 30, which is the value of ל or L, the original title of *Liber AL vel Legis* as 666 *heard* it spoken and *wrote it down*.

The first two numbers multiplied yield (4 x 6) = 24. The next two numbers multiplied yield

(3 x 8) = 24. The first "word," ABK, can be transliterated into Hebrew as A = Aleph, or Atu 0, which by the mathematics of Thelema becomes 0 = 2; B transliterated as Beth equals 2; and K transliterated as Kaph equals 20: therefore (2 x 2 x 20) = 80. Adding all of this to the next number (24) gives the Sum (24 + 24 + 80 + 24) = 152.

ALGMOR (as רעמגלא) gives the value by notariqon (1+3+3+4+7+2) = 20.

Making Y = 2 (as the I or 1 divided) and X = 4 (as the Cross of the Four Quarters), gives the algebraic form 3YX = (3 x 2 x 4) = 24 as well. The number after that is 89, and the Sum here is (24 + 24 + 89) = 137.

RPSTOVAL (ΡΠΣΤΟΦΑΛ) by στενογραφία in Greek reads as (1+8+6+7+6+1+3) = 32. This numeration counts the letter stau (the combined sigma+tau) as six, the value given to it after the letter φ replaced the obsolete letter digamma, originally enumerated as 6. Sigma-plus-Tau became equal to 6 because (Σ+T) = 500 = Φ. The ancient digamma (F), similar to our modern English "F," is equivalent to the Hebrew letter Vav.

The Sum of these Four numbers, or (152 + 20 + 137 + 32) = 341, the sum of the Mother Letters א מ ש , which equals 220 + 11², or the number of *The Book of the Law* plus 11 (the number of Magick) squared.

A slightly different slant (although one which confirms the above interpretation, as will be demonstrated below) can be seen when ALGMOR is taken as a phrase in itself, since in Hebrew אל גמור means "a complete god" (vide *Liber OZ vel LXXVII*: "There is no god but man") and is equal to the number 280. This gives the sum 152+280+137+32 for the entire code, or 601, the value of אם, *Mother*, when the letter Mem is counted in the value of its final form as 600.

This may suggest that:

א equates with *Nuit* as Air (or Space)

מ equates with *Hadit* as Water (or the Deep), and

ש equates with *Ra-Hoor-Khuit* as Fire (or the Primal Fire)

Their full sums add up to

אלף equals 111

מים equals 90

שין equals 360

$$= 561 = (341 + 220),$$

or the number of the Mother Letters plus the number of *The Book of the Law* itself .

Modern physicists claim that the numbers 5, 8, and 24 are continually turning up in string theory, and may even explain why we could live in a ten-dimensional universe analogous to the Tree of Life itself. Notice that the number 24 appears in this interpretation of *AL* II.76 five times, and $(24 \times 5) = 120$, or the sum of the numbers $[1----15]$, ה being the 15th Path.

120 is twice 60, the number of both הנה, "to behold," and מחזה, "vision"; and 120 is also the value of the word מועד, "The Time of the Decree."

24 is the smallest 5-hemiperfect number, because the sum of all positive divisors of 24 (that is, $1+2+3+4+6+8+12+24) = 60 = (\frac{5}{2} \times 24)$.

There are 4 numbers on each side of the word ALGMOR, or eight in all.

24 is the smallest number with exactly eight divisors.

The *product* of any eight consecutive numbers is divisible by 24.

Fibonacci Numbers, 1, 1, 2, 3, 5, 8, 13, 21, 34, 55, 89, 144, 233, 377, 610, and so on, contracted by *numerical reduction* into the digits 1, 1, 2, 3, 5, 8, 4, 3, 7, 1, 8, 9, and so forth, reveal a 24-fold repeating sequence of: 1 1 2 3 5 8 4 3 7 1 8 9 8 8 7 6 4 1 5 6 2 8 1 9 which, when broken in half, placed one over the other, and added, show the pattern

$$1\ 1\ 2\ 3\ 5\ 8\ 4\ 3\ 7\ 1\ 8\ 9\ +$$
$$8\ 8\ 7\ 6\ 4\ 1\ 5\ 6\ 2\ 8\ 1\ 9\ =$$
$$9\ 9\ 9\ 9\ 9\ 9\ 9\ 9\ 9\ 9\ 9\ 9\ (18)$$

...and the final 18 becomes 9 by *numerical reduction.* This sequence of 12 repeating numbers adds to 117, which equals 93 + 24.

In the symbolism of Cthulhu,

א as *Nuit* (or the Goddess of Infinite Space) represents the realm of the Mi-Go who colonized Yuggoth, and מי-גע has the numerical value of 123, the number of אהה יהוה אלהים, a name of GOD implying Kether-Chokmah-Binah.

מ as *Hadit* (or the Deep Place) represents the realm of the *Deep Ones*, who inhabit the City of R'lyeh. Its number as רלא—the final half of K'rla—is 231, the formula of the Tunnels of Set on the Nightside of the Tree of Life. The Deep Ones worship Dagon, the Archetypal Dragon to which so many young virgins (Andromeda, Persephone, etc.) were sacrificed, as K'rla is sacrificed to the Great Old Ones for Their inhumane scientific studies.

ש as *Ra-Hoor-Khuit* (or the Primal Fire) represents the Old Ones, comprised of the first life-substances to arrive on Earth from extra-terrestrial realms and ignited by the accretion of chemicals flaring from the solar nebula.[224] Volcanic outgassing created the primordial atmosphere. Much of the Earth at that time was molten because of frequent collisions with other bodies leading to extreme volcanism. The following Archean and Proterozoic Aeons produced the beginnings of life on Earth, or *abiogenesis*, circa 4.28 billion years ago.[225]

Thus, there have been Five Aeons in Earth's occult history[226], and can be read cyclically, beginning with the last one above:

0.

ש symbolizes the Aeon of the Old Ones, the first extraterrestrials to come to Earth.

1.

מ symbolizes the Aeon of the Deep Ones, in their Underwater realms on Earth.

1   3

א symbolizes a Dual Aeon (cf. "None, breathed the light, faint & faery, of the stars, and two. For I am divided for love's sake, for the chance of union." (*AL* I. 28-29) Also, see the Seal of the A∴A∴ This was the Rule of the Mi-Go, which merged into the Aeon of Isis in the occult

---

224 "Our religion therefore, for the People, is the Cult of the Sun, who is our particular Star in the Body of Nuit, from whom, in the strictest scientific sense, comes this earth, a chilled spark of Him, and all our Light and Life."—Crowley, comment on *AL* III.22

225 Chemical reactions produced in the ancient ferric-iron rich sea were made possible by the chemical molecules found in the Archean sea. This implies that metabolism may have been shaped by stellar rays projected from the Six-rayed Star.

226 "According to obscure occult traditions, the present planetary life-wave comprises seven cycles, or aeons, numbered, for the sake of convenience, Nought to Six. The current Aeon is the Fifth."—Kenneth Grant, *Aleister Crowley and the Hidden God*, Starfire Publishing, Ltd., 2013 edition, pps. 54 and following. "The fifth Aeon will be followed by that of Maat (the Daughter), and the flowering of full solar consciousness imaged by the Six-rayed star.

"The Sixfold Star of the Daughter combined with the Fivefold Star of the Son forms the Elevenfold Star of the Great Work accomplished. And this in a mystical sense, for the radiating *bindu*, or root-vibration, of the Six-rayed Star is the lunar light of Babalon, therefore a *seventh* and hidden ray to her manifested six. This Star is, then, a figure of Seven, not of Six."—Kenneth Grant, *ibid.*, p. 55.

symbolism of humanity. At this time the worship of the Great Mother
(the Goddess of Infinite Space) predominated.

4.

22. מ represents the Aeon of Osiris in the symbolism of the occult
cycles of humanity. At this time the worship of Paternal Deities took
over. Recall that, after his death, the body of Osiris in the Egyptian
Myth-cycle was hacked into pieces which were cast into the **waters** of
the Nile. Cf. Also the four corners of the square.

5.

1. ש represents the Aeon of Horus, which was announced in 1904 with
the receipt of *Liber AL vel Legis* or *The Book of the Law*. Horus, a
God of Force and Fire, is a return to the beginning, or re-commence-
ment of the Circle[227], which is why the symbolism of the Cthulhu Cult
is becoming prevalent today. The Old Ones are attempting to reclaim
Their Supremacy once again, or in other words, to *take over the Earth*
They once ruled, and our only means of fighting this can be through a
unified, controlled attempt to communicate with Them. Such means as
the group practice of *mantra japa*[228], and the K'rla Cell Rite—which
channeled a mathematics pertinent to both the Old Ones and the *93
Current*—can be our only hope.

• • •

The sum of ש+מ+א+מ+ש is 681, the number of תרועה, " battle-cry" or
"sound of a trumpet," a reference to the Seven Trumpets sounded after
the breaking of the seventh seal in the Book of *Revelation (Rev. 8: 1-2)*.

---

227 This Sevenfold Star of Babalon is the Symbol of the Double Aeon of Horus-Maat; and, counting
Nought to Seven, the Aeon of Maat will technically be the Eighth, as Atu VIII is attributed to Balance,
or Justice (Maat)—titled Adjustment in the Atus of Tahuti—and 8 forms half of the perfect Ratio 8:5,
....1.6, or the basic Ratio of the Golden Mean. שיר equals 360, the unbroken Circle.
228 *www.bibliotecapleyades.net* and *www.parareligion.ch*

Also, note that $(681 + \frac{1}{2}\Phi)\Phi^2 - (\Phi^2 + \Phi^{-2})^2 = 1776$, which is the sum of all the permutations of 251, or $(125 + 152 + 215 + 251 + 512 + 521$.

The cipher can also be counted in the Qabalah of *Liber Trigrammaton* (taking the **X** as a sign of multiplication) as:

$$(4+6+3+8+5+20+17+2+4+5+1+11+21+10+14+3+18)$$
$$\mathbf{X} \ (24+89+14+4+15+9+10+22+5+1)$$

which equals $(152 \ \mathbf{x} \ 193) = 29{,}336 = (2^3 \ \mathbf{x} \ 19 \ \mathbf{x} \ 193)$; and, adding the factors...

$$[2^3 + 19 + 193] = 220^{229}$$

---

229 $220 = 1+(1+2)+\sum[1\text{--}3]+\sum[1\text{--}4]+\sum[1\text{--}5]+\sum[1\text{--}6]+\sum[1\text{--}7]+\sum[1\text{--}8]+\sum[1\text{--}9]+\sum[1\text{--}10]$.

IV A

Liber AL II:76 Decoded

Transmission between Jeffrey Evans and Peter Levenda, emails dated March 19, 2020 (the Vernal Equinox), as this book was being prepared, concerning the enigmatic verse in *Liber AL* II:76.

From Jeffrey

Hi Peter,

Well, the Cell has made a strong Contact. Not only with the earlier material, but I believe this will especially interest you:

4 + 6 + 3 + 8 + A + B + K + 2 + 4 + A + L + G + M + O + R + 3 + Y + X + 2 + 4 + 8 + 9 + R + P + (ST) + O + V + A + L

4 + 6 + 3 + 8 + 1 + 2 + 20 + 2 + 4 + 1 + 30 + 3 + 40 + 6 + 100 + 3 + 10 + 60 + 2 + 4 + 8 + 9 + 100 + 80 + 6 + 6 + 6 + 1 + 30 = **555.**

...

Until last night, the verse was totally obscure to me for nearly 50 years!

Then, it was as if a Gate suddenly opened. That seems to be the way things *"come through."* I suddenly feel like jotting a few inspirational lines of research down, then almost automatically pick up my calculator and sometimes it produces no results. But at other times (such as last night) I fall into a semi-automatic trance state, and the material begins to flow quickly.

Witness the arrangement of the code:

4 + 6 + 3 + 8 + A + B + K + 2 + 4 + A + L + G + M + O + R + 3 = 233 = the thirteenth Fibonacci Number (by the same method of counting)

As well as Y + X + 2 + 4 + 8 + 9 + R + P + (ST) + O + V + A + L = 322 = יעצמאהוק (QV HMTzOI), "MIDDLE LINE" - !!

Σ = 555

Levenda's Response

This could work. A controversial move, using ST as the Greek stau/stigma with a value of 6, but the sum of 555 is consistent with the verse itself: "What meaneth this, o prophet? Thou knowest not; nor shalt thou know ever." In Hebrew gematria, 555 means "obscurity" according to *Sepher Sephiroth*, so that's consistent. It *was* obscure to AC.

Of course, it's also *Necronomicon*, as we both know, in isopsephy and also "separation, division" (Διακρισις) and "desire, lust" (Επιθυμια). Thus, we get "division" again, as in *AL* I:25, but with the addition of "desire, lust" you get *AL* I:29, "For I am divided for love's sake..."

In isopsephy, you also get "Foundation" and "Image" (Ιδρυμα) for 555. (As an aside, the word "stigma" itself, spelled in Greek (στιγμα) adds to 554.)

Great Work!

APPENDIX

Additional Libri

Liber 17:
The Number 17

O ne of the most cryptic things the O.H.O. said to me in our conversa-
tions over the years was, "Seventeen is going to be *a very import-*
ant number!" Why (?) I wondered, but refrained from asking him,
deciding that it might be a puzzle he intended for me to work out on my
own. Otherwise, he would have simply told me why.

The first thing I thought of, was the fact that *AL* I:57 reads "All
these old letters of my Book are aright; but צ is not the Star." 666 clearly
explains in *The Book of Thoth* why he therefore switched Atu IV with
Atu XVII in the Atus of Tahuti, so that was certainly not a puzzle for
me. I experimented with the number somewhat unsuccessfully for a
few years without much result, until one day in the mid-1980s (about
5 or 6 years after the initial Cell Rite in Ithaca) the Cell—Soror 403,
her Magickal Number as the K'rla Cell—became entranced and began
to gaze at page 17 on the holograph mss. of *AL*. Something motivated
her to begin counting the words on the page, and *there are ninety-three*
words on it! I couldn't believe it. Cross-checking her results and com-
paring with other pages in the manuscript, brought me to the astonish-
ing realization that *this is true of no other page in the holograph copy*
of the text.

That was only the first of a number of remarkable discoveries we made concerning this number over the years. The next was that the Four Celestial Hexagrams are comprised of seventeen stars *in toto*, as some of them overlap and two Hexagrams may often share a single star if it lies on the border between the two. Next, I found out that the sum of the first four prime numbers $(2 + 3 + 5 + 7)$ equals 17, and that the sum of *any other four consecutive prime numbers* is always an even number.

Not only that, but (and the following facts are of particular significance to Thelemites) the sum of the *squares* of the first seven prime numbers—from 2 to 17—gives the result

$$(2^2 + 3^2 + 5^2 + 7^2 + 11^2 + 13^2 + 17^2) = \mathbf{666}$$

This certainly suggests the infernal hebdomad of the Tree of Life itself, but notice that there are ten non-primes up to 17, and this suggests all ten Sephiroth: but together, they imply the Beast with Seven Heads and Ten Horns that appears both in *Daniel* 7 and the Book of *Revelation* (Rev.13), two of the major apocalyptic books in the bible. The Hebrew phrase **for seven**teenth, HaShaBO OShRaH, equals 952, or (17 x 56). Also, $(2 \times 17^2) + (222 + 17^2) = (16 + 17)^2$; and...

$$\Sigma\,[Fn_1 — Fn_{17}] = (10 \times 418)$$

$$\Sigma n\,[1 — 17] + \Sigma[F_1 — Fn_7] = (2 \times 93)$$

$(5 \times 17) = 85$ (the value of the letter Pe)

$17 = \sqrt{(\Sigma n[1 — 16] + \Sigma n[1 — 17])}$,
and...
$(1 + 1\} = 2\ (2 + 1) = 3$
$(3 + 2) = 5$
$(4 + 3) = 7$

$+\ \underline{\quad\quad}$

$= 17 = \Sigma n[1 — 4] + \Sigma[Fn_1 — Fn_4]$

The orbit of Pluto (which H. P. Lovecraft suggested in a letter to a friend, might actually be *Yuggoth* itself), lies out of the ecliptic plane of the other planets of the solar system, inclined at an angle of 17°, and 17 is the numerical value of the Hebrew word ChVG, "a circle, orbit" (see *Liber D*).

Mathematically, 17 is the smallest number that can be written as the sum of a square and a cube in two different ways: $3^2 + 2^3 = 4^2 + 1^3$. Also, $1 \wedge 1^1 + 2 \wedge 2^2 = 17$. $17 = 9+8$; $72 = 9 \times 8$; $1+7 = 8$ and $7+2 = 9$. ($17 \times 11) = (93 + 1 + 93)$. $481 \div \pi = 153 = (9 \times 17) = \Sigma n[1—17]$; therefore $\Sigma n[2—17] = 152$. $\Sigma n[1^2—17^2] = 1785$, and the *factors* of 1785, which are $(3 \times 5 \times 7 \times 17)$, add up to 32, the number of Paths on the Tree of Life. Also, 17×30 (the number of the **original title** of *Liber AL*) equals 510, the number of the Greek letter-name **Φι**.

The sum of the first nine Fibonacci Numbers and the first eight Decimal Numbers *interlaced* (**17** numbers in all) equals (**31 + 93**).

17 is one of the numbers used to illustrate the closest approximation to $\sqrt{3}$; $265 \div \Sigma [1-- 17] = \sqrt{3}$, and $\sqrt{3}$ is recognized as the central line in the geometry of the vesica piscis. Rehoboam, the son of Solomon and the first king of **Ju**dah after the United Kingdom split in 930 B.C., reigned for **17 years.**

Curiously, there are 17 muscles in the tongue: and the ancient Greeks acknowledged 17 consonants in their alphabet, with 9 "silent" consonants and 8 semi-consonants. The Book of Exodus is (7×17) verses shorter than **666 + 666**; and the Pentateuch contains $7^6 \times$ **17** verses. 969 $(= 17 \times 57)$ is the **seventeenth tetrahedral number.**[230]

$$17\Phi(101^{39}\!/_{99} + 46\Phi^{-1}) = \Phi^{17}$$

---

230   969 is also the 17th nonagonal number. 1 is the smallest to be both; 969 is the next smallest; and the difference between them is $968 = 2^3 \times 11^2$. $2^3 \times 11 = 88$; and $969 - 88 = 880$.

Additional notes (added 12/21/2018):

The 16th tetrahedral number, plus the 17th triangular number (153, or $\sum[1\text{---}17]$ equals 969.

In base 20, 969 is 289; $17^2 = 289$, and 17 is a factor of 969.

Methusaleh is the oldest in the bible at 969 years, and therefore that number is a reference to Saturn and Chronos as types of Time; and $969 = (6+56+156+333+418)$.

Seventeen Stars

There are four stellar Hexagons called *The Winter Hexagon*; *The Spring Triangle*; *The Summer Triangle*; and *The Northern Cross*. Information about them can be found at the following websites:

The Winter Hexagon:
https://en.wikipedia.org/wiki/Winter_Hexagon

The Spring Triangle:
https://en.wikipedia.org/wiki/Spring_Triangle

The Summer Triangle:
https://en.wikipedia.org/wiki/Summer_Triangle

The Northern Cross:
https://en.wikipedia.org/wiki/Northern_Cross_(asterism)

They correspond respectively to the FOUR HEXAGRAMS depicted in "The Lesser Ritual of the Hexagram" as it is written in LIBER 0 vel MANUS ET SAGITTAE SUB FIGURA VI, as follows:

The Winter Hexagon is the Hexagram of Earth in the South.

The Spring Triangle is the Hexagram of Fire in the East.

The Summer Triangle is the Hexagram of Air in the West.

The Northern Cross is the Hexagram of Water in the North.

They correspond respectively to the stars:

The Winter Hexagon	Rigel
	Aldebaran
	Capella
	Pollux
	Procyon
	Sothis
The Spring Triangle:	Arcturus
	Spica
	Regulus
	Denebola
The Summer Triangle:	Altair
	Deneb
	Vega
The Northern Cross:	Deneb
	Sadr
	Gienah
	Delta Cygni
	Albireo

It will be noticed that the star Deneb (α Cygni) appears *twice* in this grouping (in both The Summer Triangle and The Northern Cross: therefore there are 17 stars altogether in the four celestial Hexagons).

They have numerical values as follows by the Hebrew system of gematria and the corresponding Greek system of isopsephy, and they can be designated:

Winter Hexagon:

Rigel is לגיר in Hebrew, which has a value of 243.

Al Dabaran is Arabic for "The Follower," but in Ancient Greek it was called Λαμπαδιας, which meant "Torch-bearer." It has the value of 198, with the final Sigma counted as 31.

Capella is Latin for "Little Goat"; therefore it can be called עז (goat) in Hebrew, which = 77.

Pollux, the twin-brother of Castor in Greek mythology, is Πολλουξ = 1,280.

Procyon in Greek, "Little Dog," is Προκυων = 1,520.

Sirius or Sothis, in Greek, is Σωθις = 1,050.

*This gives a total numerical value of **4,368** for the SIX stars of the Winter Hexagon.*

Spring Triangle:

Arcturus is Greek for "Guardian of the Bear," spelled Αρκτουρος = 1,092.

Spica is from the Arabic "(Virgin's) ear of the wheat of grain," and in Greek can be "ear," σταχυ, with a value of 1,007 (combined Sigma + Tau = Stau, with a numerical value of 6).

Regulus is Latin for "Little Prince" or in Greek, Πριγκιπας = 335. (However, see my interpretation of *Liber V vel Reguli*, quite often translated as "The Book of the Prince," in which I suggest that "Reguli" in this Liber refers not to a Prince or the star in Leo, but to the Latin word for "Asp.")

Denebola is from the Arabic phrase for "Tail of the Lion." In Hebrew this is היראה בנז , which has the numerical value of 280.

*This gives a total numerical value of **2,714** for the FOUR stars of the Spring Triangle.*

Summer Triangle:

Altair is from the Arabic and means "The Falling Eagle" or "The Landing Eagle," and is possibly connected etymologically to the Hebrew phrase "To an eagle," רשנ לא, which equals 581.

Deneb is from the Arabic word for "tail." In Hebrew, בנז, with a value of 59.

Vega is spelled הגו in Hebrew, with a value of 14.

*This gives a total numerical value of **654** for the THREE stars of the Summer Triangle.*

Northern Cross:

Deneb *(vide supra)* is from Ar. "tail," in Heb. בנז, or 59.

Sadr is from the Arabic "Hen's Chest," and may be related to the Hebrew רידא ש ("Great"), as in the pronounced "puffed up" chest of the hen or cock about to crow. Its number is 515.

Gienah was the traditional Arabic name for Gienah Cygni, possibly related to the Heb. הניג, the word for "Garden." It has the value of 68.

The star delta Cygni belonged to the Arabic constellation al-Fawaris, meaning "The Riders." This is translated םיבכורה in Hebrew, with a value of 283.

Al bireo is a result of mistranslation and miscopying from Latin
of Arabic and back again into the word סיריא ב לא, which has
a value of 314. See *en.wikipedia.org* under "Nomenclature."

*This gives a total numerical value of **1,239** for the FIVE stars of the
Northern Cross.*

• • •

Thus the total numerical value for the Eighteen stars in the Four Hexagons is 8,975 or (4,368 + 2,714 + 654 + 1,239); and 8,975 = (5^2×359)—
the product of twenty-five times 359, the number of ושט, Shaitan or Set.
Counting the number of Deneb (59) only once, gives a total value of
8,916: 12 (the number of signs in the zodiac)—times the sum of 671
and 72. And 72 is the number of LAMA, the prime focus of visualiza-
tion in Kenneth Grant's development of the Typhonian Current.

The Tree of Life as 93

An Exposition of the Numerical Value
by the Mathematics of the Old Ones
and the Symbolism of the Krla Cell Rite

"Numbers," "Spheres," ספירות is equal to 756 = x "Paths," נתיבים is equal to 512 = y

equation I: $((\frac{1}{2}(x/y + (\Phi^2 + \Phi^{-2}))) + \Phi^{-2} - \Phi^2) = z$

equation II: $\frac{1}{10}(452 - z^{-1} + 16 - 74{,}798^{-1}) = \Phi$

452 = (152 + ש); and 152 is the number of Ναος, "a Cell"

16 = the *kalas* of the *vamamarg* or Left-hand Path

74,798 = (2 x 149) 251
*and, adding the first 2 factor*s = [2 + 149] = 151 is (Κρλα)
while 251 is (כרלא)

Which are The Numbers of the Formula of Krla in both Greek and Hebrew

The *Sums* of the 5 elements of each of these two equations are:

equation I: $(\frac{1}{2} + (x \div y) + (\Phi^2 + \Phi^{-2}) + \Phi^{-2} + \Phi^2) = a$

equation II: $((1 \div 10) + 452 + z^{-1} + 16 + 74{,}798^{-1}) = b$

Therefore: $((a+b) \div 10) + ((5{,}665{,}535 + \Phi^{-1}) \div 26{,}930{,}300) = \mathbf{93}$

The *ten elements* in the first two equations above define the 10 Sephiroth in the following manner:

$\frac{1}{2} \equiv$ KthR as *the "Twin Faces"* or One *divided* to become the 2 of ChVKMaH; or, KthR both *manifest* and *non-manifest.*

$x \!\!/ y \equiv$ ChVKMaH as *"the Word"* or Λογος (Sephiroth/Paths) that formulates the Tree of Life.

$(\Phi^2 + \Phi^{-2}) \equiv$ BINaH as *the Number Three.*

$\Phi^{-2} \equiv$ ChSD as *the Illusory nature of 4 Dimensions,* since Φ^{-2} $= \Phi \wedge^- \sqrt{4}$.

$\Phi^2 \equiv$ GBVRaH as *($\Phi+1$) or 4 "dimensions" plus One* = Five Dimensions.

$\frac{1}{10} \equiv$ TiPhARTh as *the Center of the Tree (or Ten Contracted).*

$452 \equiv$ NeTzaCh as *(♀ plus 152) and (♂ plus 352), both Formulae of Venus in the Krla Cell Rite.*

$Z^{-1} \equiv$ HVD *as representing the Intellectual Process formulated in Equation 1.*

$16 \equiv$ YSVD *as the 16 kalas of Kularnava Tantra.*

74,798 ≡ MaLKVTh *as the Kingdom (or World-basis) of the Krla Cell Rite. (Vide Supra). Also, note that (2 x 149) = 298, the numerical value of* צהר, *White, the color of the orisha Obatala, the Ori Inu or Inner Head of the Krla Cell. This recalls the Qabalistic Dictum that "Kether is in Malkuth, and Malkuth is in Kether, but after another manner."*

The Pisa Arrangement[231]

By means of a comparative description of the ten numbers of the decimal system to the first ten Fibonacci numbers (referred to as Fn) we can arrive at a unique comprehension of the Tree of Life, as I intend to show. Beginning with the idea of Nothing as Absolute Nothing or "Ain" (represented by the digit 0 in this outline), since the Fn *do not begin with Zero*, this idea is expanded into the concept of No Limit or "Ain Soph" as the Qabalists called it. A Positive idea, it represents Space as a Unity, and is therefore represented by Fn_1 or the first Fibonacci number, One. The interpretation of this Space necessitated its expansion into the Limitless Light or "Ain Soph Aur" of the Qabalists, conceptualized by Aleister Crowley as *the space-time continuum*, and represented in the Fn system as a second One corresponding to the number Two of the Decimal system. Therefore, the Qabalistic "Triple Veil of the Negative" as $0 + 1 + 1$ demonstrates the key equation of Thelemic mathematics, $0 = 2$.[232]

---

231 With apologies to 666. So-called because it is based on the mathematical system of Leonardo de Pisa, known popularly as Fibonacci.

232 "With the God & the Adorer I am nothing: they do not see me. They are as upon the earth. I am Heaven, and there is no other God than me, and my Lord Hadit." - *AL* I.21. Also, see *AL* I. 28—30, and elsewhere.

n   Fn

$0 \equiv 0 =$ Ain $=$ Absolute Zero

$1 = 1 =$ Ain Soph $=$ Space (UNITY)
$\} \, 0 = 2$

$2 > 1 =$ Ain Soph Aur $=$ The Space-Time Continuum

(These two Ones $=$ The Point)

$=$ Nonmanifest & Manifest aspects of   **Kether**

$3 > 2 =$ The Line $=$ **Chokmah**

$4 > 3 =$ The Surface (the Plane as the Triangle) $=$ **Binah**

$(11) \equiv 89 =$ THE ABYSS $= (11 + 0) \equiv (89 + 4) =$ Illusion and Destruction of "Ego in Maya"

(Gravity, electromagnetism, and the strong & weak nuclear forces
as perceivable) $=$ **Chesed**
$5 = 5 =$ Unification of g-force and electromagnetism
$=$ The Fifth Dimension $=$ **Geburah**
$6 < 8 = \sum[1\text{----}4] - 2$
$=$ Ananda, Bliss: "eight, and one in eight." $=$ **Tiphareth**
$7 < 13 = \sum[1\text{----}5] - 2$ $=$ Chit, Knowledge. $=$ **Netzach**
$8 < 21 = \sum[1\text{----}6] \pm 0$ $=$ Sat, Being $=$ **Hod**
$9 < 34 = \sum[1\text{----}8] - 2$
$=$ The Illusory "Foundation" of Existence $=$ **Yesod**
$10 < 55 = \sum[1\text{---}10] \pm 0 =$ Duality $=$ **Malkuth**

These two *"imaginary"* Points or Units representing the "Twin Faces" of Kether, sometimes called the non-manifest and manifest aspects of Kether, can only be measured by comparison, which allows for creation of the number Two representing the Line. Although this Two represents the second Sephirah, Chokmah, it is Fn_3 or the *third* Fibonacci number. Adding the previous One (of Kether manifest) onto it gives the number Three for Binah, representing the Plane as the Triangle.

Notice that except in the case of Fn_1, the next three numbers of the Decimal system (2, 3, 4) are *greater* than Fn_2 , Fn_3, and Fn_4, depicted by the numbers 1, 2, and 3, representing the Idealism of the Sephiroth of the Supernal Triad.

Next comes THE ABYSS, depicted by the number Eleven in the Decimal system, and the number 89 in the Fibonacci system (since Fn_{11} = 89). In the Decimal system $(11 + 0) = 11$, but in the Fn system *the number Four is illusory or non-existent*, therefore $(89 + 4) = 93$, identifying the number of Magick with the central Formula of Thelema. On the *downward path* of "The Lightning Flash" this represents the Illusion of "the Ego in Maya"; while on the *upward path* of "The Ascending Serpent" this represents the *Destruction* of "the Ego in Maya."

The non-existence of the number Four in the Fn system depicts the illusory nature of matter, and represents the physical forces we perceive as gravity, electromagnetism, and the strong & weak nuclear forces.

To the Fourth Fn is added the Third Fn, which gives us the number Five. Notice that One and Five *are the only two places where the Decimal system and the Fn system coincide*, giving us a Fifth Dimension, which unifies the previous Four that we perceive. At this stage in the spiritual evolution of humanity, the Fifth Dimension is imperceptible to all but the very few.[233] The special significance of this is that, 5 is not only the base upon which the Fn system is founded, it is also the planetary number of Mars, and therefore of the god Horus (symbolic of the forces ruling the earth at this stage); and also the number of the mathematical system of the Old Ones.[234] This is the Fifth Dimension that

---

[233] "Let my servants be few & secret: they shall rule the many & the known." - *AL* I.10.

[234] See on online resource, "The Arkham Archivist" for numerous references in the novel *At the Mountains of Madness* by H. P. Lovecraft.

Quantum physicists and String-theory physicists have sought as the unification of gravity and electromagnetism, and therefore perfectly attributable to Geburah, the Sephirah called "Strength" on the Tree of Life.[235]

Just as the Fn above the Abyss (1, 2, 3) are less than the Decimal numbers they contrast (2, 3, 4), below the Abyss and below the number Five, the Decimal numbers 6, 7, 8, 9, and 10 are *less than the comparable* Fns 8, 13, 21, 34, and 55. This is because these dimensions are "compacted" or sub-atomic at this time and are therefore imperceptible to humanity. The *outcome* of the Aeon of Horus (or the Aeon of Maat) will be the development by the species of this perception. We will become telepathic[236], and Silence will reign supreme. Cf. *AL* III.70, "I am the Hawk-Headed Lord of Silence & of Strength; my nemyss shrouds the night-blue sky." The Aeon of Maat is foretold in the two verses of *AL* III. 71-72.[237] Time will then be perceived and experienced as running in two directions, that is *both forward and backward simultaneously* (as the most advanced physicists now theorize), and humanity will begin to see in both the past and the future simultaneously.[238]

In the sequence of the Decimal system the Sephirah Tiphareth is given to Six and is the center of the Tree, but in the Fn system the Sixth Fn is 8, which is why Hadit declares in *AL* II.15, "I am eight, and one in eight: Which is vital, for I am none indeed." Notice that in *The Naples*

---

235 *https://sciencing.com*
236 "The working basis of communication with occult entities is as arbitrary as any system of algebra or geometry. As long as the system possesses an inherent harmony, an internal coherence, it is valid within its sphere of function. Reimann, Lobachewsky, Poincare, Einstein, Cantor, all constructed mathematical systems which—although at variance with each other—are consistent within themselves."—Kenneth Grant, The Magical Revival, pps. 111-112; Starfire Publishing, Ltd., London, 2010. "Jeffrey Evans has demonstrated a mathematical projection of the Tree of Life from the Star of Nuit, thereby confirming Crowley's claim that *Liber AL* contains the keys to a higher Mathematics."—Kenneth Grant, Beyond the Mauve Zone, p. 99; Starfire Publishing, Ltd., London, 2015.
237 See *AL* III: 34, ."..when Hrumachis shall arise, and the double-wanded one assume my throne and place."
238 *www.ancient-code.com*

Arrangement Tiphareth is called "The point: now self-conscious, able to define itself in terms of the above." Mathematically, $8 = \sum[1\text{----}4] - 2$, or minus the space-time continuum, making $\sum Fn\ (1 + 2 + 3) = 6$, and $Fn_6 = 8$....The experience of the Point (8) as Bliss (Ananda). By gematria, $8 = $ ABH, "to will," or "to intend," which is why Hadit (the Point within the Circle) says " *'Come unto me"* is a foolish word: for it is I that go."[239]

The Seventh Sephirah in the Decimal system is the number 13 in the Fn system, and 13 is the number of AchD, "Unity," and so the Point's Knowledge of itself as a Unit equates with the Buddhist concept of Chit.

The Eighth Sephirah Hod (since $Fn_8 = 21$) is the Point's idea of Existence in its identity with Tiphareth, since $\sum[1\text{----}6] = 21$; and the Decimal number 9 (Yesod) = Fn 34, or $\sum[1\text{----}8] - 2$, being the illusory nature of all systems of attainment: there is "nowhere" to go, only the need to *realize* that we are *already There*. This is the accomplishment of the Great Work. Since $34 = (2 \times 17)$ and Atu XVII is "The Star," this also highlight's the exclamation of Nuit[240] "Thus ye have star & star, system & system; let not one know well the other!"

The Decimal number Ten equates with Fn 55, or $\sum[1\text{----}10]$, and the illusion of Duality symbolized by the *doubled* Five.

---

239 *AL* II.7
240 *AL* I.50

Liber V
vel Reguli

A Qabalistic Interpretation by Frater Shemsw-nn-Ast, 576∴
of the K'rla Cell Lodge of the Typhonian O.T.O.

Frequently "translated" by commentators as "Book 5 of the Prince," they point out that "Regulus" is the star which marks 0° of Leo. The ritual is not, however, Liber Regulus, but Liber Reguli. "Prince" in Latin is regulus, but also regis filius ("son of the king"), princeps, regimen, regnator, and regula, as well as a number of other designations. Latin is a very inflected language and can be difficult for those who do not know that it has three distinct genders, seven noun cases, five declensions, four verb conjugations, four verb principal parts, six tenses, three persons, three moods, two voices, two aspects and two numbers. Realize that there is also an Old Latin, a Classical Latin, a Vulgar Latin, a Medieval Latin, a Renaissance Latin, a New Latin and a Contemporary Latin. To anyone who does not grasp these distinctions, I suggest taking two or three years of a High School Latin class.

Reguli easily translates into English as "Asp," a serpent-type, therefore the Liber should most likely be read as "Book 5 of the Asp." If that were not enough proof for a reassessment of the title, in Hebrew "asp," עהפא equals 156, and BABAΛON is an earthly form of the goddess Nuit, pictured on Atu XVII, "The Star," to which is attributed the letter ה. It has the numerical value[241] of 5, and is the Mother-Daughter letter of Tetragrammaton.

As "The Ritual of the Mark of the Beast," the star that it ought to refer to is not Regulus in Leo but the star γ Geminorum (Gamma Geminorum) at approximately 9°06′ of Cancer, very near to Sothis and within the celestial Winter Hexagon, depicted as the Hexagram of Earth in LIBER O vel MANUS ET SAGITTAE SUB FIGURA VI. It has an orb of 2°20′. Gamma Geminorum was called al hanah by Arabian astronomers, which means "a brand, or mark," on the neck of a camel or some other beast of burden.[242] In other words, a mark of the beast. It transliterates into Hebrew as

האנאה לא

which equals **93**

Liber V vel Reguli, "Being the Ritual of the Mark of the Beast," is a publication in Class D, signifying it as an official ritual or instruction, described as "an incantation proper to invoke the Energies of the Aeon of Horus, adapted for the daily use of the Magician of whatever grade."

It is comprised of Three Gestures, yet called Liber V or "Book 5." 3 and 5 are the fourth and fifth Fibonacci Numbers. 3 is the primary sacred number of Eleggua/Eshu (Horus/Set) in the Afro-Cuban cult of Santeria (widely practiced in S. Florida and elsewhere) and 5 is the planetary number of Mars, signifying Horus. Note that $(3 + 5) = 8$; the sixth Fibonacci Number. These three successive numbers are the Sephiroth of the Pillar of Severity on the Tree of Life, and 5:3 followed

---

241 By gematria.

242 *See Star Names—Their Lore and Meaning,* by Richard Hinckley Allen (online at http://penelope.uchicago.edu/Thayer/E/Gazetteer/Topics/astronomy/_Texts/secondary/ALLSTA/ home.html , under "Gemini."

by 8:5 are two successive ratios in the development of the limit of the Golden Mean. 8:5 = 1.6, the basic Golden Mean ratio.[243]

The number of the Liber, V (Roman Numeral for 5), is the number upon which the Geometry of the Golden Ratio is based. Mathematically, the Golden Ratio (or Golden Mean) is glyphed by the Greek letter Φ (pronounced "fee"), which has the numerical value 500 by isopsephy. By numerical reduction, 500 equates with 5, and in Liber 777 (col. LIII, line 5) Φ is given to Geburah, the fifth Sephirah.

The First Gesture

The Oath of the Enchantment, which is called the Elevenfold Seal.

The First Gesture is made up of five subsections: the first one divided into 3 Sub-subsections; the second one divided into 3 Sub-subsections; the third one divided into 6 Sub-subsections; and the fourth containing only 1 Sub-subsection. The sum of these is $(3 + 3 + 6 + 1) = 13$, the sixth Fibonacci Number. The First Gesture, subtitled "The Oath of the Enchantment, which is called The Elevenfold Seal," contains 6 Divine Names, followed by 5 Words of Power. $(6 + 5) = 11$, the number of Magick, and $11 = (\Phi^5 - \Phi^{-5})$. The first subsection, "The Animadversion Towards the Aeon," begins (with Sub-subsection 1) having the Magician "robed and armed as he may deem to be fit," turning "his face towards Boleskine[244], that is the House of the Beast 666." ("...as he may deem to be fit" means "according to the Grade for which the performer is fitted").

The Elevenfold Seal refers to the numerical analysis by 666 hinted at below; the 6 Divine Names united with the 5 Words of Power given

---

243 3 and 5 are the 4th and 5th Fn, 5:3 = 1.666....; 8:5 = 1.6, the basic Golden Mean ratio in the first decad of Natural Numbers.
244 Lat. 57.14 N; Long. 4.28 W. Calc: $(((((\Phi+^{100}/_{1557})\div60)+21)\div60)+13)\cdot4.28 = 57.14$

in the text; and the Magickal Formula ABRAHADABRA which seals (or closes) The First Gesture with its 11 letters.

Sub-subsection 2 instructs:

Let him strike the battery 1—3—3—3—1.

This is the sound-sign of the Elevenfold Seal. The Sum of these numbers is eleven.

In Sub-subsection 3 the instruction is:

Let him put the Thumb of his right hand between its index and medius, and make the gestures hereafter following:

I have seen it stated in other comments to this rite that "It is not clear from this description whether the right hand should be open or closed," however Crowley was certainly not slovenly in his magical writings, as I shall now demonstrate. The pareidolia he refers to is the fig-sign of the Illuminati. The Fig tree is the third tree mentioned in the Book of Genesis, the leaves of which Adam and Eve used to sew garments for themselves after the Fall, when they realized that they were naked (Gen. 3:7). Also, "a sign of figs," מיהנאת זמיס equals 666.

The first subsection, "The Vertical Component of the Enchantment," instructs the Magician or Sorceress (in Sub-subsection 1):

*Let him describe a circle about his head, crying **NUIT!***

Sub-subsection 2 instructs:

*Let him draw the Thumb vertically downward and touch the Muladhara Cakkra, crying, **HADIT!***

LIBER V VEL REGULI

Sub-subsection 3 instructs:

> *Let him, retracing the line, touch the centre of his breast and*
> *cry RA-HOOR-KHUIT!*

The third subsection, "The Horizontal Component of the Enchantment," instructs (Sub-subsection 1):

> *Let him touch the Centre of his Forehead, his mouth, and his*
> *larynx, crying AIWAZ!*

Sub-subsection 2 instructs:

> *Let him draw his thumb from right to left across his face at the*
> *level of the nostrils.*

Sub-subsection 3 instructs:

> *Let him touch the centre of his breast, and his solar plexus,*
> *crying, THERION!*

Sub-subsection 4 instructs:

> *Let him draw his thumb from left to right across his breast, at*
> *the level of the sternum.*

Sub-subsection 5 instructs:

> *Let him touch the Svadistthana, and the Muladhara Cakkra,*
> *crying, BABALON!*

Sub-subsection 6 instructs:

> *Let him draw his thumb from right to left across his abdomen,*
> *at the level of the hips.*

(Thus shall he formulate the Sigil of the Grand Hierophant, but
dependent from the Circle.)

Numerically, the Divine Names tally:

NUIT   = *56 (as נו or NV)*

HADIT   = *10 (as דאה or HAD)*

RA-HOOR-KHUIT   = *463 (as אר-הוור-כוט or*
RA-HVVR-KVIT)

AIWAZ   = *93 (as זיוע or OIVZ).*

Note that עי is 80, Mars, and זו equals 13, which is the number of Unity.
A unification of Ajna & Vissudha is implied.

Also, זו means "here"; "this."

THERION   = *666 (as Το Μηγα Θεριον or TO MEGA*
ThERION)

BABALON   = *156 (as Βαβαλον or BABALON)*

$(56 + 10 + 463 + 93 + 666 + 156) = 1444 = (2^2 \times 19^2)$; by addition of
factors, $(2^2 + 19^2) = 365$; the number of days in the year of the Gregorian Calendar; and this Ritual was performed at the end of the year
according to the Gregorian Calendar in 1980 in order to open the first
of the 39-year series of K'rla Cell Rites (as of this date, it now being
2019 e.v. or anno CXIV). Note that **39** is the reverse of **93**.

The fourth subsection, "The Asseveration of the Spells," states:

Let the Magician clasp his hands upon his Wand, his fingers
and thumbs interlaced, crying:

LAShTAL! *(= 93 as 31 + XX+XI + 31)*

ΘΕΛΗΜΑ! *(= 93 as ThELHMA)*

FIAOF! *(= 93 as וזאיר)*

ΑΓΑΠΗ! *(= 93 as AGAPH)*

ΑΥΜΓΝ! *(= **93**: with **A** and **U** as silent breathing = 0; vocalized vibrations...MGN = 93)*

*93 + 93 + 93 + 93 + 93 = 465 = (3 x 5 x 31); and ∑[3 + 5 + 31] = 39, **the reverse of 93.***

The Magician or Sorceress cries **FIVE** Words of Power, thus indicating (along with the number of the Liber, (V or 5), that this is in truth an expanded ritual of the pentagram, intended for use as a Ritual for Banishing the Forces from Outside (or the Great Old Ones) that threaten to overtake earth today. 465 is the Sum of the numbers 1 through 30; the number of the letter **L**, which was the original title of *The Book of the Law*, or *Liber L vel Legis*. See holograph manuscript). Liber V is a Ritual of Protection.

The sum of these Divine Names and Words of Power add to 1909, the year of the first volume of "The Equinox." (i.e., 56 + 10 + 463 + 93 + 666 + 156 + 93 + 93 + 93 + 93 + 93 = 1909).

The fourth subsection, "The Proclamation of the Accomplishment," reads:

Let the Magician strike the Battery: 3—5—3 , crying
***ABRAHADABRA** (= 418)*

This is "The Word of the Aeon" and *a Key of the Pentagram* (see Liber D), being an 11-lettered formula comprised of **5** letters, **A, B, D, H,** and **R,** representing the Crown, the Wand, the Cup, the Sword, and the Rosy Cross: the traditional Weapons of the Magician or the Sorceress. Hence its central significance in Liber V. These letters also represent Amoun: Thoth: Isis: Horus: and Osiris,and by notariqon A + Th + I + H + O = 1 + 9 + 10 + 5 + 6 = 31, or one-third of ninety-three.

418 is the value of זיכשלוב, or Boleskine, toward which the Magician or Sorceress faces during the performance of Liber V. The Formula of ABRAHADABRA unites the 5 and the 6, or the Pentagram and the Hexagram. For all these ideas vide Liber D under the number 418. Note that A+B+D+H+R in Hebrew equals 215, a temurah of 251, the number of K'RLA. 215 is 5 times 43, the number of Challah (הלח), which is translated in Liber D as "to make faint," i.e. to put into a trance: to turn into a Prophetess or a Seer in a Ritual. The second half of the formula of the K'rla Cell (152) is her energy or Power, and *AL* III: 7, "I will give you a war-engine," is **the 152nd verse of the Book as a whole.**

152 is the number of איצומה, "expend," or "bring forth," and the One brought forth is the Child or "magical child" with which magicians throughout human history have been preoccupied. On page 106 of *Beyond the Mauve Zone* (Starfire Publishing, Ltd., 2016 edition), Kenneth Grant writes:

> It should be evident from the material presented in these trilogies that Crowley, Leadbeater, Parsons, Evans, and others, known and unknown, have been attempting to utilise such a formula. The inevitable question is surely: has such a magical child been brought to birth within the current Aeon? Crowley may not have failed, for the Star envisaged by Cameron Parsons [note: See Hecate's Fountain (Grant) Part I, ch.3.] yet struggles in the birth pangs of an aeon that is nameless, perhaps because the child of its bowels has not yet emerged. Perhaps Evans, Nema, [n: See Outside the Circles of Time (Grant), ch. 12, and chapters 9, 10, and 11 of this present volume] and others are labouring to bring forth not a single entity but a composite stellar complex of Powers, such as Lovecraft

may have glimpsed in the shadowy gulfs of dream. The Great Old Ones, the Deep Ones, the Outer Ones: may they not be entities or gods such as those described by Crowley as "certain vast"stars" (or aggregates of experience)'? [n: Introduction to *The Book of the Law* (Crowley), O.T.O., London, 1938]. He claims that "one of these is in charge of the destinies of this planet for periods of 2,000 years."[n: Ibid.]

The Mathematical formulae inherent in *The Book of the Law*, which are indeed the Mathematics of the Old Ones, may give us a clue. It's basis is the truly unique number Phi, that is, the Golden Mean, and its properties are such that it displays within its very structure the Triple functions of:

$\Phi - \Phi^{-1} = 0.61803398875....$ ≡ the dwarf-child of which Besz and LAM are prototypes;

$\Phi = 1.61803398875....$ ≡ the potential of creation in the act of Love under Will, and\

$\Phi^2 = 2.61803398875....$ ≡ the Mother-Goddess who bears that Child.

Phi is indeed a unique number, for it is the *only* number the powers of which are *identical* to its additives! It is inherent throughout all Nature, from the spiral shapes of whole galaxies to the structure of our own DNA. (And, note: the number of those letters, whether counted by gematria or by isopsephy is 55—the "Secret Number of Malkuth." It forms a geometry of the square root of Five, a math of Lovecraft's Great Old Ones, a geometry of the Spiral, and a geometry of *The Book of the Law*. A curious run of qabalitic "coincidences" can be found in these numerical relationships. 74 is the number of Lamed, the symbol of the upcoming (or, rather, **in**-coming) Aeon of Maat, and:

74 + ((152 + Φ^{-5})/400)= x =   74.380226875 .... which is 74°22'48.81675, or 74 degrees, 22 minutes, 48.81675 seconds: *the declination of Gamma Geminorum in decimal notation!*

$$(x+((5{,}000{,}017{,}391{,}363 \div 10^{10})+\Phi) = 576,$$

while...

$$((80-x) \div 10)+(x \div 10) \qquad\qquad = 8$$
$$(80-x)+ x \qquad\qquad = 80$$

and:

$$(80-x){\cdot}x \qquad\qquad\qquad =418$$

The sum (8+80+418) = 506; a form of the "word" of Nuit (see *AL* I:24), and also the union of 500 (the qabalistic value of the Greek letter Φ) plus the value of stau: a combined sigma plus tau that took on the numerical value of 6 after the letter phi replaced the obsolete digamma for the "f" or "ph" sound-value. Digamma looked like F—similar to our modern "F"—and originally stood for the number 6, equating with the Hebrew "vav." The letter "digamma" can be found in Liber 777, col. LIII line 16. Its later replacement, stau, does not seem to be in the column.

The Ritual of the Pentagram and The Lesser Ritual of the Hexagram opened the first K'rla Cell Rite in Ithaca, New York, at the mundane new year by the Gregorian calendar over 1980—1981 (anno LXXVI); and 76 is the value of the word זויבח , "put away," "a hiding-place"; and also of דבע , or "slave."[245] The K'rla Cell in the Rite is the terrestrial female abducted by the Agents of the Old Ones to become one of the captive slaves that serve Them in Their campaign to overtake the

---

245 See *AL* II:58. This is the 124th verse of the Book as a whole, and 124 is the value of דחע , "pleasure," and is (93 + 31) or Four times Thirty-One, therefore they turn themselves into the Guardians of the Gates of the Quarters (*dikpalas*) in their roles to save humanity from the alien invasion by the Old Ones.

earth They once ruled: to become Their telepathic means of communication with humanity by teaching mortals both Their verbal language and Their mathematical language. By isopsephy, Ithaca is Ιθακη = 48; and as 418 is a numerical formula of the Great Work, so 48 can be read as a numerical formula of the *completion* of the Great Work, that is, 418 minus it's central Unity or the Dissolution of Ego (inner sense of "self"). Confirm this by the fact that the K'rla Cell is a feminine Magickal Machine, and "a woman" (as ליה) has the numerical value of 48, which is also the number of "Mercy," הלודג , or the Sephirah from which the Holy Guardian Angel guides the Sorceress across the Abyss in which her limited ego experiences that dissolution. The female captured by the Agents for deliverance to the

Old Ones must seek Mercy (Gedulah). It can be the only point from which to begin the Crossing. Any other would be exceedingly perilous, as Magical History shows.

By isopsephy, ΑΒΡΑΗΑΔΑΒΡΑ equals 221, and (418 + 221) = 639 = (9 x 71). Therefore it is a Formula of LAM in relation to the numerical reduction of the Fibonacci numbers as a series of nines. Spelled in full (in Hebrew) it equals 2843, which equals the formula of the K'rla Cell (403) times 7—the seven lower Sephiroth below the Abyss—plus 22, the number of the Paths that connect the Ten Sephiroth. Also, $2843 = ((\frac{1}{3}\Phi^{-4} +152) \div \Phi)\Phi^{19}-(2 \cdot 93)^{-1}$: and 152 represents the driving Force of the formula of K'rla; 19 is the Feminine number par excellence; and twice 93 is the Formula of the Aeon as the Number of both Love and Will.

Has anyone ever noticed that the number of years from the completion of the *Malleus Maleficarum* ("The Hammer of Sorceresses," or "Witches' Hammer") in 1486 to the receipt of *The Book of the Law* in 1904, *is 418* ?

That abominable book was second *only to the Bible* in terms of its popularity for nearly 200 years, and the vast majority of those prosecuted were women and girls. It was believed that females were more carnal, more lustful, than men. The Latin title *Malleus Maleficarum* is in the feminine form, demonstrating the idea that it was women who should be be accused, tortured and prosecuted. In the Latin grammar, the feminine form Malefic<u>arum</u> would only be used for women and girls, and so they inevitably became the victims.

A similar rationale exists among the Agents of the Old Ones in modern times. In their practice of Alien Abduction, they take terrestrial females to the hiding place of the Old Ones in the star Ibt al Ghauzi where They have been imprisoned by the Elder Gods in order to prevent Them from Their plan of taking over the earth. The Old Ones have begun their nefarious plot by capturing earth's females to experiment with their sexual natures and use that Power to turn females into the form of Their Silent Brides (המוד,"silent" and הלכ, "bride," both have the numerical value of 55: the Secret Number of Malkuth or Earth and *the sum of the numbers One through Ten*. It is also the tenth Fn or Fibonacci number). Maleficarum translates into Hebrew as תופשכמ with the numerical value of 846, the sum of (403+40+403)[246] or the Union of the K'rla Cells in the bondage of their enslavement as תופשכמ of the Old Ones. 846 is also (3 x 251) + 93; and 418 plus 428. The number 428 signifies "The breakers-in-pieces," or the Qliphoth of Chesed ready to tear the girl of earth apart as the Agents carry her into the abyss of space toward the star alpha Orionis (Betelgeuse).Her only hope can be to focus on the star gamma Geminorum (*al hanah*), *the Mark of the Beast*, which is the House or Fortress[247] of the Elder Gods. The Priestess presiding at the Opening Rite of the K'rla Cell was instructed to focus on the star Ibt al Ghauzi, or Betelgeuse: this analysis comprises much of the essence of the material she received via the trance-state induced in her by the Rite.

---

246 403 = K'rla Cell; 40 = לבח ("a rope"; "to bind").
247 See *AL*III: 3--- *AL*III: 9.

More than three times as many women were tortured and prosecuted as sorceresses in the Middle Ages than men were as sorcerers.
In the twentieth century, over twice as many women as men were
abducted as victims for intense sexual experimentation by the alien
Old Ones. In both cases, the victims were unwilling. The female cap-
tives of aliens often had intense sexual experiences followed by preg-
nancies that would be terminated in a follow up abduction several
months later, and occasionally her alien kidnappers would show a girl
an apparently human/alien hybrid, which she would sense was her
own. These female abductees experienced intense sexual "tortures"
just as the female sorceresses abducted by the Inquisitors of the Middle Ages experienced intense physical tortures. Is this a return to the
Middle Ages when the Catholic church was attempting to take over
the earth, just as the alien Old Ones are attempting to take over the
earth in modern times?

The ratio of female to male Alien Abductees is 68.34 percent
female to 31.55 percent male (go to *www.syracusenewtimes.com* for
these figures). Notice that the decimals, 34 and 55, are the 9th and 10th
Fibonacci numbers, and have the ratio 1.617647059,,,,, or, 1.618 (= Φ).
Also, $(((68 \div 31) + 1) \div 10) + 3 \approx \sqrt{11}$.

The mantra of the K'rla Cell in her plight is given by Kenneth
Grant in the eighth volume of his *Typhonian Trilogies*, the book titled
Beyond the Mauve Zone, in chapter six ("The Rite of the K'rla Cell").
Her mantra is KR-LAM-KRAL-NIA-MA-RLA-KA-RLA, and its
numerical value is 1127,the number by isopsephy of κλειτοφαλλικος:
clitoris[248] or, more properly, clitorophallic. The mantra, with her focus
on *al hanah* ("the Mark of the Beast") is her only salvation. In this way
she will fight against the Great Old Ones and Their agents with Their
preoccupations of her own sexual nature, as the females prosecuted as
"sorceresses" in humanity's own past were unable to fight. Inquisitors

---

248 κλειτ ("clit") means "key" (Gk.)

once sought the "Mark of the Beast" on their captive victims. The captive of the Old Ones must now seek the celestial Mark of the Beast and focus on the Elder Gods to save herself from the sexual tortures of the Old Ones; and she will once again rise supreme as the whore BABALON, but as Babalon Triumphant over the animal nature, as Babalon is astride the Beast in Atu XI of *The Book of Thoth*, and *She* will Rule the earth once again.

418 times five (the number of the female as the letter of Atu XVII) equals 500 (the value of the Greek letter Φ) plus 1127 (the Cell mantra) plus 463 (the number of RA-HOOR-KHUIT).

The Priestess presiding in the first Rite of the K'rla Cell was a member of the now-defunct Typhonian O.T.O.[249] headed by Kenneth Grant, but she was also a Priestess of Isis (initiated into the Aset Shemsw or "Retinue of Isis" of Olivia Robertson[250] on October 7th, 1980) named Deborah Davis. Her name, Deborah, was the name of a most famous prophetess of the Torah, "Deborah of the Palms",and after Ms. Davis willingly functioned in the role of Priestess in the Rite of the K'rla Cell she began to utter a strange mathematics believed to be "the mathematics of the Old Ones" *and the mathematics of The Book of the Law*. She discovered an equation for the Golden Mean (also called the Golden Line and the Golden Balance, and "the Cut" or "the Section" by Greek esoteric mathematicians. She discovered this in *AL* I:25, where Nuit exclaims "Divide, add, multiply, and understand." In Hebrew,"Golden Line," or בהזה וק , has the numerical value of 125. Similarly, "The Golden Balance" in Hebrew is בהזה ווזיא, which equals 93. "Golden Line Numbers" is בהזה וק מירפסמ, which has the numerical value of 555, indicating that this may be the true basis of

---

249 Under the Magical Motto K'rla-Naos, 403˙˙

250 Olivia Melian Durdin-Robertson, known as Olivia Robertson, (13 April 1917—14 November 2013) was a co-founder and High Priestess of the Fellowship of Isis, an international spiritual organization devoted to promoting awareness of the Goddess.

the mathematics of the Old Ones[251] (the numerical value by isopsephy of Their sacred book, Νεκρονομικον, is 555); and the Greek word for "Cut," or "Section," is Τομη, which is equal to 418. The color Gold appears in *The Book of the Law* more times than any other color: in *AL* I:60; *AL* II:50; *AL* III:30; *AL* III:31; *AL* III:32; and *AL* III:65.

The notable thing about these facts is that before functioning as Priestess in the K'rla Cell Rite in an attempt to contact the Old Ones; discovering this equation in Liber *AL* I:25; and receiving its follow up systematic development; *she had no previous mathematical knowledge or ability whatsoever*. It was thus truly a Received Mathematics.

In *Beyond the Mauve Zone,*[252] Kenneth Grant points out that specific magical rites were performed in New Isis Lodge on March 22, 1951. This was the day of the occult New Year or the Vernal Equinox, and 30 years before the beginning of the K'rla Cell Rituals in 1981, on the day of the New Year by the Gregorian Calendar—and 30 is the number of the letter Lamed, or *L*, which was the original title of *The Book of the Law. MARLA* was the word received by the Priestess presiding at the time of the Nu-Isis Rites. In his analysis of the formula, Kenneth Grant notes:

> In the course of this analysis [infra] it will become evident that K'rla was adumbrated in the workings of New Isis Lodge, and even earlier, for in 1943 were received by Aossic The Chronicles of Kr[alnia]" adding (in a footnote) "An intricate interrelatedness

---

251 A mathematics based on the number 5 and all its properties, numerical as well as geometrical, as can be evinced from any perusal of the works of H.P. Lovecraft. Einstein himself spent the latter part of his life searching for a key to the Fifth Dimension, and many M-Theory physicists today claim to have found it. And as Kenneth Grant writes in *The Magical Revival:* "The working basis of communication with occult entities is as arbitrary as any system of algebra or geometry. As long as the system possesses an inherent harmony, an internal coherence, it is valid within its sphere of function. Reimann, Lobatchewsky, Poincare, Einstein, Cantor, all constructed mathematical systems which—although at variance with each other—are consistent within themselves" (pps. 111-112, Starfire Publishing, ltd,, 2010 ed.).

252 Starfire Publishing Ltd., Spring Equinox 2016.

becomes apparent between these events and the author's involve-ment with Jeffrey Evans and Ruth Keenan several decades later.

The analysis of *MARLA* aforementioned reads:

> Marla, 272, without its "phonetic"[253] (i.e. as M'rla), becomes 271, which is the number of NHIRV (LVX); of AVR NVGH, "shin-ing light," and of GANZIR—'The Gate of the Shadows and the Shells'[254] This is "the Gate that leads to the seven steps into the Frightful Pit and the shrieking of the God on the Throne of Dark-ness.'[255] This is reminiscent of the

> > Thrones underground
> > And the Monarchs upon them
> > who are to be Invoked in Darkness Outside the
> > Circles of Time.

> M'rla, therefore, glyphs the light of Consciousness (LVX) shining in the Darkness (NOX) in the Tunnels of Set.

> ....as K'rla glyphs the light of Her Nature (SEX) glowing in the Dark Kingdom (REX) of the Dungeons of Teth (the Serpent or ASP).

Mr. Grant continues,

> The Evans-Keenan Cell Workings in the Tunnel of Niantiel[256] established contact with the Old Ones in the specific form of

---

253 Kenneth Grant notes: "With the phonetic, Marla = 272 a form of Apophis, the type-name of the Ophidian Current. The instruments of this Current are the Phallus and the Kteis, the initial letters of which, Kappa + Pi, when spelt in full, equal 272."

254 *The Necronomicon* (Schlangekraft ed., p. 16)

255 The "Throne of Darkness" parallels the Iron Chair in the Dungeon of the Inquisitors. The "Mon-archs upon them" were the innocent accused women who were Queens in their own Right.

256 The Tunnel of Niantiel is the Nightside Path of Nun, a fish. Fish was added to the seder plate in honor of the Prophetess Miriam, who thus became associated with Water in the Jewish tradition, and so with the water-Beast Leviathan, cognate with the Makara of Sanskrit mythology, whose number is 263.

KRLAMKR. This formula has the specific formula of 511, or 93 plus 418, thereby revealing at its heart the 93 Current—Aiwass.[257]

And as 403 plus 15 (the androgynous yod-he of tetragrammaton) equals 418, so 418 plus 93 equals 511: the formulae are steps up, or Grades of Initiation for the K'rla Cell.

We should also note that, as OIVZ (or Ayin + Yod + Vav + Zain = 93) is the true spelling of Aiwass in Hebrew, so also by isopsephy AIΓAΣΣ equals 418.

The quote from the Necronomicon above reflects the Inquisitors' Iron Chair in the Dungeon and the Regal, truly innocent victims who were forced to Confess in Darkness Segregated from the view of the public. Now (which is eternal) is the Time for Woman to regain Her suppressed Monarchy and repel those forces which threaten the earth today. She must work **with** the Elder Gods in *al hanah* to keep the Old Ones banished in Ibt al Ghauzi. The student must turn to Kenneth Grant's book *Beyond the Mauve Zone* (and the books in the *Typhonian Trilogies* which precede it) for a fuller exposition of these ideas.

The Second Gesture.

The Second Gesture is made up of 23 subsections and 9 Sub-subsections. 23 is the number of חיה, which means "life," but also "as an animal," i.e., as a Beast. See above, in reference to the star לא האנאה, "the Mark of the Beast"[258]. The 9 Sub-subsections reflect the nonuple nature of the Fn series.

(N.B. Footnotes by 666 are not reproduced here, or commented upon. For these footnotes, refer to Liber V itself).

---

257 *Beyond the Mauve Zone,* p. 95. (Starfire ltd. ed., Spring Equinox, 2016).

258 For, "Every man and every woman is a star." (*AL* I:3). The Prophetess K'rla Naos, 403 became focused on the star al hanah.

The Enchantment.

1. Let the Magician, still facing Boleskine, advance to the circumference of his circle.

2. Let him turn himself towards the left, and pace with the stealth and swiftness of a tiger the precincts of his circle, until he complete one revolution thereof.

The tiger is of the lion family, therefore attributed to the letter teth, which means "a serpent," and the asp is a serpent. In sections 18 and 23 (infra) the Magician performs a **spiral dance**, and the noted qabalist Isaac de Luria (הירא , "the Lion") devised a Spiral Tree of Life. Also, the Fibonacci system produces a spiral geometry.

3. Let him give the sign of Horus (or The Enterer) as he passeth, so to project the force that radiateth from Boleskine before him.

4. Let him pace his path until he comes to the North,; there let him halt, and turn his face to the North.

5. Let him trace with his wand the Averse Pentagram proper to invoke Air (Aquarius).

6. Let him bring the wand to the centre of the Pentagram and call upon NUIT!

The formula of NUIT is here **56**, as previously.

7. Let him make the sign called Puella, standing with his feet together, head bowed, his left hand shielding the Muladhara Cakkra, and his right hand shielding his breast (attitude of the Venus de Medici).

8. Let him turn again to the left, and pursue his Path as before, projecting the force from Boleskine as he passeth; let him halt when he next cometh to the South and face outward.

9. Let him trace the Averse Pentagram that invoketh Fire (Leo).

10. Let him point his wand to the centre of the Pentagram, and cry, HADIT!

The formula of HADIT is here **10**, as previously.

11. Let him give the sign Puer, standing with feet together, and head erect. Let his right hand (the thumb extended at right angles to the fingers) be raised, the forearm vertical at a right angle with the upper arm, which is horizontally extended in a line joining the shoulders. Let his left hand, the thumb extended forward and the fingers clenched, rest at the junction of the thighs (Attitude of the God Mentu, Khem, etc.).

12. Let him proceed as before; then in the East, let him make the Averse Pentagram that invoketh Earth (Taurus).

13. Let him point his wand to the centre of the pentagram, and cry THERION!

The formula of THERION is here **666**, as previously.

14. Let him give the sign called Vir, the feet being together. The hands, with clenched finger and thumbs thrust out forward, are held to the temples; the head is then bowed and pushed out, as if to symbolize the butting of an horned beast (attitude of Pan, Bacchus, etc.).(Frontispiece, The Equinox I. number III.)

15. Proceeding as before, let him make in the West the Averse Pentagram whereby Water is invoked.

16. Pointing the wand to the centre of the Pentagram, let him call upon BABALON!!

The formula of BABALON is here **156**, as previously. Note that BABALON is followed by *two* exclamation points, not merely one, thus emphasizing the extremely feminine form of this ritual.

17. Let him give the sign Mulier. The feet are widely separated, and the arms raised so as to suggest a crescent. The head is thrown back (attitude of Baphomet, Isis in Welcome, the Microcosm of Vitruvius). (See Book 4, Part II.)

18. Let him break into the dance, tracing a centripetal spiral widdershins, enriched by revolutions upon his axis as he passeth each quarter, until he come to the centre of the circle. There let him halt, facing Boleskine.

This Spiral dance is what is known as a **Fibonacci Spiral** mathematically, that is, it is a spiral based upon the special geometrical mathematics of θελημα and of the Great Old Ones[259]. The dance, it should be noted, is a counter-clockwise spiral. See works by, and about, noted Qabalist Isaac de Luria (1534—July 25th, 1572) for views on a spiral form of the Tree of Life in Sacred Geometry.

19. Let him raise the wand, trace the Mark of the Beast, and cry AIWAZ!

The formula of AIWAZ is here **93**, as previously. The Mark of the Beast is the special pareidolia of the star al hanah (לא האנאה), or Gamma Geminorum.

---

259 That is, a five-fold mathematics, or the mathematics of Leonardo de Pisa ("Fibonacci"), which he learned from an Arabian astronomer in the Dark Ages, the "mad Arab" Abdul al-Hazred.

20. Let him trace the invoking Hexagram of The Beast[260].

21. Let him lower the wand, striking the Earth therewith.

22. Let him give the sign Mater Triumphans (the feet are together; the left arm is curved as if it supported a child; the thumb and index finger of the right hand pinch the nipple of the left breast, as if offering it to that child). Let him utter the word ΘΕΛΗΜΑ!

The formula of ΘΕΛΗΜΑ is here **93**, as previously

23. Perform the spiral dance deosil and whirling widdershins. Each time on passing the West extend the wand to the Quarter in question, and bow:

    a. "Before me the powers of LA!" (to West.)

    b. "Behind me the powers of AL!" (to East.)

    c. "On my right hand the powers of LA!" (to North.)

    d. "On my left hand the powers of AL!" (to South.)

    e. "Above me the powers of ShT!" (leaping in the air.)

    f. "Beneath me the powers of ShT!" (striking the ground.)

    g. "Within me the Powers!" (in the attitude of Phthah erect, the feet together, the hands clasped upon the vertical wand.)

    h. "About me flames my Father's face, the Star of Force and Fire.'

    i. "And in the Column stands His six-rayed Splendour!'

(This dance may be omitted, and the whole utterance chanted in the attitude of Ptah.)

---

260 The unicursal Hexagram.

The dance, however, should not (in my humble opinion) be omitted, but instead seen as an integral part of the Liber. Note that the initial spiral is widdershins (or counter-clockwise), yet the final spiral is deosil (or clockwise) performed with a widdershins whirl. It is thus a spiral-within-a-spiral; while the initial spiral is performed with a centripetal step. It thus marks a Triple Spiral, as if the magician or sorceress performing the Liber were manifesting the energies of The Triple Veil of the Negative and earthing those Energies into Malkuth (the Kingdom). It is an assertion of the inherent Royalty of Humanity and the fact that "Every man and every woman is a star." (*AL* I: 3).

The Final Gesture.

This is identical to the First Gesture.

Since this Gesture is identical with the First, it shall not be repeated in this Qabalistic interpretation. However, the numerical details of this Ritual are of vital importance to the development of the Rite of the K'rla Cell, as I will show. The First Gesture is comprised of six Divine Names which have the numbers 56, 10, 463, 93, 666 and 156, the Sum of which is *1444*. They are followed by five especially significant formulae, each one having the numerical value of 93: and (5 x 93) = 465.

1444 plus 465 = 1909, the year of the publication of Equinox I, number I. 1909 was also *five years after the receipt of The Book of the Law*. When the number 418 is added to this, the Sum is 2327, which factors into (13 x 179), and 179 is the number of הדקע or *self-sacrifice*, which Crowley translates into Latin as *ligatio*, or "bond." The Priestess in the Rite of the K'rla Cell must be a Willing victim to the Alien Abductions by the Old Ones for Their sexual experiments and torments. The unfortunate girls convicted of being Sorceresses in the Middle Ages were certainly *not* willing.

The Second Gesture is comprised of *five Divine Names* with the separate numerical values of 56, 10, 666, 156, and 93. The Sum of these numbers totals 981, or (481 + 500). 481 was the Magical Number of Jeffrey Evans as Frater Khephra-ma-Ast in the Typhonian O.T.O. headed by Kenneth Grant (see *Beyond the Mauve Zone*[261]) and is a temurah of 418; and 500 is the numerical value of the Greek letter Phi, used by modern-day mathematicians to represent the Golden Mean. The Divine Names in the Second Gesture are followed by the number 93 plus a six-fold grouping of the number **31**, which can be seen as 9 times 31, equal to the number 279 (the number of וריגס or SGIRV, the Aramaic form of the word "leprosy." In the Torah it does not refer to a skin disease, but to sins which require "banishment" from the community. Moses was said to have leprosy on his hand, for speaking badly of the Israelites. The symbolism also figures heavily into the story of Miriam, one of the seven greatest prophetesses mentioned in the Torah. Moses, Aaron, and Miriam were the Three who led Israel out of bondage, and Miriam was "afflicted with leprosy" after speaking badly about her brother Moses. She also taught women the Torah, as Moses taught the men.

In ancient Jewish practice, a piece of fish was added to the Seder plate in honor of Miriam, who is associated with Water. Based on ancient teachings, Moses was associated with Earth; Aaron with "Clouds of Glory"; and Miriam with Water, and so the lamb (earth), egg (air), and fish (water) in the seder symbolize these three prophets respectively. They also refer to the three monsters in Jewish mythical tradition: the land beast Behemoth, the bird Ziz, and the sea beast Leviathan; the last of which is equivalent to Makara, " the Beast of the Waters" or "Dragon of the Deep" which becamea symbol of Set.[262]

---

261 See *Beyond the Mauve Zone*, p. 97, n. 26 (pub. By Starfire ltd., Spring Equinox, 2016).
262 And, Kenneth Grant notes that "The Evans-Keenan Cell Workings [were performed] in the Tunnel of Niantiel." As he told us in a private conference dealing with the Lodge of the K'rla Cell, the Rite "is a tantric form of the Death Posture."

The sum of 981 and 279 is 1260, and the previous sum (2327) added to 1260 equals 3587; and since The FINAL GESTURE is identical with The FIRST GESTURE, 3587 + 2327 = *5914*.

5914 equals (1127 x 5) plus 279, or the number of the mantra of the K'rla Cell times Five, plus 279; and 279 equals 9 times 31, but 279 spelled in full it equals 120 + 73 + 20 + 510 + 12 = 735, which is Five times 147: The Four Names in the Lesser Ritual of the Pentagram:

אלגא היהא ינדא הוהי

Yahweh Adonai Eheieh Agla, or
YHVH MY LORD SHALL BE WONDROUS!

Acknowledgments

To Thelemites everywhere who have Worked to keep the 93 Current strong, especially Steffi and Kenneth Grant for bringing through the Typhonian recension of the Current. To Michael Staley, for selflessly working to keep the books of Kenneth Grant and others available to the public through the operation of Starfire Press, Ltd., in the face of immense obstacles; and to Jan and Mike Magee for graciously allowing me to stay in their flat on my first visit to the U.K.

To Nema, Michael Bertiaux, and Mikhailovic-Slavinsky, who each contributed to a revitalization of the Current in their own unique ways; and to Bill Seibert, for allowing me and my magical partner to stay at his Math of the Chrystal Humm in Ithaca, New York, when we officially opened this working.

There are too many people I would like to like to acknowledge but who would not wish to be known by their names. They will recognize themselves by their initials: D.V.; C.K. and L.B.; and I.K. and B.G., for teaching me so much about theater in my early years as an actor.

To my family, especially to my mother and father, Virginia Davis Evans and Donald Nelson "Nick" Evans; and to my brother and sisters.

Finally, to my acting mentors Karl Redcoff and his wife Kay Daphne Redcoff; my good friends Mindy Myshrall Katz and her husband Steve Katz; and to Mitch Poulos, an actor who made himself a professional success in a very difficult field.

—Jeffrey D. Evans

• • •

I would like to thank Birol Koç of *EyePhi.com* for his permission to use the excellent Pentagram diagram in Chapter Eleven.

Thanks also, of course, to Yvonne Paglia, who believed in this unbelievable manuscript. And to Jeffrey D. Evans, for his patience through the sometimes-mind-numbing labyrinth of seemingly endless tasks that accompany the publication of every book.

—PETER LEVENDA

Bibliography

Allen, Richard Hinckley, *Star Names: Their Lore and Meaning*, Dover, New York, 1963.

Atallah, Hashem & Geylan Holmquest, trans. *Picatrix: Ghayat al-Hakim: The Goal of the Wise*, Volume II, Ouroboros Press, Seattle, 2008.

Avalon, Arthur, *The Serpent Power*

Beatty, Charles, *Gate of Dreams*, Geoffrey Chapman, London, 1972.

Berlitz, Charles, *The Bermuda Triangle*

Blavatsky, H.P., *The Secret Doctrine* Theosophical University Press, 1952.

Budge, E.A., *Egyptian Hieroglyphics*

Charpentier, Louis, *The Mysteries of Chartres Cathedral*, Research Into Lost Knowledge Organisation, Hammersmith (UK), 1972.

Clarke, Arthur C., "Hazards of Prophecy: The Failure of Imagination" in *Profiles of the Future: An Inquiry into the Limits of the Possible,* Harper & Row, New York, 1962.

Coleman, Loren, *Mysterious America*, Faber & Faber, London and Boston, 1983.

Crowley, Aleister, *777 and Other Qabalistic Writings*, Weiser, New York, 1977.

Crowley, Aleister, *The Book of the Goetia of Solomon the King*, Magickal Childe, New York, 1989.

———, *The Book of Thoth*, Weiser, New York, 1969.

———, *The Confessions of Aleister Crowley*, Arkana Books, London, 1989.

————, *Liber CCXXXI*, in *Equinox* I, vii., Weiser, New York, 1993.

————, *Magick in Theory and Practice*, Dover, New York, 1976.

Czaplicka, M.A.,"Shamanism and Sex" in *Aboriginal Siberia: A Study in Social Anthropology*, Oxford: Clarendon Press, 1914.

Dehn, Georg, *The Book of Abramelin: A new translation*, Ibis Press, Lake Worth (FL), 2015.

Derleth, August and Donald Wandrei, *The Outsider and Others*, Arkham House, 1939.

Devereux, George, *Psychoanalysis and the Occult*, New York: International Universities Press, 1953.

Dobson, Eleanor, "Cross-Dressing Scholars and Mummies in Drag: Egyptology and Queer Identity," in *Aegyptiaca* 4 (2019).

Eliade, Mircea, *Shamanism*, Princeton University Press, Princeton (NJ), 1974.

————, *Yoga: Immortality & Freedom*, Princeton University Press, Princeton (NJ) 1971.

Gleason, Judith, *A Record of Ifa: Oracle of the Yoruba*, Grossman, New York, 1973.

Graham, Sharyn, "Sex, Gender , and Priests in South Sulawesi, Indonesia," in *IIAS Newsletter*, #29, November 2004

Grant, Kenneth, *Beyond the Mauve Zone*, Starfire Publishing, London, 1999.

————, *Images & Oracles of Austin Osman Spare* , Weiser, NY, 1975.

————, *The Magical Revival*, Samuel Weiser, New York, 1972.

————, *Nightside of Eden*, Skoob Books, London, 1994 (1977).

Kepler, *Johannes Kelpius Gesammelte Werke*, Band XVI, Briefe 1607-1611, Herausgegeben von Max Caspar, C. H. Beck'sche Verlagsbuchhandlung, Munich, MCMLIV.

Krishna, Gopi, *Kundalini: the Evolutionary Energy in Man*, Shambhala 1971.

Kuhlmann, Klaus P., "Throne" in *UCLA Encyclopedia of Egyptology*, 2011.

Lambropoulou, Voula, "Reversal of Gender Roles in Ancient Greece and Venezuela," in B. Berggreen & N. Marinatos, eds., *Greece & Gender*, Bergen, 1995.

Lawlor, Robert, *Sacred Geometry: Philosophy and practice*, Thames & Hudson, London, 1982.

LeShan, Lawrence, *The Medium, The Mystic, and the Physicist*, Viking Press, New York, 1974.

Levenda, Peter, *Stairway to Heaven*, Continuum, New York, 2008

————, *Tantric Temples: Eros and Magic in Java*, Ibis Press, Lake Worth (FL), 2011.

Livio, Mario, *The Golden Ratio*, Broadway Books, New York, 2002

Lovecraft, H.P., *At the Mountains of Madness & Other Novels*, Arkham House, Sauk City, WI, 1964

————, *The Dunwich Horror*, Lancer Books, New York, 1963.

————, *The Lurker at the Threshold*, Beagle Books, New York, 1971.

————, *Selected Letters*, Vols. I-V, Arkham House, Sauk City. WI, 1976.

Mack, John E., *Abduction: Human Encounters with Aliens*, Ballantine Books, New York, 1995.

Massey, Gerald, *The Natural Genesis,* Weiser, New York, 1974

Michell, John, *The View Over Atlantis*, Ballantine Books, New York, 1973.

Parker, R.A. and I. H. Lesko, "The Khonsu Cosmogony," in *Pyramid Studies and Other Essays Presented to I.E.S. Edwards*, The Egyptian Exploration Society, London, 1988.

Perro, Robert and Michael Grunley, *Atlantis: the Autobiography of a Search*, Bell Publishing Company, New York, 1970.

Peterson, Joseph, ed., *The Clavis or Key to the Magic of Solomon*, Ibis Press, Lake Worth, 2009.

Pike, Albert, *Morals and Dogma of the Ancient and Accepted Scottish Rite of Freemasonry*, Charleston, 1871 (1947).

Plato, B. Jowett, trans. *The Dialogues of Plato*, Vol. Two, Random House, NY, 1892 (1920).

Plotinus, *The Enneads*, Stephen MacKenna, trans. Faber & Faber Ltd., London, 1917–1930.

Powell, James N., *The Tao of Symbols*; Quill, NY, 1982.

Pregadio, Fabrizio, trans. *Commentary On the Mirror for Compounding the Medicine: A Fourteenth-Century Work on Taoist Internal Alchemy*, Golden Elixir Press, Mountain View (CA), 2013.

Reymond, Eva A.E., *The Mythical Origin of the Egyptian Temple*, Manchester University Press, New York, 1969.

Rhine, J.D., *Extra Sensory Perception*, Bruce Humphries, Boston, 1954.

Roscoe, Will, "Priests of the Goddess: Gender Transgression in Ancient Religion," in *History of Religions*, Vol. 35, No. 3 (Feb., 1996).

Sahasrabudhe, N.H. and R.D. Mahatme, *Secrets of Vastushastra*, Sterling Paperbacks, New Delhi, 1999.

Satyr, "The Black Lodge of Santa Cruz." In: Biroco, Joel, (ed.). *KAOS 14: Supplement* [PDF Edition] London: The Kaos-Babalon Press, 2002.

Scholelm, Gershom, *On the Mystical Shape of the Godhead*, Schocken Books, New York, (1962) 1991.

Schwaller de Lubicz, R.A., *The Temple in Man: Sacred Architecture and the Perfect Man*, Inner Traditions International, Rochester (VT), 1977.

Scott-Elliott, W., *The Story of Atlantis & The Lost Lemuria*, The Theosophical Publishing House, 1968

Shiels, Tony *"Doc," Monstrum! A Wizard's Tale*, Fortean Tomes, London, 1990.

Simon, ed., *Necronomicon*, Schlangekraft, New York, 1977.

Skinner, Stephen, *Sacred Geometry: Deciphering the Code*, Sterling, NY, 2006.

Spare, Austin Osman, *The Book of Pleasure (Self-Love): The Psychology of Ecstasy*, self-published, London, 1913.

———, *The Focus of Life*, London, 1921.

Stoker, Bram, *The Jewel of Seven Stars*, William Heinemann, London, 1903.

Taylor, John G., *Black Holes: The End of the Universe?* Avon, New York, 1975.

Temple, Robert, *Egyptian Dawn*, Arrow Books, London, 2011

Temple, Robert with Olivia Temple, *The Sphinx Mystery*, Inner Traditions, Rochester (VT), 2009.

Ullman, Montague and Stanley Krippner, *Dream Telepathy: Experiments in Nocturnal ESP*, with Alan Vaughan, Macmillan, New York, 1973.

Vanderbroeck, Andre, *Al-Kemi: A Memoir*, Lindisfarne Press, Hudson (NY), 1987.

Webb, James, *The Occult Establishment*, Open Court, LaSalle (IL), (1976) 1991.

Wei Wu Wei, *Posthumous Pieces*, Oxford University Press, 1968

Wilkinson, Toby, "Before the Pyramids: Early Developments in Egyptian Royal Funerary Ideology," in *Egypt at its Origins, Studies in Memory of Barbara Adams*, S. Hendricks, Friedman, Ciałowicz, Chłodniki, eds. (Leuven: Peeters, 2004).

A Note to Our Readers

IBIS PRESS / NICOLAS HAYS is dedicated to to providing the finest spiritual literature available today. We specialize in publishing books from both classic and modern sources that outline the basis and development of the world's Mystery Traditions. Our subjects include Depth Psychology, Alchemy, Astrology, Magick, New Age thought, Women's Mysteries, and the many other paths of human striving for union with the Infinite. For more information, contact us us at *info@ibispress.net* or *info@nicolashays.com*

Distributed by Red Wheel/Weiser, LLC.
65 Parker St. • Ste. 7 • Newburyport, MA 01950
www.redwheelweiser.com